Everything you ever wanted to know about college – a guide for minority students™

Dr. Boyce Dewhite Watkins
Professor of Finance

Blue Boy Publishing Company

Published by

Blue Boy Publishing Co.
P.O. Box 691
Camillus, NY. 13031-0691

Printed in the United States of America

First Printing: February, 2004

ISBN: 0-9742632-0-6

Designed by Budgetbookdesign.com

For information on speaking engagements or questions, go
to www.boycewatkins.com or contact Blue Boy Publishing
Company directly.

This book was written based on the personal experiences of the author and are reflections of his opinion only and not those of Blue Boy Publishing. Neither the author nor the publisher assume responsibility for errors. The author and publisher specifically disclaim any and all liability resulting from the use or application of the information contained in this book.

To my daughter, Patrice. I hope that one day you will know that I wrote this book for you. I also dedicate this book to my "adopted children" David, Carmen, Mia, Dominique, Monique, and Thaiisha, all of whom inspire me with their love.

Table of contents

Acknowledgements

I would like to thank my parents, Robin and Larry and my grandmother Felicia. Without their wisdom, I would be nothing. I am especially thankful to their patience and guidance as I toiled through the years of ups and downs on my path to the PhD. My brother Lawrence and sister Latanja have always shown me tremendous support through the years. My Uncle Donald was the closest thing to a big brother for me, and he has always shown me tremendous loyalty.

My mentors, Dan Black and Tommy Whittler have both provided great protection and help through the years, particularly on professional matters. I would like to thank Sheri Mitchell, Lakisha Clark and Leah Gunning for help with editing and formatting issues
.

Finally, I would like to thank the Black Achievers Organization in Louisville, KY for opening the door for me to obtain a college education. Had they not taken a chance on me, I would not be where I am today.

Foreward

By Dr. Tommy Whittler

The Undergraduate Years

In April 1993, a soft-spoken black college student knocked on my office door. I was an associate professor in the Department of Marketing at the University of Kentucky and served as faculty advisor for Beta Gamma Sigma, the distinguished, nationally recognized business honorary. Perspective students were sent invitations to join the honorary and Boyce had been elected into the honorary. I was pleasantly surprised that he had performed so well in the classroom. During my 16 years at the university, I believe only three black students were selected into the honorary: Now-Judge Pamela Goodwin, now-attorney Braxton Crenshaw, and now-Ph.D. Boyce Watkins, the same young man who was sitting in my office wondering what this honorary was all about.

I told him about the honorary and how he should be very proud of what he had accomplished. He told me that next year he would graduate with three business degrees: Finance, economics, and management. What made this feat more impressive was that he would earn the degrees within a four-year time span and a 3.94 (out of a possible 4.0) cumulative grade point average. Since I was a marketing professor and Boyce took other majors, our paths would not have crossed. He talked with a soft voice, but he seemed as curious to see a black professor at the university as I was to see bright young male excelling in the classroom.

The induction ceremony for Beta Gamma Sigma was in a few days and I asked Boyce if he and his parents were attending the banquet. Sadly, he said it was unlikely that they would attend since he had not told them of his honor;

he also had studying to do that night. After all, he did have three majors! He never made it to the induction ceremony, but from that point on we became friends. We played numerous games of one-on-one basketball (He never beat me in a seven-game series!). We often talked about education, race, and politics.

Doctoral Studies

Boyce showed an interest in academia. He often asked questions about my research, publishing, and teaching at the university. I was surprised to hear a young person show so much interest in college professors' responsibilities. Initially, he told me that he planned to earn degrees in law and the Masters of Business Administration (MBA) and "make lots of money working on Wall Street." But our talks sparked his interest in academia. He often asked "why" about publishing and research. He even helped me collect data for an experiment. The fall of his senior year, Boyce took the GMAT examination and scored high enough to be offered a fellowship at Indiana University, Bloomington. Boyce was a mere 21 years old!

At Indiana, Boyce performed well enough in the classroom, earning a 3.54 g.p.a. on a 4.0 scale. However, he felt that his mathematical skills were not proficient enough for the Ph. D. in Finance. Boyce decided to return to Kentucky to take classes in statistics and mathematics. Within two and a half years, Boyce earned a master's degree in mathematics and nearly another degree in statistics. He was now prepared to finish what he started - the Ph. D. in Finance. This time Boyce would attend the University of Rochester, a top-five university in the finance area. To the best of my knowledge, he was the first African-American PhD student in the *history* of the entire business school!

Again, he did well in the classroom. The qualifying examinations posed a different hurdle. These examinations must be passed before one can proceed to dissertation work. Some frustrations with the examinations led Boyce to change institutions. He chose to complete his qualifying examination and dissertation at The Ohio State University.

On November 26, 2002, Boyce defended his dissertation and became Dr. Boyce D. Watkins! I don't know who was more proud of Boyce's accomplishment – him or me! Of nearly 300 students being granted doctorates that day, Boyce was the only African-American male *in the entire group.* Although a few of my former students had earned professional degrees (e.g., law, MBA degrees), Boyce was the only black student at Kentucky to earn a Ph. D. In fact, within the last five years, Boyce was one of just five black doctoral students in the country to earn a Ph. D. in finance. His intellect, hard-work, and persistence in the face of an extremely difficult, arguably racist profession paid off handsomely. Today, Boyce is an assistant professor in the Department of Finance at Syracuse University. He makes more money than I make and he gets to break ground in new areas of research. Boyce just turned 31 years old in June of 2002.

In addition to conducting research on stock equities, mergers and acquisitions, Boyce teaches finance to college students. He is a gifted communicator who understands how young people learn. He connects with young people because he is not much older than they. He also has a sister who recently completed college and a brother who is a sophomore in college. I expect him to make quite a name for himself in Finance.

About this book

When Boyce informed me of this endeavor, I applauded him. During my years at Kentucky and now at DePaul University in Chicago, I have seen so many black students get sidetracked from their educational goals. At Kentucky, I taught a course that introduced first-year students to college life. I was disappointed that I never had more than two black students in my courses. Often, I had no black students. This course taught students about time management, how to study, how to read college textbooks, how to prepare for exams, and how to talk to professors. It also talked about alcohol and drug abuse, date rape, and sexually transmitted diseases. Not many black students heard these important messages.

Boyce Watkins wants this group in particular to receive vital information that prepares them for college life. I wish that Boyce had completed the book before my young nephew began college last fall. That summer, my nephew and I spent a few days talking about issues such as class attendance, preparation for examinations, and the allocation of study time. We also talked about contraception, date rape, and respect for others and their property. Sadly, those talks went unheeded. Perhaps my nephew did not "connect" with his older uncle. Perhaps he would have had a more promising college beginning had he read the Boyce's book. Academia can provide young black students with a tremendous learning experience, but it also affords great freedom and responsibility. This book talks about those responsibilities. Perhaps through the use of this ground-breaking new book, minority students around the country will have opportunities to reach the greatest heights of academic, professional and personal success. Accomplished individuals like Boyce are a critical part of that learning process.

Introduction

This book is a no nonsense guide to everything a minority student needs to know in order to succeed and dominate in college. If you want to be a winner, and you want great things to happen in your life, then please read this book. If you are not interested in paying the price to become the best that you can be as a student, then you may want to put the book right back on the shelf and find something else. I have always wanted to be a winner, and I've defined myself as a winner. I have written this book to seek out other people who either are winners already or just need to know what it takes to be an academic champion. I don't care how smart or how dumb you think you are. I don't care where you come from. I don't care what your parents did for a living. I don't care if you graduated at the top of your class or at the very bottom. I only care about what YOU want from your life, and what you want from yourself. I also care about what price you are willing to pay to be a high achiever and a lifetime winner.

Winning and succeeding is not easy. It's like buying a pair of pants at the mall. You can't go into the mall with $20 and expect them to give you the $150 outfit. You also can't be successful and get all the rewards that come with greatness if you are not willing to work like a dog to make it happen. Sometimes people get lucky, but luck does not carry you through this world, only gut-wrenching, butt-kicking hard work.

I happen to be a college professor. My PhD is in Finance. I have taught thousands of students over the course of 10 years, and I have also been a track coach. Sometimes when you read this book, I am NOT going to sound like a coach, a parent or a professor. I am going to sound like the thing that I've been since I was born: A young black man who doesn't believe in B.S. So, if you are taken aback by my language, my analogies, or the way you see things expressed here, then this book is not for you.

However, if you want to know what college success is all about without any fakin, frontin or holdin back, then this is the place to be!

The book is cut into sections, some of it having to do with the academic side of college, some having to do with the financial side, some of it related to the social side. Some of it talks about what you should do before and after college, some of it during. Some of it is for women and some for men. If there is a section that doesn't fit your needs or interests, then feel free to skip around and get what you need. The goal is to provide you with all of the intellectual ammunition that you need to succeed as a college student. So, load up your gun and get ready to go to war, for the victory is already yours.

Why should you do that ol college thang anyway?

Before we sit and tell you all the great things about college, what is going to happen before, during and after, what you need to do to get the most out of it, the ups, the downs, the in-betweens, the loopty-loops, and all that, we should start with a very basic question: why do you want to go to college anyway? I mean, you could be doing a lot of things: playing in the NBA, bustin rhymes with your boys on stage, acting in Hollywood, or just plain old "kickin it". More realistically, you could also just jump right out and get a job after high school. There was a time when that wasn't such a bad thing. My grandmother always tells me stories about the days when a high school diploma went a long way, when a house cost 8 cents, when dogs didn't bite and police loved to whip the crap out of black people...wait, I guess they still do that, scratch the last part. But a lot of things have definitely changed since then, and a person must adjust to the times.

If you want to increase your chances to getting a good job one day, then getting a solid education under your belt is a great place to start. Once, I asked a friend if she was going to college. I think that she was the kind of sister that wanted to make the quick money, rather than spend 4 years investing in her education. In her mind, it was all about "getin paid" right away, and college would be a waste of 4 years for her. When I asked her if she was going to go to college, she said "I like money too much to go to college". I said to her "I like money too much *not* to go to college!" So the fact is this: you need degrees to get to the cheese! To lay it down in concrete terms, a census bureau survey showed that college graduates earn nearly one million dollars more during their lifetime than people with high school diplomas. What would you do with your extra million?

Sure there are exceptions. I went to college with guys who never graduated and left early for the NBA to make more money than most of us will ever make. However, this is clearly the exception. For every Kobe Bryant or Allen Iverson, there are literally millions of other students who

1

are not quite good enough to make the big money. For every Vivica Fox or Halle Berry, there are a lot of sisters out there in Hollywood with roaches crawling across the bathroom floor. I am not saying this to stamp out the dreams you may have, it's a reminder that you should pursue higher education *no matter what you decide you want to do.* This guarantees that you will have something to fall back on in case your plans don't turn out quite the way you thought they would.

One thing that we are taught to do is to think of college as optional. It's something that we do if we feel like it, but if we don't do it, then nobody gets too mad at us. But sometimes, that can be the wrong way to think. When you finished the 8th grade, did you think about not going to high school? When you finished the 5th grade, did you consider not going on to the 6th? Well, the only difference between the 12th and other grades is that you can stop if you want to. But would you have stopped going to school after the 8th grade if you didn't have to keep going? Maybe the answer is yes (I probably would have too), but you are probably glad you did go to high school. Without going to high school, the only fast food restaurant you could eat from would be McDonalds, not because it's good, but because they have pictures of the food and you don't have to be able to read to place your order. Without going to high school, you would have never met your friends, you would have never had a chance to play sports, and you would never have had some of your best experiences as a person. As you think about whether or not you should keep going to school after the 12th grade, you should realize that stopping *should not even be an option.* After you finish high school, you probably don't even have a good trade to earn a decent living, so your ability to survive in this world and get all the things that you want would be severely limited. College is not the only way to financial success, but it is one of the ways that works if you want it to.

Ok, now you know that if you want a better future for yourself, then you should probably keep going to school. The second nice thing about going to college is that it gives you the chance to get a job that you really like. If you are lucky, you might even end up with a job that you love. Usually, only the people in the NBA or NFL could say they love their jobs, but if you get the right kind of education, you might be able to find something that you love also. Unlike the NBA or NFL, you can work till you are 65, instead of having to quit when your body wears down. What if you love history and get to be an Historian? What if you love science and find yourself curing diseases for a living? What if you love computers and find yourself working as a computer scientist or video game creator? What about becoming an astronaut and going to the moon? That is the beauty of an education. It gives you the chance to mold yourself into whatever you want to become. You get to stretch, bend and twist yourself like silly putty and turn yourself into the person that you've always dreamed of becoming.

The world is probably a lot bigger than what you see right now. When I got to college, I found out about careers that I had never heard of, making more money than my mama and daddy put together. This was exciting, and if I had never stepped on the campus, I would never have known what else the world had to offer.

I almost never had a chance to find out about the good life. The summer before I went to college, I was not a very good student. My GPA was just 2.2, and I almost failed senior English, which would have kept me from graduating. My teacher gave me a D- in her class, barely keeping me from being held back another year. She let me pass mainly because she wanted to get rid of me. I had no money, and on top of all that, my girlfriend was pregnant. Life wasn't exactly looking up. My counselor also told me that I was not "college material", and that I shouldn't even think about trying to go to school after the 12th grade. But I never listened to what people told me anyway, so why start with her? I went to college because I had nowhere else to go, but I honestly didn't think that I was going to make it.

An organization called "The Black Achievers" seemed to think that I had potential, so they gave me a partial scholarship. I found that I liked the set up of college much more than high school. First, I could set my own schedule, which meant that I could get up at 10 or 11 o'clock every day if I wanted to, instead of 6:30 A.M. like high school. Second, I only had 2-3 classes a day, which was a lot different from the 9-10 hour grind of high school. Third, no one told me what classes I had to take or when I had to take them. I just had to complete the classes for my major, either in my freshman year or later on. The best part was that I didn't have nearly as much homework. I had more stuff to study, but not some stupid homework assignment that I had to turn in every day. High school felt a lot more like babysitting than anything else. In college, I was given the flexibility of an adult, and it fit my personality a lot better.

In my freshman year, I got the first 4.0 of my life, outperforming every single African-American freshman on the entire University of Kentucky campus, including those who had been offered full scholarships. I had NEVER IN MY LIFE come close to doing very well in school. Basically, I had put my mind to something, and succeeded at it. It is amazing what you can do when your mind decides that it is going to happen. The fear of having a child on the way and no future in front of me pushed me to use this college education as a chance to find my way out of the dismal future I had created for myself. After earning a 4.0 during my first semester, good grades came easy. Bill Cosby was right when he said "Good study habits are like an airplane. It takes a lot of fuel to get it off the ground, but once it's in the air, you can turn the engines off and just coast." The first semester was a grind, but the rest was like coasting.

So, the point is that even if you don't feel that college is right for you, it might be if you give it a chance. If it doesn't work out, you can always go back to whatever you wanted to do in the first place. But if it does work out, you will get a chance to see and do things that are beyond your wildest dreams.

The fun of college

One other thing about college that you should know......it's fun!!!!!! I'm not lying, joking or exaggerating. I had more fun in college than I've ever had in my life. Imagine living in a building with all your best friends, with no parents to tell you what time you have to come in or go to bed. You can get up at 2 am and go swimming with your friends, you can visit your buddy or your boyfriend/girlfriend across the way, you can get together with your friends to go to the library, go to football and basketball games, go shoot hoop with your boys, all that. It's really just a fantasy world of thousands of people the same age as you, and I guarantee that when you're done, you will never have the chance to live like that again.

Many people think that when you go to college, you have to make a choice between having fun and making good grades. That isn't true at all. I graduated from college with a 3.9 GPA and 2 Bachelors degrees (all in 4 years), and I had a ton of fun. The best part was that I was also planting the seeds for a great future, so in some ways, the best part was just beginning. So, if you work hard and play hard, college is going to be a great experience.

What you can expect to read here

The rest of the book goes through everything I can think of that you need to know to get ready and to navigate the collegiate process successfully. We are going to talk about the academic stuff, the social stuff, the athletic stuff, the financial stuff, the psychological stuff, and the spiritual stuff that you want to be prepared for in order to get through. I want to be your guide to help you watch out for the traps and land mines that catch minority students along the way through this jacked-up system. I want you to get past the very same problems and issues that made me into the only African-American male to receive a PhD from Ohio State University on the day of my graduation. It's not that there weren't other brothers out there who were smart enough. It's not that there weren't others who tried. It is that there are traps and hurdles along the way that push you to the limits of human mental endurance. They mess with you and screw with your brain and your spirit to the point that you are tired and want to quit. They distract you, manipulate you, chastise you, harass you, violate you and barricade you to the point that you end up feeling that there is no hope. But the thing for you to remember on this day and never forget is that THERE IS ALWAYS HOPE IF YOU BELIEVE. You must believe in yourself through the wind and rain, the torture and pain and all the hell that breaks loose in front of you. You must know that others have gone through worse and survived, and that you must find a way to keep going, even when it seems that the world has come to an end. I will say this now and again later: Your obstacles have limits, so if your persistence is unlimited, you can do anything.

Do not feel that you have to read this entire book. Just read what you feel applies to you. I try to make sure that all situations are included here, so if something is not for you, just skip to the next section. However, I recommend that you read as much as you can, so that you can learn from my mistakes, as well as the things that helped make me successful. We are all going to make mistakes in our lives. They winners are those who learn from their mistakes and use them to make themselves stronger.

Where to get the money for college

OK doc, where am I supposed to get the money from?

The first thing to remember when it comes to paying for college is that it is probably not as expensive as you think. Some people hold onto a myth that leads them to believe that college is not affordable to most of us. This is not true at all. If you want to go, you can definitely find a way to get there without making your mother sell the house.

Even if you don't happen to have a million dollars in the bank, there are schools out there that don't cost a lot of money to attend. Usually, state universities (i.e. The University of Oklahoma, Wichita State University, etc.) have pretty low tuition in comparison with private schools, mainly because state schools are funded by the government. Even if you have the money to pay for an expensive private school, it may be a waste if you can get a good education at a less-expensive state school. I definitely feel that you should think twice before straining yourself and your family to pay for one of those really expensive colleges. They are good if you have the dough, but not good if you have to eat bologna sandwiches to get there.

Consider community college

One other alternative for those who don't have the money for a 4-year college is to consider attending a community college first. Community colleges are usually much less expensive than larger institutions. Also, they can be excellent stepping-stones to getting into a larger school one day. Besides offering 2-year degrees, they can also help students finish the first two years of their four-year program. For example, if you want to become a nurse at a four-year college, then you may want to cover the first two years of general classes at a community college, while taking your more specialized classes at a 4-year institution.

The main thing to remember is that what you do in college is more important than where you do it. For example, a student at "Cheap As Hell University" who makes straight "A"s can probably get better graduate school and job opportunities than a student at "Break Yo Self U." who made all "C"s. Your education is what you make of it. What I know for sure is that a college education is better than not having one at all, no matter what school you go to.

Let's break it all down right quick

Let's go blow-by-blow to figure out where a person can get money for college. The best route is the one that everyone knows the best: scholarships. First, you should make sure that you DO NOT FORGET that scholarships are not just for people with ten brains in their head. You don't have to have a 4.0 GPA or be the superstar of the math team. Sometimes, you can be a regular Joe Blow or Jane Doe and get the real dough too. There are some scholarships for smart people, for athletic people, for minorities, for women, for people who go to a certain church, for one-legged Protestants who speak Chinese, for 7-foot Siamese twins with big lips, the list goes on and on. You have to look around to find out where this stuff is hidden.

To increase your chances of getting some money for school, make sure that you put your name on EVERY APPLICATION YOU POSSIBLY CAN, even if you don't think that you are going to get the money. There are some scholarships that go unclaimed every year, just because no one applied for them! Second, turn over every stone to find out where the scholarships are: check the Internet, books in the library, books that are sold on finding scholarships, etc. Just going to the website www.google.com and typing the words "finding scholarship money" can produce a ton of references that you can start with. But to do this, you have to put in the time and do your homework, you can't be lazy on this one.

Minorities have the inside track

Minorities have a special inside track when it comes to getting scholarships. This may change in the future, since there is a lot of jealous backlash against Affirmative Action. However, there are a lot of universities that believe in the value of diversity and are willing to work hard to offer financial aid to minority students. Find out where this money is and check schools across the country to find out what they might have to offer you. You can start with the school in your home state, plus any other schools you apply to. You can get this information by asking the minority affairs office, the financial aid office, or the admissions office for the school that you are thinking about going to. Also, if you know any other minority students who have attended the school you are going to, talk to them. If you don't know anyone, then go to campus and try to meet someone. It's easy, just go up and say "Hi, my name is Luscious P. Broke-as-Hell, I was wondering if I could ask you a few questions." Talking to these people can sometimes help you find out what campus resources exist for minority students and where you can go to get them.

Thought about the "Lawud" lately? Try your church!

If you belong to a church, then this would be a good time to allow them to do some of the Lord's work. Most decent-sized churches have scholarship programs for members. If your church doesn't have one, this would be a great time to start! Sometimes if you ask the minister nicely and explain your situation, the church might take up a collection for you. Most good folks want to help young people who are doing good things for themselves. The ones who don't can go to hell (just kidding, but I HAD to say that). The important thing to remember here is that you don't have to get all your money from one place, you can get it from several places, as long as the little pieces add up to the big piece.

Save your cheesecake

Saving your money isn't just something that you should do once you start college. It is something you have to do before you consider going to college at all. I know it's hard, since saving for me is like having my teeth removed through the crack of my butt. I HATE SAVING MONEY! It has never been fun, and it never became fun. But you know what? Being broke became even less fun. I got tired of living from paycheck to paycheck, having to beg, borrow and sell my internal organs to keep up with my bills. So, I eventually learned that in life YOU EITHER PAY THE PRICE NOW OR YOU PAY IT LATER. The difference is that if you pay it now, you get to enjoy life later. But if you pay it later, then the suffering never seems to end and it can go on for the rest of your life.

You can think of college the same way. You are investing in yourself financially and educationally. It is not easy now, but in the long run, things are going to be easier, and they are going to stay that way in your 20s, 30s, 40s, 50s, 60s and 70s. So, be smart: save and invest your money. Also, save and invest in yourself.

It is never too late or too early to save. Even if you are still in high school, you can save 15% of that money that you make flipping burgers or cutting grass, and you would be surprised what that will do for you in the long run. The summer before you leave for school is a great time to pay most of your tuition for the following semester. For example, let's say that it's the summer before college and you are trying to save your own dough. Putting aside $400 a month toward school may seem difficult, but that is less than most people pay in rent. A person working for $6.00 an hour for 40 hours per week is going to bring home about

$650 each month after taxes, so you could afford this if you budget your money right. To make yourself save, you should try sending the money right to the school that you are going to attend and have them put it into your tuition account. That way, you can knock one or two thousand dollars off the cost before you step foot on campus. This may not cover the entire bill, but even if you have to go to school part-time, at least you are there. Getting your foot in the door and keeping it there till graduation is what matters, nothing else. Being on campus is fun, and it would give you a chance to be in the mix of college students, even if you can't go to college full-time right away.

Working while you're in school

If you are like I was, you may have to keep a job the entire time you are in college. There is nothing wrong with that, and a little hard work never hurt anybody. Also, the extra money you make from a job beats the heck out of the little chump change that your parents might send you. Besides that, making your own money is the quickest way to make sure that people are out of your business. It's easier for your parents to tell you what to do if they are paying for you to do it. Consider it one of the first and most important steps in growing up.

Don't work a 9 to 5

But if you decide to look for a job on campus or off campus, don't just get any job. The worst kind of job to have while you are going to school is a nine to five. That is a job that makes you work during the day, all day long, four or five days a week. These jobs make you feel like you are a worker first and a student second. You don't want that. You want a job that understands that you are a student first and a worker second. It is your education that is going to create the future that you are trying to have for yourself.

Day jobs make it tough for you to take the classes that you need for your major, which are usually going to be offered during the day. You also miss out on a lot of fun stuff if you are working all the time. These jobs suck, so don't do it if you don't have to.

The best job to get while you are in school is a job that lets you study while you are working. These might be security guard positions, or jobs sitting at the front desk in one of the dorms, etc. These are the best jobs because they let you kill two birds with one stone. You can get all your studying done while you're at work, and then you can use that extra time to either chill or find a second job, whatever you want to do.

The next best job to get is one that offers flexible hours and a good tuition assistance plan. United Parcel Service (UPS) and Federal Express tend to offer these kinds of plans, and you can probably check around in the town that you are going to college in to find out who the major employers are in that area. You should make sure that your hours are either flexible, or placed at a time that is convenient for you to still be able to go to class. But don't go to any workplace just because they claim to offer tuition assistance, a lot of places will tell you anything to get you there. Find out the details of the program, how much they pay, what classes they cover, and how long you have to work there to be eligible.

Getting a job on campus

The next best option would be a job with the university. You see, this is kinda tricky. The reason is that a) these jobs can be hard to get, and b) a lot of schools are really sneaky about only offering their tuition benefits to full-time people, who are less likely to use them. The LAST thing they want is for all of their students to know that they can get around paying tuition by working for the university. The reason that this option is third, rather than first or second is because many of these jobs require you to work all day long, which is going to get in the way of your class schedule. So, I recommend that you only consider this option when you have no place else to get the money.

So, how do you pull it off? First, you have to scope out the target. That means you have to get the information on the types of jobs available, and what kinds of plans they offer their employees. Most major universities have large human resources offices that you can apply to and they also keep a list of all the different jobs available. Apply for the position before you are enrolled as a student, and then use the tuition benefits to help you pay for school. It is not a sneaky way to rip off the school, but is instead a way for you to pay your tuition with labor rather than money that you don't have. I recommend applying for these jobs before you start the semester so you don't have as much competition.

Part-time jobs and the grave yard shift

The next two jobs in my rankings would be a) a part-time job with flexible hours, and b) a full-time or part-time job on the graveyard shift. The graveyard shift is another name for any job that makes you work at night, when the rest of the world is sleeping. A lot of these jobs don't let you off work till the next morning. These jobs can be tough on your health, since sleeping at night is something that we've been used to doing since we were little babies. Also, a lack of sleep can cause depression, so these shifts can have an impact on your mental health as well. There are a list of "Coco Rules" (My mama calls me Coco, like she did when I was a baby. Well, now I'm her "whittle Doctor Coco") below for those who are thinking about working the graveyard shift. A regular part-time job is the best option of the two, since it would let you make some extra money and still stay in school. Flexible hours would give you the chance to make it to your classes. I think that the graveyard shift should be a last resort, unless you really need the money. A lot of employers are looking for people who can work these shifts, but you should think carefully before you do it.

The really last resort

The last job on the list is the one that I mentioned above, a "full time nine-to-five". Or you could call it a "bull-swine shuck and jive" (you see, that was supposed to rhyme. If it wasn't funny, just chalk it up to the fact that I am a REALLY CORNY PERSON). A full-time 9 to 5 is exactly what it sounds like: a job that requires you to work a regular 9 to 5 shift, where all your hours are during the day. You would then have to go to school at night and on weekends. This is not the way to go as a college student. Some might disagree with me, but the fact is that most people who put themselves in this position are asking for trouble in the long run. You can very easily find yourself spending more time with work than with school. This way, school ends up on the back burner, rather than the front, where it belongs. If you can avoid putting yourself into that position, stay away. Let's do a quick recap:

Coco ranking on the types of jobs that you should look for in college:

1) A job that lets you study while you work.
2) A job with flexible hours that offers a good tuition assistance plan.
3) A job with the university that lets you take classes for free
4) A part-time job with flexible hours.
5) A full-time job on the grave yard shift
6) A regular job (9 – 5, 40 hours per week.....I recommend this one the least).

Coco Rules on how to work the graveyard shift:

1) Do it only if you have to. It may seem easy at first, but it's tough to do over a long period of time.
2) Make sure that your class schedule is open enough so that you have at least 5.5 hours free between the time you get off work and the time you have to go to class. Also, make sure that you don't have a long day of classes on the days after you've worked all night. You need time to rest and get a good, solid sleep.
3) Take your vitamins, since staying up all night can affect your immune system.
4) Don't keep this job for a very long time. Try to find something different after 3 or 4 months.
5) If your job gives you time to study, get all your studying done so that you can sleep later on and chill out if you want to. You might as well get something out of these crazy hours! Working could even help your grades get better if you manage your time properly.
6) Make sure you leave time open to get plenty of sleep before you go to work. You might be bubbly around 11 P.M., but by 4:30 A.M., life ain't too good!
7) Try to only work shifts less then 4 or 5 hours per night.
8) Don't work every night, give yourself some time off so that your body can recover.
9) Since a lack of sleep can cause depression, make sure that you always keep a positive attitude! Remember: YOU are your own best psychologist!

Other Ways to get the cheese that you need

As I mentioned before, there are a million and one ways to get the money that you need for school. State grants are another option that is readily available for almost any student who doesn't come from a high-income family. This is basically money that the states have put aside in their budget to help people pay for college. They don't usually cover all of your expenses, but they can cover most of them, depending on how much you get. The amount that you can get in the long run is usually limited, but it definitely helps.

All the information that you need on grants is usually available in your school's financial aid office. Since they want money, the schools tend to be good at helping you figure out how to get the money that you need. Sometimes, being poor is a great way to get the money for college, since there are many things out there in the world for a motivated person who wants to be somebody.

They always need a few good men and women

Another way to get money is through military service, which I don't recommend. But this is my personal opinion. The reason that I have a problem with this option is because the military tends to make things look a little better than they are. There is a *reason* that they usually recruit young kids who don't know their butts from a hole in the ground (excuse my French, but sometimes, French is the best language to use). It's a lot harder to get an old stubborn person to follow orders than a young, naïve person. If you are trying to figure out who to send off to possibly get killed, who would you rather pick? Someone who knows better, or someone who listens to everything you say? The other reason that the military loves young people is because they are the strongest and most energetic, the best to fight with in a war.

If you sign with the military, even in the reserves, you are giving *another person the right to send you off to die if they decide that is what they want to do.* That's what it is, plain and simple. If you talk to a recruiter, they are not going to highlight the chance that you might DIE. Instead, they are going to talk about all the wonderful things about being a soldier, all the glory, the money and all that. If you tell them that you are looking for the money as a way to go to college, they are going to tell you about how wonderful it is going to be when they give you the gillions of dollars they promise that you will receive for the GI Bill. There are a lot of older folks in the world who will lie to you and say whatever they need to say to get you to sign on the dotted line. They tell you all this with the clear assumption that you are surely going to be alive and healthy when your time is done. They don't tell you that you may come home in a wheelchair, in a box, or not at all.

I am not saying that the military is not an option for anyone. If it were not for those brave souls who did join the military, we would not have a national defense. What I am saying is that you should *join for the right reasons.* Don't join because you think the military is your only way to college. Also, you need to make sure that you think carefully about the risks of what you are doing. Would you go out and work as a drug dealer just for the money? Would someone recruiting you to sell drugs tell you the bad things about the job? No. They would highlight the fast money, the jewels, the cars, and the glory, and would forget to mention the sight of your mother crying over your casket, or you rotting away in somebody's jail cell, wearing the cute bunny slippers that your 400 pound cell mate bought for you. The thing about the military is that they, like the drug dealers, will only highlight the glory of the uniform, and the chance for fast money. They are not going to talk much about the bad things that can happen.

There are a lot of people who have served time in the military and don't have a single regret. But there are many who are either dead, crippled or severely traumatized from their experience. If military service is not for you, find the money some other way.

Make yourself a resident

One thing about a lot of state schools is that they have one price that they charge people who are from that state ("state residents"), and another tuition that they charge to people who are not from that state ("non-residents"). Usually, the non-resident tuition is about twice as high as the resident tuition. This is done because the state government doesn't want to give college money to people who are not from that state and don't pay taxes.

One of the things that a cash-strapped college student can do is find out how to become a resident of the state that the university resides in. This could really lower the tuition bill. Some states have rules that say you have to work in the state for 6 months without going to school, some places say that you have to be there for a year, etc. A clever student can find out what the rules are and work them to their advantage. If they require you to work for 6 months without going to school, then you may want to do that, but only as a last resort. The best option for the cash strapped student is to go to school in their home state.

Now for the trump card: student loans

I mention student loans as the last subject of this section for two reasons. First, you obviously want to go after the FREE money first, stuff that you don't have to pay back. Secondly, this is the trump card, like in spades. This is the place you can get much of the money that your scholarships couldn't give you. It is tough to get loans if your parents make a lot of money, but if they have that kind of loot, then maybe you can skip the whole financial aid section of this book!

Basically, the idea behind student loans is really simple: You sign some papers, they give you the money. That's about all there is to it. The hitch is that you can't think of this as free money, because it's definitely not free. You have to pay it all back, and if you don't, your butt will be in a sling.

Are you afraid of borrowing money?

Some people think that borrowing money is a bad thing, under any conditions. You might have to hear your great grandmother, who was born during the Great Depression, take you aside and say in her wrinkled little voice "Baaaaaaaaaybeee. You don't wanna borra all dat munee. You have to pay it back!" What she is saying makes sense. But the thing is that if you don't have the money to make the investment, then you are worse off if you don't borrow than if you do. For example, imagine if you had a friend who said that you could open a kool-aid stand and that there are 70 kids in the neighborhood that want to buy 4 glasses of kool-aid a day for 50 cents each. That means that you could make almost $1,000 per week. But what if you don't have the money to open the stand? Would you rather just let that chance go to waste, or would you consider borrowing a little money from your pops to pay for the first few pitchers of kool-aid, till you get on your feet? That's how you have to think about student loans. Having a college degree with a bunch of loans is better than having no loans and no degree at all.

Nearly every great American corporation was created by borrowing money from somebody else. Without borrowing that money, the company could not go out and do the things they do to make cash, like make computers or cars or hamburgers. People borrow money all the time for a house, a car or a new boat. Why not borrow money to go to college? The thing about borrowing money is that it's not bad, *as long as you make enough money to pay it all back.* DO NOT EVER LET A FEAR OF BORROWING MONEY KEEP YOU FROM GOING TO COLLEGE.

Other ways to borrow money if you have to use them

Federal loans are great because the interest rates are really low. But sometimes, they can be hard to get if the government thinks that you make too much money. If you can't get student loans to pay for school, then a high-priced borrowing option might be credit cards. If you have a job and can keep good credit, then credit cards might be a good way to pay the bills till you get more money. Saving money for the fall semester isn't too hard, since you've got the whole summer to work. But saving money for the spring might be tough, since you don't have as much free time during the fall to work and save. Credit cards can help you through these times. Now, when it comes to credit cards, there is some good news and bad news. The good news is that they can come in handy when you are in a bind. Also, there are a lot of companies out there that love to give credit cards to college students. I guess they think that if the kid doesn't pay the money back, then their mother will. That is usually true for the kids with money, but my mother just laughed at them and hung up the phone. The bad news is that these companies really grease you up by charging you very damn near criminally high interest rates. You sometimes feel like you are dealing with the mafia instead of a reputable company. Also, bad management of credit cards is a good way to make trouble for your self. You can ruin your credit, or you could end up with so much debt that you have to sell your first 3 kids into slavery. Be careful when using credit cards and avoid them if possible.

Getting ready to be a butt-kicking college student

Scholastic preparation and getting your butt ready to kick some butts

Obviously, if you want to go to college one day, then you have to try to be as prepared as you possibly can. Don't get me wrong, you can still get there if you are older and didn't prepare the first time around, but the sooner you get the educational background you need, the better off you are going to be.

First, there is the academic side of things. Since college makes you use your brain, you are doing yourself a favor by making sure that your mind is ready. One of the first things you can do on the academic side is to try to take a set of classes that will prepare you for what you need to know to get through college. This is what they call a "college preparatory curriculum". Your counselor should be able to guide you to the classes that you need to prepare for college, and these classes will also help you to perform well on the ACT and SAT when you are ready to take them.

If you have a specific college in mind that you would like to attend, you should probably try to find out what classes you need to take in order to get into that particular university. You can get this information either by calling the school, talking to your counselor, looking on the internet, or having the college send you information. The more specific you can be in terms of where you want to go, the easier it is to design a plan that is going to get you there.

Once you start gathering information about what you need to be admitted to the school of your choice, you should start keeping records of all this information. Keep a file or notebook that has all the requirements that you need to get ready for college. Add to the file whenever you find new information. It is up to you to make sure that you are taking the classes that you need in order to get ready for college, since many minority students are not taught what they need to know at the high school level. If you are not sure, then find an adult that may know, a teacher, or someone at a local community center. Email ME if you have to! But find a way to make it happen, no matter what the cost. If you believe it, you can achieve it. Remember that.

Get those grades up!!!

The second thing you should do academically is to *keep your grades as high as possible*. This might sound like a simple thing to say, but the higher your grades are, the easier things will be for you later. Even if it means sometimes taking an easier class over a harder one, grades are very important to college admissions boards. Sometimes getting an "A" in an easy class means more to the university than getting a B-minus in a harder class. Don't ask me why things are like this, but that's just the way it is. So, keep the grades up at all costs, and if the college prep curriculum is too tough, either start working harder or take easier classes so that you can have a high GPA. Either way, good grades are better than bad ones.

Get involved in activities

The next thing you should do is to stay involved in extracurricular activities. Get involved in a lot of things, but not so much that it hurts your grades. Also, if you have a part-time job, make sure that you clearly state this on your college application. However, keep your working hours down, since colleges tend to reward after school activities, as opposed to things that are non-scholastic. I recommend being involved in at least two after school activities at all times, one of them physical and the other mental. For example, you can be on the basketball team and the chess club at the same time, or on the track team and the Student Government Association. Being involved in activities shows colleges that you are well rounded and not just someone who sits with their nose in a book all the time. Also, being involved in mental activities shows that you are not just a dumb jock who can run and jump, but you are also someone who can show intelligence in a lot of different situations.

If you can get into leadership positions, this really stands out on a college application. Of course, not everyone can be student body president, but there are plenty of leadership opportunities if you look all around you. You could be president or vice president of a student organization. You could even start your own organization and make yourself president! If you go that route, you should make sure that it is legitimate, but every organization has to be started by someone! You may find that there is no Christian Organization at your school, there is no team in the sport that you like, or there is no organization to play chess in competitions. You could go down in history as the person who started the first "Booty-shaker Computer Engineering Club" at your school! Don't be afraid to be a leader!

Those *&(%$ Standardized Tests!

Standardized tests such as the ACT and the SAT are given to students all over the country who are interested in going to college. For some people, they are considered a pain, and for others, they are a chance to show that you are smarter than your grades might signal. Either way, they should not be the only factor that determines whether or not you go to college. Some students do very well on these kinds of tests, and some do not. But the key factors that determine what you are going to be able to do in college are HARD WORK AND MOTIVATION. If you don't work hard, you are probably not going to do very well in college, no matter how smart you are. I've known a lot of valedictorians, Super-bionic, I-think-I-am-smarter-than-God Award winners, Straight As plus tax, IQ over 8,000 type students who are now 30 years old living in their mama's basement. They didn't understand that no matter how smart you are, not working hard at anything is the quickest way to end up as a squashed bug on the soul of life's shoe. Life will take you NOWHERE if you do not learn the value of working as hard as you can.

These tests can be intimidating, but there is no reason to let them scare you. You should NOT, however, take them lightly. These tests can make or break you in college admissions, so I recommend that you prepare the very best you can. If you happen to be a great student, a good score on these tests can confirm to the university that you are as smart as your grades say. This distinguishes you from the other students who make good grades at other schools. No matter what your test score, you should not let your grades slip, because a high test score with low grades may also make them think you are a lazy person who happens to be smart. Most colleges would rather have a hard working student with average intelligence than a highly intelligent student who doesn't want to work hard.

Study for the standardized tests before you take them

When it comes to the ACT and SAT, you should not take theses tests cold turkey. You need to study and be as prepared as possible. Most bookstores sell preparation books for the ACT and SAT, and the books are not very expensive. I recommend going through one of these books and taking as many of the practice tests as you possibly can. This will help you to become familiar with the test before you even take it. Being familiar with the tests will strengthen your performance because you don't have to waste time reading the directions, and you will already be familiar with the types of questions you will face.

A company called Kaplan, Inc. (www.kaplan.com) has a class you can take that will get you ready for your standardized tests. If you can afford it, I highly recommend taking one of the Kaplan courses to get ready for the SAT and ACT. The courses are not perfect, but they don't hurt either. The downside is that they can be kind of expensive. But if you save money from your job or borrow the money from a relative, it is definitely worth the cost. However, if you cannot afford these classes, don't worry about it. Buying the books and studying on your own can work just fine.

Getting someone to let you into their university

Getting into college can be a tough task, depending on what type of school you want to go to. It requires as much organization and advanced preparation as possible, so I recommend that you think carefully about this stage of the game. Most schools require that you send them an application that also includes current transcripts, written essays, letters of recommendation, etc. If you don't spend a lot of time talking to your high school counselor, then you probably should pay a visit to his/her office. If you can't work with your counselor, then try to talk to anyone who might know what you are about to go through that can also be supportive and encouraging. Sometimes the college that you are thinking about attending has people that can help you.

The key is to be as familiar with the process as possible. Start by contacting as many schools as you can and getting them to send you information. You can do this through the Internet, by telephone, by visiting the school (if it happens to be near by), etc. Then, go through the manuals that they send you and get information on the application process. If a college recruiter visits your school, go see him/her and ask as many questions as you possibly can, even if you are not interested in attending their college. If you hear of a trip that your school or organization is taking to visit any university, always take advantage of this opportunity. If the school is within driving distance, you can call the university yourself and ask for a campus tour and a meeting with financial aid officers and admissions counselors. You want to take as much initiative as possible to ensure yourself a solid future, even if there aren't a lot of people who want to help you get there. The only person that you need is a very determined Y-O-U!

Get the information as early as you can

You should get all of your college and application information during your Junior year of high school, not your Senior year. The fall semester of your Senior year is when the applications have to be submitted, so you want to be ahead of the game, not behind. By the time the spring semester of your Junior year hits, you should have a list of schools that you are strongly interested in, all of your test scores, and some idea of how you are going to get your transcripts mailed to the schools. Test scores are usually are sent to the schools by the companies that administer the test. Transcripts are sent by your high school guidance counselor. Keep a lot of schools on your list, but not more than 25 or so.

Alright Doc, I know that I want to go to college, and I've got the money. How in the world do I know which school is best for me?

Picking a school that works for you

Now you know that you're ready to do the college thing after you graduate from high school. They're about to hand you your diploma and they give you those age-old words of wisdom "I don't give a damn where you go, but you gotta get the hell outta here!" Where do you go? What do you do? How do you do it? How do you know what choice is the right one for you?

Well, first, I should tell you that sitting around idle is almost always a VERY BAD IDEA. You should be doing something, even during the summer before you head off to college. It is really true when they say that "an idle mind is the devil's workshop", because people who don't have anything to do are usually the first ones to get into trouble.

HBCUs vs. Predominantly white universities

So, let's talk about some of the college options that exist for you. Since you may very well be a black or Hispanic student, we should start with HBCUs (Historically Black Colleges and Universities). HBCUs arguably provide the kind of environment that many minority students are most used to: one in which nearly everything and everyone is also a minority. That can be a luxury, since there are millions of minority students who go to school their entire lives with nearly 100% white teachers. I was one of those people. HBCUs can provide the kind of support a student is looking for, or at the very least, give them the chance to see a familiar face.

One benefit of HBCUs is the fact that everything and every office is established with minority students in mind. That doesn't usually happen on predominantly white campuses, where black and Hispanic students can sometimes blend in like a few grains of pepper in a big ol bowl of mashed potatoes. Also, at an HBCU you are probably less likely to encounter the traditional forms of racism that exist in America. The chances that a black or Hispanic teacher is going to mistreat you because you are a minority are pretty small (although there are some that make you wonder). Added to this is the fact that the chance of finding friends with a common background is usually much higher when you are around people of your same ethnicity. Another HBCU benefit is the fact that many corporations that are seeking well-qualified minority employees will recruit at HBCUs. There are programs such as Florida A&M (FAMU), Spelman and Morehouse that have used these business connections to establish themselves among the premier universities in the world.

Now, let's stop the bus right here. HBCUs can be wonderful places to go to school, but they are not perfect. But then again, what kind of school is perfect? There is also the fact that being in an all-minority environment for the entire time you are in college may not be good preparation for the real world, which tends to be controlled by white men. Some would say that being in a *diverse* environment is the best kind of preparation. Also, there is a sad fact about human nature that says that even if there isn't racism on the campus, there are going to be other kinds of discrimination: the rich against the poor, the greeks against the non-greeks, the good-looking people against the butt-ugly ones (I was captain of the butt-ugly squad when I was in college), all that mess. So, the fact is that no matter where you go, the same kinds of problems seem to pop up everywhere. Finally, one nice thing about a predominantly white school vs. an HBCU is that there can be fewer distractions for you. HBCUs may give you a chance to have a fuller social life, but sometimes that's not always a good thing. For example, some HBCUs are known to have female-to-male ratios as high as 25-1! If I had that kind of ratio at my school, I might not have ever made it to class! One other unfortunate disadvantage of HBCUs is that they tend to have less funding than the

31

larger white schools. This is no fault of their own, but rather an outcome of the past 400 years of discrimination. This might mean that there is not as much technology on campus, the professors are overworked and underpaid, there may be fewer scholarship options, or the football and basketball teams are not going to be as good.

Large cheese factory or small?

Beyond the HBCU vs. white-school question lies the small vs. large question. Do you want a small school, with small classes, where all of your teachers know you by name, and most of the students do also? Or, do you want one of the great big, mammoth schools, where your life is just a megabyte on some Earth-size supercomputer?

The good thing about large schools is that they tend to have lots of money, which means that they can have lots of "stuff". Their computer systems are usually more modern and efficient, and they have more specialized classes that will let you learn more about your field. If you are going into something that is highly specialized, like Advanced Urbodynamic Hyperbolic Anti-Molecular B-Chain Physics, you may want to take that into account. Also, some people don't want everyone knowing their name and being all up in their business. I personally liked being part of a large group, and I also liked the fact that my teachers never knew if I was in class or not. That way, only my performance on the test mattered when I got my grade, and my work was more likely to be judged on it's quality rather than whether or not the teacher liked me.

A smaller school environment might fit your personality if you enjoy individual attention, or are intimidated by large institutions. Smaller schools are known for having a more nurturing environment than larger ones, where the student/teacher ratio is usually a lot lower. One problem with small schools is that if the school happens to be all-white, you may be the only minority in all of your classes. At least at a large school, even a 1%

32

minority student population can add up. For example, if the school has 40,000 students, 1% means that there are 4,000 minorities on campus. I don't recommend one type of school size over another. I just say that you should find something that best fits your goals and personality.

Home or away?

Next, there is this question: "Do I go out of state for college, or do I stay close to home?" That's a big question, particularly for your mama. She may not want to see her baby head off so far away, and her baby (meaning you) may not want to head off either. I don't have much of an opinion one way or the other, but I can give you some facts that will help you decide which option is best for you.

First, if you go out of state for college, be sure to bring your super-fat, stanky large, ultrabionic money clip. Most state-funded universities double their tuition for students who come from out of state. So, if a school charges double the tuition of the school that you could have attended within the state, then you better be sure that the out of state school is at least twice as good. Some students want to leave the state just to get away from home. Their goal is to get as far away from mama as they possibly can. That's a STUPID reason to go to school out of state. Not only are you wasting your parents' (or your) money, but you are probably going to really miss your family when they are no longer nearby. Also, when the cash flow is running low, it might be good to have family close so that you can bring home your laundry. I am not saying that you should not go out of state, but you should do it for the right reasons.

Usually, when it comes to the out-of-state vs. in-state question, you can have one of two types of students. First, there is Ms. Independence. She is the one that says "I can't wait to graduate so that I can get as far away from home as possible". Ms. Independence may live in Florida, but she wants to go to school in LA. She thinks she knows it all and that she is ready to get as far away as possible for as long as possible.

The other extreme is Mr. Underwing. This dude won't leave his parents for anything! He thinks that going to school at Down-the-street-University is the best of all worlds, because he doesn't have to leave his family, his friends or that love-of-his-life girlfriend who is creeping with some other dude behind his back. He doesn't even want to move out of the house, so his plan is to save money by living with his parents for the entire time that he is in college.

Now, while Ms. Independence and Mr. Underwing may very well go on to college and do just fine, they might also be setting themselves up for trouble. Ms. Independence did leave for college, getting that admission to UCLA. She kissed her mama and her girls goodbye and headed off, never to be seen again. A few things happened to her when she got there. First, after a couple of months on campus, she started to find out that she actually did miss her mama more than she thought she would. She also missed the rest of her family and friends. She couldn't visit them until Christmas though, and after that, not again until summer. That meant she would be seeing her family twice a year for the next four years. Not good. She also realized that the support network she had taken for granted for so long can be pretty crucial after she fails an exam or starts getting lonely and out of place in LA. She's a Florida sistuh, and these Cali-types just don't match her personality. This awkwardness, as well as the standard struggles of college and not being able to see her family eventually make Ms. Independence homesick. She heads out the door with the latest crop of freshman dropouts. Leaving college felt good to her, since it gave her a chance to be back in the same familiar territory that she was so anxious to leave before. As a result, she never came back to college again.

Mr. Underwing had it made, right? Well, not exactly. He stays in his mama's house, while going to school at the same time. Money is cool, and he's not even paying rent because he gets to live at home. The first thing that Mr. U finds is that studying at home can be tough with your little brother blasting his music in the next room, and your mother coming in every 10 seconds to nag you about taking out the garbage or cleaning the kitchen. Second, he realizes that being in the same city around the same old people is not only boring, but unproductive. Rather than mixing more with the university and meeting smart, productive people like himself, he finds himself dealing with the same old people, like his boy Refus, who is happy to be out of jail this week. Refus has been his boy since second grade, but his life is headed in the wrong direction. By refusing to move forward to a new environment, Mr. U misses the chance to grow and deal with higher-achieving people. He also puts himself at risk.

So, if Mr. U graduates, another thing that he is going to find is that staying with his mama and staying in the same city through college might severely stunt his growth as a person. When you become an adult, that is a time for you to stake out into the world and make a claim of your own. Why would you ever work hard to have good things for yourself if your Mama is always taking care of you? You never learn how to pay your own rent or bills, or even to do the basics to take care of yourself. So, while your friends are growing into responsible adults, you're still living like you did back in high school. Before you know it, you're 30 years old, sittin in your mama's living room on a Tuesday afternoon playing Playstation in your underwear. Not cool.

I'm not trying to diss Ms. I and Mr. U. I am also not trying to say that staying close to home or moving far away is a recipe for disaster. There are tens of thousands of students who go far away or stay close to home and do just fine. I'm simply saying that one extreme or the other might make sense right now, but for the long run, it is probably not going to work. The best strategy is to logically and realistically evaluate your college opportunities and decide what you should do then.

I can give you an example....Ms. Moderation. Ms. Moderation was pretty mature for her age. She understood the need to balance her desire to grow as a person with her desire to stay close to her family. She also knew that going far away to school would be expensive in travel and tuition. So, what did she do? She signed up to attend State U. State U. was 80 miles down the road. Far enough to be away from home, yet close enough to come home in a little more than an hour. This gave Ms. Moderation the chance to have her own crib, meet new friends, and save money. At the same time, she had the opportunity to keep in touch with her girls back home, visit her mama whenever she wanted, and run that laundry back to the crib if she found herself a little broke.

Ms. M had a rewarding college experience, full of fun, learning and growth into an adult. She understood that college is about more than just getting an education, it's also about developing as a human being. After graduating from college, she married a nice guy that she met in college and went on to medical school. She is now living large as a high-paid physician, making over $12,000 per month and buying a new luxury car every year.

Don't think that the choices of Ms. M, Ms. I or Mr. U are the wrong ones or right ones for sure. Sometimes, it makes sense to go to school across the country, or it could also make sense to stay near home. The point is that whatever decision you make, be sure to think it through and know that you are doing it for the right reasons. Also, make sure that you know what you are getting into. If you decide to stay home and go to school, you may want to live on campus anyway, even if your parents give you the chance to stay at home. That would let you hang with your friends and establish your independence gradually, without having to go too far away. It would also put you close to the library so that you can get your studying done without distractions.

If you decide to go far away to college, make sure that you are clear and realistic about how often you are going to be able to get home. Also, try to visit the school and make sure that the environment works for you. Going far away to school is like taking a trip to Mars: once you are there, you're kinda stuck, at least for a while. Make sure that you know what the deal is before you make a snap decision.

Public vs. Private school

There is also a choice about whether or not you want to attend a public school or a private one. Some think that there is a big difference in the quality of education that you get from each type of school, but I personally think that a college education is what you make of it. Private schools tend to cost more, and also tend to be smaller, although this is not always the case. One thing about private schools is that you wouldn't have your tuition doubled just because you came from out of state, while public schools charge much higher tuition for non-state residents. But on average, private school tuition tends to be much higher than public school tuition, so they get you either way.

Since most of the public schools are tied to the state, they tend to have rules that relate to supporting the state. For example, a lot of state medical schools give first priority to students who come from the same state. Also, if the state government has a budget crunch, that usually leads to an increase in the tuition at state-sponsored universities. This can sometimes lead to state universities having an admission bias in favor of state residents.

State schools tend to admit a wider range of students, whereas private schools can sometimes be a little more selective in who they choose to admit. Also, they are allowed to have religious themes for their admission or focus on specialized interests (like Catholic or Christian schools, or schools that are all male or all female). If you are low on cash, the public state school is usually going to be your best bet. However, there are a lot of great private schools to choose from, and they might even offer you scholarship money.

Rural vs. Urban Campus

The demographics of where you attend school can be important. There are college towns that are practically owned by the university, medium-sized cities, and cities that barely know that your school is there. The kind of place you choose to do your college thing depends on your preferences as a person.

The college town tends to cater nearly everything to college students. The town is usually pretty small, and there isn't much going on when school is out. Much of the town's population also works for the university, and the local college owns a big chunk of the town's land. Once you graduate, it's not exactly the place where you want to try to stay and look for a job. The rent is usually pretty cheap in these places, since there are a lot of apartments right near campus where the landlords focus on recruiting college students to live in their buildings. The crime rate is usually pretty low, although there are exceptions. These schools seem to be pretty good at providing the kind of true-blue college atmosphere that you see in the movies.

Then, there is the medium-size town, not very big, and not very small. Even if the university is big, it doesn't absorb the entire city. There are people in the town who actually have nothing at all to do with the university. The rent is usually not much more expensive than a college town, but it depends on where you live. It's also the kind of place where you could definitely raise a family after you graduate and even find a job, but not the best kind possible. The crime rate may also be higher here than in college towns, depending on where you live.

Finally, there is the urban campus, located within a large city. Here, the campus usually has a lot more concrete and less grass than other places, although there are exceptions. In the largest cities, the rent can be sky-high, and you could find yourself paying 800 dollars per month to live in a cardboard box. There tends to be a lot going on in the city, whether school is in session or not. The crime also depends on where you live, but big cities are usually places where you have to watch your back. You want to also be careful about having too many distractions that could keep you from focusing on your education.

The type of campus you choose depends on your preferences. The key is that you make sure that you visit a lot of different schools so that you can see what you are going to get first hand. The worst feeling in the world is to arrive some place that you are going to have to be for 4 years, and then find out that you hate it. You don't want to end up in a dangerous area, or Klan country and not even know what you are dealing with!

What are you going to study in college?

Some people think that choosing a field of study is something that you absolutely, positively have to do long before you head off to college or even think about going. This couldn't be further from the truth. First, most people switch their major several times once they get to college. So, even if you rush to choose a major in advance, you are probably going to change it. Second of all, once you get to college, you are going to be exposed to careers that you never even knew existed. This is going to change your perspective a great deal, to the point that the world is not going to look the same to you as it did when you were in high school. So if you are already locked into a certain career without being open-minded, you are not going to be able to see these opportunities. Now, this doesn't mean that you shouldn't think about your major before you head to college. It just means that you should keep an open mind and not panic if you don't have a major yet. Most schools don't even allow students to start taking courses deep within their major for at least 1-2 years. That means that you have plenty of time to choose.

One mistake many students make is that they wait TOO LONG to choose a major. Believe me when I say that this is the quickest way to make sure that you are in college for 5, 6 or 7 years. I knew some people in undergrad who were so old that they started college with Jesus. You have to have some degree of focus to know where you are going. Imagine that you are driving on a trip and your goal is to land in New York City, Los Angeles or Miami within 3 weeks. And then imagine that you don't take any time to look at your map. Each morning, you just get up and drive any direction, without thinking about where you are going. Do you think that you are going to make it to one of those cities within 3 weeks? Probably not, unless you are extremely lucky. Chances are that you would end up driving all day and all night for weeks and end up just running out of gas. Life works the same way. Those who are without focus just go round and round until they run out of gas and give up. So, if you don't know where you are going, you should definitely spend some time thinking about it.

A good rule of thumb is to try choosing your major by the middle of your sophomore year. This is roughly the time when you are going to start having to deal with the classes in your major, and it is also when the college academic counselor is going to start pushing you in a certain direction. They keep their "undeclared" category for students who have not chosen a major. That is not a good group to be dumped in, since they basically make you take a bunch of classes to pass the time until you decide what you want to do. Make sure that you get out of the "Undeclared" category by the middle of your sophomore year.

Think about why you are in the major that you chose

Another thing about choosing a major before you start college is to make sure that you understand why you are choosing the field that you are going into. A lot of kids make the mistake of choosing a field just because their mother, father or Uncle Willy wants them to do it. If you think you want to be a doctor, try to write down the reasons WHY you want to become one. Is it the money? The prestige? The chance to see blood and guts all day? Because you love science? Because you want to help people? All of the above? Speaking of becoming a doctor, I wouldn't want to become one just for the money. The path to becoming a physician is rough: paved with bloody body parts, long nights, a lot of studying and very little sleep. That is a yucky path to walk just for the chance to make a little dough.

When I was in high school, I wanted to become a lawyer. I really thought that this profession was made for me. I one day realized that I didn't really want to become a lawyer. I just wanted to do it because my father said that it was what I should do, and black people are always proud when their kids become lawyers. Some lawyers make a lot of money, and they also get to dress nice and carry brief cases. People with brief cases always look more important than everybody else, and I wanted to be important. But those were the wrong reasons for me to become a lawyer, which is why I am glad that I never became one. Don't get so caught up in the glamour of a profession that you forget what the profession is really all about. Money is nice to have, but if you look hard enough, you will probably be able to find something that pays you well and still gives you a happy life. There is no feeling worse than having to get up every morning and go to a job that you hate. Even if you make a million dollars a year, that may not be enough to compensate you for the stress and unhappiness of picking a job that you don't enjoy very much.

If you think that you know what field you want to work in, go talk to people who work in the field. Try to "shadow" someone who works in your area. For example, if you would like to become an engineer, find one, introduce yourself, and ask him/her if you could follow them around for a day or two, in order to see what they do on a day-to-day basis. Perhaps you can ask if they will give you a job in their office. You may even want to consider volunteering, since everybody loves a free employee!

Be sure to pick a school that is good in your field

If you do have the fortune of knowing what major you are going to pick, be sure that the university you attend is strong in the area that you are going into. The way to find this out is to look at News Week or Business Week rankings, or just word of mouth. You can ask the professors at that school, talk to your high school counselor or any adult you might have access to in that field.

Also, make sure that the school has a strong ability to help people in your field get jobs. Some schools are good at training students to do certain types of work, but they are unable or unwilling to find jobs for them when they graduate. You want to go to a school that works hard to help its students get jobs doing what they've been trained to do. Don't take the university's word for it (since they are all going to SWEAR that they are the best in the world at job placement), try to go directly to the career placement office of that school and ask how many interviews most students in your area tend to get. Take a look at the list of companies that are interviewing at your school and which ones have interviewed in the past. Also, try to talk to graduating seniors at the school who are in your field, and professors too to find out what options are available to them when they leave. You have to do your homework on this one and do it carefully, since some recruiters will tell you anything just to get you to attend their university.

You have to dig dig dig to get the information. Don't be afraid to present the same question to a lot of different people, since all of them are going to have a different perspective to add to what you need to know. Also, try to find out what the starting salaries are for graduating students in your area (at your chosen school), and what parts of the country they are getting jobs. For example, if you are trying to get a job in California, you might want to think twice about going to school in Alabama!

Four year college vs. Technical or Community College

There are some people who think that not all students are ready to go right into a 4-year college. I personally believe that it doesn't hurt to at least try. It is a big myth that college students are smarter than everyone else. There are a lot of beer-drinking frat boys who can't count to ten who go to college mainly because that is what their parents expect from them. And guess what? They graduate! So, they end up going through life with this piece of paper that makes everybody think that they are smart, even if they are not. You don't have to be Einstein to have a place in college. You just have to believe in yourself enough to know that this is going to work for you.

Technical School

Just in case you are interested in the other options out there besides a standard 4-year college, or you feel that you are not yet ready, there are some alternatives that you can consider. First, there is technical school. Technical schools tend to take less time and teach actual trades, rather than broader educational stuff. For example, in college, you usually spend 2 years learning a lot of things that don't have much to do with your major. Some people consider this a waste of time, but there is value to this "extra stuff". This "extra stuff" makes it easier for you to do the things that are important for success in life: being able to hold an intelligent conversation, being able to read effectively and understand what you are reading. This "extra stuff" you learn in college may be what you need to impress the rich dude that you are trying to convince to buy something from you.

The good side of technical school is that you get done faster, usually in 1-2 years, and you get to hop right into the "meat" of your trade. If you are training to become a plumber, they have you plumbing right away and don't spend any time doing much else. They are also pretty good at placing students into jobs.

The downside of technical school is that it just isn't as much fun as college. There are no intramural football teams, no fraternities, no parties, no dormitories and you are not encouraged to take classes outside your field of study. The long run salary is usually not as high for technical school graduates as it is for college graduates. I know many college graduates who make over $100,000 per year, while it is hard for me to say the same about my friends who have graduated from technical school. Not that it is impossible, it's just more difficult. Also, my friends who graduated from college seem to have careers that are much more fulfilling and not nearly as physically demanding as technical school jobs. There is a difference between working construction all day and sitting at a desk in an office. Not to say that one is better than the other, but if you are not interested in work that is going to drain you physically until you are 60, you may want to try going to college.

2 – year community college

Another option would be the 2-year community college. There are some benefits to this option: first, the cost is usually lower for community college than either technical school or 4-year college. So, this is a great route to go if you don't quite have the money for college or you aren't sure what you want to do. You can take the first two years of classes at your community college, and then transfer your credits to a 4-year institution.

Second, the classes are a nice "bridge" for those who are afraid to hop right into a 4-year college. What I mean is that if you don't feel that you are ready for college just yet, community college classes tend to be a bit easier, and also start off on a lower-level than 4-year college classes. This gives the student a chance to catch up and learn a few things before they head off to college.

The downside to community colleges is that once you are done, you are expected to finish up your training at a 4-year college. The more times you transfer, the longer it usually takes for you to graduate. Although many 4-year colleges accept most of the credits of community college students, there may be a lot of classes that don't transfer and have to be taken over again. This can eat away at your time, and before you know it, you could end up spending 5-6 years in school.

The second downside is that, like technical schools, community colleges just aren't as much fun. Many of the students aren't going to be in your age group, and there aren't the same frats, dorms, and other fun stuff that colleges have. I recommend going this route only if you have a good reason. Don't go this route just because you are afraid of college or think that it is just as good as going right into a four-year institution. In my opinion, it is not.

If you decide to attend community college, do it with a very clear plan for what you want out of the future. This is your chance for a fresh start, even if you didn't do so well in high school. Making good grades at the community college level can open many doors for you when you apply to a 4-year college. Also, you may want to check in advance with the university you have in mind to ensure that they are going to accept your credits when you leave the community college. You don't want to have to take classes twice. DO NOT simply take the word of your community college when it comes to which classes are transferable. Some of these schools may tell you anything to get you to take more of their classes and spend more money. Remember, their goal is to get money out of you, whether you get educated or not. So, after checking with the community college counselor, make a phone call down to the 4-year college that you are planning to attend to get details on admission. If the class isn't going to transfer, DO NOT TAKE IT YET.

Part-time and distance learning programs

A final option that I believe should be a last resort are night, part-time or distance learning programs. I only recommend this approach if you absolutely cannot go to school full-time. Going to school full-time may be expensive, but it's worth it because you can get done faster and still make money on the side if you manage your time properly. I am not one to say that a person should not work while going to school. In fact, I think it builds character. What I am saying is that you should make the job your *second* priority, and school should be the first. There is a big difference between a student who works and a worker who is also a student. For the student, school assignments are taken care of first, and the job second. For the worker, it is the other way around: assignments get neglected and grades are low. If something goes wrong financially, this person is probably going to drop a few classes, let their grades fall and take even longer to graduate (if they ever graduate). To be honest, going this route really SUCKS. You end up spending half your life in school, and you never get the chance to get your education or make any real money. So, if you are planning to work and go to school, just make sure that you do it the right way. Don't be afraid to borrow to make more time for studying. You can pay the money off in the future without much trouble. Which would you rather have, $15,000 in loans and a $50,000 job, or no loans and a $20,000 job? I would rather make $50k.

The bottom line when it comes to choosing a school is that you should think carefully about every decision that you make. Don't step out too far, but don't be afraid to step out. If you really want to go to college and create that kind of future for yourself, don't let anyone put limitations on you. Minorities have always been limited in terms of what we are told that we can accomplish, but the truth is that you can do anything you put your mind to.

Family status and other considerations

Family is an important factor when choosing a school to attend. While the weight that you give to family is a personal decision, things like marital or family status (if you are a parent) can play a tremendous part in what you should do with your life and your time. Also, different people have different levels of family attachment.

The first thing to remember is to try not to let family define you or tell you what you need to do with your life. Your life belongs to YOU, not your mother, father, sister or brother. Therefore, you should make strong decisions that incorporate their advice, but you should make the final choice.

Family can also come in handy if one of your relatives is an alumnus of a school you are trying to attend. An alumnus of a school is someone who has graduated from that school in the past. This person might know someone at the school who can help you get admitted, or maybe this will make you eligible for certain scholarships. However, this is a long shot.

Another family consideration might be whether or not you already have children. If you don't have children at this point, then you should wait a while before starting a family. As a college graduate, you will have the rest of your life to decide if you want to get married and have kids. Trying to do all that before or during college is really a big pain in the butt. Talk about stress! Life can creep up on you when you aren't looking, so you have to make sure that you think carefully about every little step along the way.

If you happen to already have children, you want to come up with a careful plan so that you can reach your personal goals and still do a great job as a parent. The first thing to remember is that you can do it! Secondly, you may want to make sure that you have a well-defined support network so that you can get through school in a short period of time. You are probably going to be eligible for tax breaks and larger loans because you have children, use this to your advantage. Even if you have to borrow a little more, it is probably worth it to do so, since you can get through school quickly and also take care of your child in the mean time. On top of all that, your child is going to experience the long-run benefits of your education. When I was young, my mother had 2 children and worked her way through school. She didn't graduate until she was 29 years old, but her education helped plant the seeds for my own development and led to my eventually obtaining a PhD. All of her children are very well educated because of the sacrifices she made when we were young.

The main squeezie-wheezie

Another family consideration that you might want to take into account is whether or not you have a significant other nearby. That boyfriend or girlfriend is something that we can't ignore, and you are the only one who knows enough about your relationship to know where it's going. Well, one thing I have to tell you is that most of the boyfriend/girlfriend relationships that start during high school don't last through college. There may be a lot of love in the beginning, but once you get to college and see all those pretty girls and handsome guys, things start to change. Also, people grow and change during college. The first year is probably one of the greatest years of personal growth in your life, and that can affect your relationships.

Don't think that I am saying you should throw your boyfriend or girlfriend in the toilet. I am simply saying that the more realistic you can be about your decisions, the better off you are. You can keep the relationship, but don't let that keep you from getting your education, and don't let it convince you to do something stupid. Also, you should not be afraid to go away to school if that is what you want to do. If they love you, they are going to be supportive and come see you whenever they can.

Close knit families

I had a friend who won a scholarship to go to any school in the United States, but her mother didn't want her to leave home. Her mother begged her and begged her to stay in their hometown. So, she gave in to her mother's wishes and turned down the chance to go to any school in the country and atteneded a school down the street from her house. While her decision partly makes sense, the fact is that she lost a lot by being forced to stay home for no apparent reason. Leaving the nest is a natural part of your growth process as a human being. If your goal is really to help your family, then you should realize that by leaving the nest and getting out on your own, you are going to be much stronger when you decide to come back. If you never leave, you will always be handicapped and limited in what you are able to accomplish. There is an old saying: "Your ship will never get the chance to discover new lands if you are always afraid to leave the shore." Remember that.

Once you are in college.....then what?

The Freshman year

The freshman year is the most eye-opening year of college, in my opinion. This is also the year of highest risk. That is when you are in a make-or-break situation, do-or-die. The habits that you start this year are probably going to affect you and stay with you for the rest of your college career. My life changed dramatically during my freshman year of college. I was scared to death of the campus, but I just figured that I should do everything I could to make the most of my opportunity. Well, I did my best, and that semester, I made the first 4.0 grade point average of my life. After that, it was easy to get straight "A"s, but it seemed impossible before. I still can't say why it suddenly became so easy, but I can say that it changed my life forever. I guess it's like when Michael Jordan won his first NBA championship, or when Serena and Venus Williams made it to their first "all-sister" grand slam title. It took forever to get the first one, but after that, the rest came easy.

Start with the right mindset and prepare yourself for success!

When you head off to college, you have to have a mentality that is geared and designed for success. A lot of minority students enter into their first year of college either worried or intimidated by the fact that there may be no other minorities around. You shouldn't think like that. You should be proud of who you are and not afraid to walk into this situation with strength, focus and the desire to be the absolute best you can be. Racism might be everywhere, but racism cannot stop you if you really want to succeed.

Make sure that your school supplies are ready. Go to the bookstore early in the year, and find out how everything works. Also, find out where your professors' websites and resources are, and what materials they would like for you to

51

have. If you don't have a computer, find out how you can get access to one. Find out where the computer labs are, and the hours of the lab. Then find out when the least people are going to be in the lab, so that you can always get a computer first. Go meet your teachers right off the bat, introduce yourself and present yourself as an ambitious student who wants to do well in their course. Sometimes, the teacher will remember you and like you from the very beginning. They are also more likely to remember you if you attend a predominantly white institution, since minority students tend to stand out in their minds. You just have to have confidence in yourself and remember the importance of first impressions.

Next, you want to be organized. Extremely organized. The more organization you have in any situation, the less stress you experience. That's a fact. Try to get copies of the syllabus for every class as early as you can so that you can map out your way to an "A" in each class that you take. Analyze the syllabus like you're Johnny Cochran getting ready for a big case. Go through every little detail and find out EXACTLY WHAT YOU NEED TO DO TO GET AN "A" IN THAT CLASS. Do not aim for "B"s or "C"s. Do not settle for second-rate grades, you have a right to be the best. Getting straight "A"s is like having an undefeated football season: you just win one game at a time. In college, you focus on each class individually and get one "A" at a time. Before you know it, you have all "A"s. Focus on each class as if your life depended on it. Make sure that you have plenty of notepads, pens, folders and everything else to keep yourself organized. Also, try to get two planners: one for appointments, and another one for homework assignments and exams. Make a big chart on your desk that has a list of all the times and dates of the exams, quizzes and homework assignments for the entire semester. Having a big chart allows you to visualize all your classes at once and doesn't let anything surprise you. Keep going back to your calendar to remind yourself of what you have to do during the semester to stay on top of things.

Beware of those weeks where you have 2 or 3 exams at once. Such a situation requires advanced preparation, more than just working a couple of days before the test. If you have a week full of tests and you wait till the last minute to study, you are going to have a whole pack of stress and a whole bunch of bad grades to go with it. Remember the karate dude Bruce Lee? He had no problem fighting 60 dudes in one fight, but he always fought them ONE AT A TIME. If you have 3 or 4 exams during one week, you have to start at least 3 weeks before the exams so that you can conquer them one by one. If you wait till the last minute, you will be as doomed as Bruce would have been if he fought all 60 dudes at the same time. Why didn't they ever figure that one out?

Do not fall behind and find a way to get ahead

The quickest way to screw your self in college is to fall behind. Avoid this at all costs, because you will then have to work twice as hard for half the rewards. In fact, get ahead if you can. You may even want to start your studying a week or two before the start of the semester: if the textbooks for your courses are already available, get them for yourself and start reading the chapters. If you can't get the syllabus early, then go see the professor and ask him/her what chapters they are going to start with. I put my syllabus on my web page a good 3 weeks before the start of my classes, and any ambitious person could easily read every chapter for my class before the semester even begins.

Get used to the campus

The next thing you can do to save yourself time and headaches is to learn your way around campus. You don't want to compound the stress of the first day of classes by not being able to find the class you are looking for. The campus can look massive when you see it for the first time, and you are going to waste a lot of time asking people for directions who may or may not know how to give them properly.

Here's what you do: get a map of the campus and spend one hour going through it. Find out where all your classes are, and look for each one. Then, figure out where your dorm is in relation to the buildings that hold your classes. After that, go out (before the first day of class), and walk to each of your classes. Do it with a new friend, it'll be fun. Then, you can get an accurate gauge of how far your classes are from your dorm, how to get right to them, how far they are from one another, whether or not there is some elevator you have to wait for (since everybody and their mama ends up waiting for the elevator 5 minutes before class, you may want to take the steps and get some exercise). You can find all that out in advance so that nothing surprises you.

Study the map to find out where the important resources are: places to eat, libraries, computer labs, minority student offices, etc. College campuses can be amazing places, since they have a ton of resources that a lot of students don't even use. Most campuses have radio stations, places to shoot hoop, churches, all that. Whatever it is you like, a decent-size campus probably has it. A lot of campuses are nothing but little cities themselves. The best way to find out what your campus has is to read up on it all before you even get there.

Putting together a class schedule

At some point, you have to put together a schedule of the classes that you are going to take. You should choose a schedule that gives you room for flexibility and perhaps margin for error. Don't overload on classes, since you want to spend some time getting used to college. Also, make sure that you schedule your days properly. Most students don't like to have Friday classes. They suck, so avoid them if you can.   Avoiding Friday classes is tougher for Freshmen, since they don't have the same options as the older students.   Also, some majors like Chemistry and Engineering require a lot of extra lab meetings that are held on Fridays.   So, getting a free and clear Friday might be possible, maybe not.   I never liked going to school on Fridays, since that gave me the chance to rest up and start my weekend early.   Also, if I wanted to go home to visit my family, I could do that too.

Make sure that as you set your schedule, you are aware of the times of recitations, labs, etc.   Labs and recitations are the little things on the side of the class that you have to go to when you are not in the actual lecture. They are usually run by the Teaching Assistant (TA), and they are a good time to ask questions and apply what you have learned.   Try to make these extra sessions fit within the flow of your class schedule without taking you out of your way.   It really stinks to have to get up at 8 am on a Friday morning for just one stupid recitation section when you don't have another class for the rest of the day.   Your temptation to skip out on that class is going to be way too high! Avoid it if you can, but sometimes, that can be tough to arrange.

When putting together your schedule, ask yourself some questions: Am I a morning or an afternoon person? Do I want all my classes together, or do I want a break in between? How many classes do I want to take during my first semester anyway? Make sure that you put aside time between classes for eating, napping, studying, whatever. Don't try to have all your classes back to back to back without making time to rest or grab a sandwich. That kind of routine can get old real quick. My preference in college was to have no more than 3 hours of classes without a break. If I decided to have all of my classes on the same day, I would make sure that there was at least a one and a half hour break between the first 3-hour block of classes and the next class. Remember that there are going to be days when you are sick or bored and want to chill. If you have a ton of back-to-back classes that you have to go to, then you are going to be tempted to skip class. Skipping class is a bad habit to get into and a tough habit to break.

Check out the professors before you sign up for their class

Do a little research on the reputation of the professors that you are considering taking classes with. That makes a difference because there are some professors who are not going to give you nearly as much grief as their colleague down the hall who believes that all students should be beaten and tortured. I'm not joking. There are seriously some professors who are *actually offended* when students make good grades in their classes. I am not sure why, but some take pride in the fact that in their class of 200, only 5 people got "A"s. Avoid teachers like that, if you can. You want a teacher that is going to be fair and give you the grade you deserve. You don't want someone that is going to give you an easy A, since you are not going to learn anything. But you want someone that is going to give you a shot at getting the grade you deserve.

How do you find out which teachers are good and which are bad? Ask other students who have taken the class. They can probably give you a real quick feel for which teachers people like and don't like. You may want to go see the teacher, but you have to be careful, since everybody acts pretty nice when they first meet you. Also, a lot of professors don't like it when students avoid their course, so they are going to almost always encourage you to take their class. You also want to take a look at the syllabus before hand, and perhaps even take a couple of visits to their class if you happen to be on campus the semester before you take a class from them.

Don't overload during the freshman year either. Sometimes, we can be TOO ambitious. You should always shoot for the stars, but if you turn your rocket ship on too high a gas level, it's just gonna blow up. There is a saying that goes "You can try to do so much that you get nothing done". That is when a person does 2% of 100 different things, and gets credit for nothing. At the same time, your boy down the hall is doing just 2 or 3 things, with 1/3 of your energy level, and they are getting more credit than you are. A student taking 5 classes and getting a 3.5 GPA is going to get much more respect than another student taking 8 classes and getting a 2.7. So, just take your time with your classes and make sure that you can do them the right way.

Get good advice and get those general classes out of the way

When deciding what classes to take, get advice from more than one source. Don't rely on just one academic advisor, one parent, or one "lil homie" to tell you what classes to take. Don't even rely completely on yourself. Talk to a lot of people about what classes you should take during your freshman year, but don't let anybody make those decisions for you. Just let them provide you with enough information so that you can make an informed decision for yourself.

My opinion is that you want to take as many of the general university courses as you possibly can during your freshman year. There seem to be a million goofball requirements, cross-cultural this, global that, whatever. These are the classes that every school requires all of their students to take so they can be well-rounded individuals. Unfortunately, many white schools don't require their students to study minorities, so you may want to take a couple of African-American, Native American or Hispanic studies courses along the way. Get all of your general classes out of the way early for three reasons. First, you probably have to, since most schools don't even let you take classes in your major until all the general requirements are done. Second, the general classes don't commit you to any particular major, just in case you decide to switch. Most college students switch majors at least 2 or 3 times during their college career. Third, you don't want these little classes hovering over your head when it's time for you to graduate. It can be a pain sitting in some freshman Art class during the last semester of your senior year, looking like somebody's grandmother. I have seen a lot of students get stuck in that position.

Register as early as you possibly can

Another thing that some Freshmen don't know is that because you are new, you are usually put right at the bottom of the registration list. That means that you get to sign up for your classes long after everybody else gets done picking all the good classes with the good times. So, that means you might find that all the 11:00 am classes are closed, but the 8 am and 3:30 pm sections are wide open. That doesn't mean that you can't still get some good classes on your schedule, but it does mean that you have to at least make sure you are ahead of the other freshmen. Don't be silly and register later than you are already forced to.

There are a few ways that you might be able to get around the late registration problem. First, you may want to begin your freshman year by taking classes that are meant for freshman. Sophomores and Juniors are not going to be fighting to get into these classes, so you are at less of a disadvantage. Second, I would try getting on the waiting list of certain sections. A lot of freshmen make mistakes, register for the wrong classes, drop out and change their minds. So, if you get on the waiting list early, there may be a chance for you to get into the course that you want. Finally, if there is a particular section that you really want to get into, try going to the professor and asking him/her to sign a form letting you into the class. That is a dicey approach, but you might as well ask and see what happens. Sometimes, if you are the first one to ask, they may go ahead and let you get away with it.

Make sure that you register with the big picture in mind of where you eventually want to go. Be sure that you know exactly what your program is asking from you before you are allowed to graduate. You should be thinking about these things any time you put together your class schedule, so that everything fits into your long run objectives as a student. Students who just register for stuff and don't think about where they are trying to go end up taking class after class, staying in school for a million years. Seriously, you can easily find people who seem like they have been in school since the Civil War. You have to be focused and make sure that all the little pictures fit into the big one.

Make time for something fun

The final point on making your first class schedule is to sign up for something that is fun and/or interesting. There are physical education classes, karate classes, all kinds of stuff that you can take that will give you a chance to accomplish some other goal you have that is not related to school. Do you want to lose weight? Have you always wanted to learn to cook? Do you want to know karate or get better at basketball? You can do all that, and not miss a step as far as graduating is concerned. That is because most universities offer students the chance to take general electives, which let you pick whatever class you want.

One thing you should be careful about is making sure that the elective you choose fits with your other classes. Some classes require you to go all the way across campus to the gym, and maybe even change clothes. So, don't schedule classes so close together that you have 10 minutes to travel two miles across campus, stinking like an old fish. Schedule yourself time to get home, take a shower, change clothes and maybe even get a nap before your next class. Fridays are a good time to schedule the fun extra classes, since these days are usually open.

The Freshman Beat-downs and how to deal with them: an introduction to some of the things that happen to all of us during our freshman year

The first day of class

The first day of class is really, really critical. You should be soooooo excited. This is the first day of the rest of your life.....or, maybe you could say the last day of the beginning of your life......or the day before the first day of the rest of your life that starts tomorrow....something like that. What I'm trying to say is that this day is important. Try to make it as stress free as possible and only full of happy memories. You can do this by being prepared and executing your strategies with precision. Remember: when it comes to your life, you are the fortune teller.....the choices you make today determine what kind of future you are going to create.

You should get up and out in the morning with 30 minutes of extra prep time. So, if it takes 30 minutes to get up, get ready and get to class, then you should give yourself an hour. That way you're covered in case something goes wrong. You will find that the parts of campus that were barren and empty during the weekend you moved in have suddenly become full with people that you didn't even know existed. This can make things interesting and also make it tougher to find your classes. As you begin the first day, there are many things that you have to think about in order to make your transition to college a successful one.

Watch out for oversleeping

Oversleeping sucks, especially on exam days. Oversleeping can make your day a bad one from the get-go. You hop up out of bed, realizing that the clock says 10:18 and your class started at 9:30. You are in ABSOLUTE SHOCK. You wonder how your alarm clock could have betrayed you, sneakily turning itself off in the middle of the night and making sure that there was no buzz to wake you up the next morning. Normally, you would skip out on the class, and just roll over to go back to sleep. But you have to make this particular class, because there is an important exam on this day. So, you jump out of bed, (tired as all get out because you were up late last night cramming for your test) and jump in the same drawz ("drawz": aka "underwear") you had on the night before. Showering is a luxury you cannot afford at this point, and eating isn't an option either. So, the only choice now is to head to class smelling like the raw version of something you would have eaten for breakfast. You don't get to eat any bacon, but at least you SMELL like a pig. You grab your stuff, hoping you don't forget anything (which you probably will), and you run to where ever you've got to go to catch the last 20 minutes of that test. You get to the classroom, and it feels like the whole class is staring at you. You also feel like you're the biggest fool on the planet, since the other students are turning in their exams at the same time you are walking through the door. You go over to the professor, and she also looks at you like you have two heads growing out of your neck. She is busy, so the last thing she has time to hear is some lame excuse as to why you didn't get to the test on time.

Needless to say, you probably aren't exactly feeling like you're on top of the world: you are tired, hungry, fonky (for the lay-person, "fonky" is not equivalent to "funky". "fonky" is a heightened sense of funk that occurs when you are not only unshowered, but you are wearing yesterday's drawz), and you are going to get an "F" on your exam or quiz, or so you expect. It's not a pretty picture. The stress has you sitting on the toilet for the rest of the week.

How to deal with this situation

Let's do the rewind.......start from the beginning of the day, when you first got up and realized that you and your alarm clock are not getting along. The first thing you have to realize is that this sense of horror you feel is not uncommon. It has happened to EVERYONE at least once. As you sit there staring at the alarm clock, you wonder how in the heck you were getting so deep into that dream about the sexy girl down the hall that she made you not hear the alarm clock and miss your final exam. She and your alarm clock have conspired to cheat you out of the good grade that was part of your destiny, and it really burns you up. But as you sit there, you probably want to plan and strategize; figure out how to make this situation better. There ARE ways to get around this, believe me.

Next, do not panic. Panicking does nothing to make the situation better....nothing. It only makes you feel worse than you already feel, and perhaps more likely to make a critical mistake. Don't get me wrong, this isn't exactly something that you should be HAPPY about, but it's not worth committing suicide or having a nervous break down. Also, no matter what the situation, the cooler your head, the better you are going to be able to make the right decisions to help you deal with the situation before you.

Exactly what you do next depends on who you ask. But I recommend this. While you're sitting there staring at the clock, take a second to reflect on the situation: How late am I? How important is this test? What kind of teacher am I dealing with here? Has this happened to me before (this may affect how sympathetic they are)? What options do I have in terms of taking the test at another time? What should I do now to make sure that I get out of here as soon as possible? Should I get a ride instead of taking the bus? How far away is the class?

These are a lot of questions to ask, and you can pick the ones that you want. The point is that you should take a second to think carefully about the situation before you freak out and start running around like a chicken with your head cut off. I mean, you've got time, right? Rather than waking up at 10:43, you could have kept on dreaming and got up at 10:50. So, using a few minutes to collect your self is not going to make or break the situation.

Then, after you've made a plan as to what you are going to do, execute the plan. Sometimes, the plan might involve calling the professor or TA so that you can either tell them what happened or make up some little white lie

63

that will cover your butt. I don't condone lying to your teachers (since I am one), but sometimes you gotta do what you gotta do! However, you will probably find that telling the truth will usually make everything all right.

Then, get yourself a quick shower, less than 5 minutes. You don't want to be funky or fonky, since that will only make you feel worse. Put on today's "drawz", not the ones from last night. Tie the hair up (unless you're bald), grab a little sandwich and be on your way. You can eat and think while you walk. If you have a cell, you can call that professor on your way, or you can call the professor's secretary to find out what you should do.

The thing is that professors understand that things happen to people. We are not nasty, behemoth, mean M-Fs who don't give a crap about the students.......well, some of us are, but most of us are not. Professors only act mean sometimes because they have to maintain strength and credibility in the classroom, or they will be taken advantage of. One of the ways that some professors maintain credibility is to make it completely clear that students receive no excuses at any time for any reason. Some professors make allowances before missing exams, but many do not. Imagine if you had 200 students all give you their little excuses for why they can't make the test? It would be a complete headache. Dealing with one little issue with one person is much different from dealing with one little issue apiece from 200 different people.

So, in a case where you really have a valid excuse, the professor will probably listen. If they try to tell you something like "Everyone who doesn't make this test gets an automatic zero", that's probably not true. The rights of students on nearly every campus in America give you some type of recourse for this kind of situation. It would be nice if professors like me could have that kind of power, but obviously, it's not to the benefit of the students. Don't fall for the hype. If someone says you can't make up an exam for any reason, they are most likely bullying you, since professors know the game and student's don't. You have to remember that most of your teachers have been dealing

64

with someone just like you for the past 20 years. They already know how most of you think and they know that most students are going to walk into the classroom thinking that the professor is all-powerful. None of that is true. Professors do have some power, yes. But they are not all-powerful. In fact, a professor can look really bad if the students consistently give the professor bad evaluations. They can even be fired. But this is not to say that you should try to go into the classroom and bully the professor either. We know how to hold our own. You should think of the professor as a judge in the courtroom: You don't mess with judges, but if they get out of hand, they can be overruled.

Back to the issue at hand, you overslept. The professor probably has a way out for you, and he/she may reveal it to you once you have bothered them long enough. Try to talk to them in private in their office, not in the class, where they are busy and probably a little annoyed. If you are nice enough, many of them are going to understand your situation and work something out. Just make sure that you are humble, apologetic and willing to do whatever is necessary to fix the problem at hand. After all, you were the one who messed up.

One way that some students deal with oversleeping for the exam is to not show up for the test. If you know that you are going to arrive to your 2-hour exam with only 20 minutes left, it may not make sense to come in that late. You could be putting yourself into a bad situation, because obviously, your grade is going to be crap. The scary thing is that the professor probably doesn't want to give make-up exams, so they may make you keep the crappy grade you got by only having 20 minutes to work on the test. If you can't make more than 75% of the class, You may want to bag it and call the teacher for a makeup later.

What if the teacher doesn't want to give you a make up test? That is when you exercise your rights and go see the academic ombudsman and department chair. Make sure that you read the rights that you have as a student and know what the heck you are doing. As I once heard someone say,

"You better be 100% correct, because if you are only 95% correct, they will use the bad 5% to discredit the correct 95%."

How to avoid all this in the first place

I assume that you don't want to be an intentional drama magnet while you are in college. I mean, who wants to deal with that kind of stuff if you don't have to? So, let's talk about how you can keep yourself out of the kinds of mess that can cause you to make a mess in your pants.

Every night when you go to bed, plan the next day carefully, especially the important ones. Make sure that you have your good "drawz" out, you've already taken your shower, you know what you're gonna do with your hair, all that. You may even want to put together some food for the next morning, or a plan to get some. Be prepared to get up early enough to handle all your business without rushing. Rushing only makes you feel stressed and nervous, which is the last thing you need right before an exam.

Go to bed early on exam and quiz nights, getting as many hours of sleep as you possibly can. If you can't do that, then make sure you don't get less than six hours. There is scientific evidence that says that we can't usually remember as much when we are tired. So, getting that extra two hours of sleep might help you remember some things you might otherwise forget. NEVER put yourself in a position to stay up all night, or only get a little sleep. Your exam preparation should begin several weeks before the test, not the night before. Staying up all night can put you in a tough situation, because when you are in your deep sleep, you may not be able to hear the alarm clock the next morning.

Speaking of alarm clocks, get at least two of them, even three if you want to be sure. Alarm clocks are cheap, so you can buy a bunch of them if you have to. Make sure that at least one of them runs on batteries, so that it will

66

wake you up if the electricity is out. Each clock needs to be loud enough to wake you up in the morning. Do not put any of the clocks right next to your bed, since you are going to just slap it to the floor and go right back to sleep. Put them across the room so that you have to roll out of bed and walk over to turn them off. Also, get a friend or two to make a wakeup call for you on quiz and exam days. Make sure that the phone is on with the ringer turned up loud so that you hear their call. It works to make an agreement with a friend that the person who wakes up first is going to call the other one.

If you do these things, then you should be cool in terms of getting up in time for exams, quizzes and regular classes. You may want to do this every day, but you don't have to. But this procedure is mandatory if you have an exam or quiz the next day, these are not the times to screw up! Remember: an ounce of prevention is worth a pound of cure!

Watch the Frats and Sororities

Fraternities and sororities are a very strong tradition on almost every college campus in the U.S. A lot of students have family members who also pledged, so they feel inclined to do the same when they get to college. That's all cool. BUT IT'S NOT A GOOD IDEA TO PLEDGE DURING THE FRESHMAN YEAR. This is a critical make or break year for a lot of people. If you don't work hard during the first year, then surviving in college suddenly becomes scarier than being butt-naked in the middle of Afghanistan. Remember, GETTING to college is not the same as GRADUATING from college. There are millions of people who spent one or two semesters in college, but most people never graduate. Don't put yourself in that position. Pledging takes way too much time and it can get in the way of what you came to college for in the first place. It's a nice extracurricular activity, that's it. The frats and sors aren't going anywhere, so just wait until you are in your Junior or Senior year.

I had a friend in undergrad who wanted to join a fraternity badly, and he wanted to join right away. Even though I told him that he shouldn't pledge during his first year of college, he did it anyway. He eventually graduated and did O.K., but his GPA hit rock bottom like a crack-head with no tennis shoes. He then spent the next 3 years making up for the poor academic performance of his freshman year. Luckily, he finally graduated, but his GPA was nothing close to what it would have been if he had waited before joining a fraternity. The pledging process is much too time-consuming, it interferes with classes, and some people seem to think it's OK to make you do things that are going to interfere with your ability to study. That's bull. You are in college FOR ONE THING: To get your damn education! If ANYONE tells you anything different, they are on the wrong page in the book of life. It is well within your rights to have a blast in college. Go to the movies, play the guitar, shave your head, eat raw fish, join the booty-shaker marching band, whatever floats your boat. But make sure that you get your education, and always keep education as your top priority.

Try not to work during your Freshman year

Some people have no choice but to get a job during their first year of college. That's fine. But if you are one of the students who has the fortune of not having to work during your first year, then don't do it. Getting used to college can take time, and being able to put all your energy into it will give you a great advantage. It doesn't mean that you can't work at the same time, but if you don't have to do it, then don't.

If you really need money right away, then consider getting more grants, student loans, or even borrowing money from parents or credit cards to get you through.

Also, think carefully about what you *really* need and what you *think* you need. "Needing" a lot of stuff is how folks end up with bad credit.

When you do start working, make sure that you find a job that either lets you study while you work, or is at least right on campus and will work around your schedule. Try not to work off campus if you can, even if it's for more money. Places on campus understand that students have things to do, and they are more likely to let you off work when you have a test coming up.

Try to get a major early and stay with it

The sooner you know what you are there for, the faster you can get out. If you don't have a major chosen by your freshman year, don't panic. However, you should definitely put energy into finding a major. Go around asking professors and friends what the benefits are of different majors. Go to the library and find books on the different majors. Make sure that the books are updated, so that you aren't getting information from 1982. Use the Internet to find stuff on various majors. A simple search on google.com or some other search engine with words like "choosing a major" will probably spit out a ton of links that you can use to find out everything you need to know.

Here are some questions you should ask yourself when choosing a major: How much do these people earn? What are the work hours? Do I get to travel? Is there job stability in this field? Do I like this field? What level of education do I need to have before I am able to get a decent job in this field? What is the demand for people in this field right now (i.e. are there a lot of jobs available?)? How is the demand predicted to change in the future? What are the different things that a person can do in this field with this type of educational background? You have to think of these things to be sure that you don't end up majoring in something that is going to make you unhappy in the long run. Ask all the questions, and even try to see if your school has a shadowing program for people in different fields. If they don't have one, then create one yourself: go out into the community and find someone who does what you do. Then ask if you can follow them for a day. If you offer to help them get some of their work done, they may not mind. If they say no, then ask someone else. Eventually someone is going to say "yes". Meeting this person may also lead to an internship, part-time job, or even a full time position one day. Make the best first-impression you can and then see where things go from there. Again, they may say "no", but eventually someone is going to say "yes".

Make some friends

A lot of people get to college during their first year and are as scared as they can be. It is natural to feel that way, since everyone has been in that position at some point. If you attend school in a different state, you are going to have some cliques already formed by people who are from the same town or went to the same high school. Don't let any of that bother you.

Making friends is as easy as introducing yourself to other people. The last thing you want to do is crawl up into your shell and hide. One of the great things about college is that there is always somebody for everybody. Even if you are as weird as you can be, with multi-colored hair, a thick neck and long purple boots, there is probably somebody who is gonna look at your boots and say "I love ya shoes girl!" Now, I can't guarantee that everybody has the same number of friends (if you are too weird, then it might be tough to find lots of others who are just like you), but I can say that college offers more chances for free expression than high school. There are thousands of people, and at least hundreds of other minorities that you can try to identify with. Even if you are different from someone you meet, that doesn't mean that you can't be friends and learn from one another's differences. Some of the best friendships can be formed between a black person from South Chicago and an Asian person from Southeast China. You're going to see all kinds of people with many backgrounds when you head to college. That is part of the beauty of the experience.

Stay focused and attack

The freshman year ABSOLUTELY PIVOTAL. It is when you have to be as focused and determined as you've ever been your entire life. You have to attack attack attack from day one so that you can get on top of things and dominate all through college. Think about it like running the 100-meter dash. If you don't get a good start, then it's hard to catch up. But if you come out of the starting blocks full speed, you are going to get so far ahead that everyone is going to have a hard time catching up with you!

Professors are different from the teachers that you knew in high school. Many of your professors are not going to care if you pass or fail. Some of them are going to think that because you are not white, you are PROBABLY going to fail. Don't expect much love from the profs. If you can get some love, congratulations. But you should not spend too much time being worried about whether they love you or not. Why? Because you have a more important type of love: Love for YOURSELF. If you have that, then it doesn't matter what the profs think about you. Just go into their class, get what you came for, and move on to the next class after that.

At the beginning of the semester, all the other students are tired and lazy from the summer. So, this is your chance to shine for the teacher. If you are really ambitious, read 4 or 5 chapters before the first day of class. Also, study like your life depends on it. Don't study just for the tests, study for each CLASS. That will give you a strong advantage over the other students. Reading the material in advance gives you a chance to make intelligent comments. Most teachers LOVE good class participation, and you don't have to say anything brilliant to be noticed in a favorable way. Most students are afraid to talk, so speaking up will make you stand out to the professor. At some schools, being a minority will make you stand out as it is. Use it to your advantage.

Finally, NEVER let anything discourage you. You should say to yourself from the very beginning that you are going to always do your best, no matter what happens to you. That means that if things are going good, you should continue to do your best. If things are going bad, you should continue to do your best. That should be your attitude at all times. Take it from me: If you are always giving 100%, great things are going to happen in your life.

The sophomore and junior years

Congratulations!!!!

The second year of college is about to begin. Since you have kicked so much butt during your freshman year, you move into your second year of college with all the confidence of a fat man walking into McDonald's. Life is good and you are feeling good, or so I hope you are. If you weren't too careful during your freshman year, then the second and third years might be spent mopping your face up off the floor. That is when you need to read the sections of my book on how to clean up an academic mess. But either way, you are on your way. The important thing is, no matter how good or bad things go, you can never ever quit, not in a million years. Quitting is the only way to make 100% sure that you fail. Never EVER give up on your self.

Getting yourself out of that fonky, fonky hole

If you are in the hole, here is a quick tip to get yourself out of it. First, you have to reassess your work ethic to determine if you are really a lazy butt. You have to be honest with yourself and figure out if you are really putting in the time. Do you just THINK that you are putting in the time, or are you REALLY putting in the time? A lot of students think that because they were sitting at a table for 6 hours, that they did 6 hours of studying. Some of them do 6 hours of socializing, browsing the Internet, watching TV or reading a magazine. If you think you are studying, make sure that you are really doing that and not something else. The sooner you are honest with yourself, the more control you are going to have over your academic problems. There is nothing more frustrating than to think that you are working your hardest, yet things are not working out for you.

Who do you kick it with?

Think about who you roll with. Are you kicking it with the brother who has trouble spelling his own name? Does your study partner like to smoke blunts while she's reading the physics book? Does your best friend have a double major in Q-Dog and Tequila? Don't hang with people like that. You may want to consider spending time with people who are similar to the person that you want to be. That means, find study groups and friends who are going to help you to become the person that you want to become, not hold you back and keep you from growing.

Get a tutor if you can

Consider getting a tutor. Most schools have some kind of program that is set up to make it easy for students to get tutors. They really have a lot of programs for minority students, since some schools don't think (incorrectly) that we can survive without one. Use this to your advantage. Find a way to get help in your courses, even if you have to pay for it yourself. A tutor isn't that expensive, you can usually get 1 –2 good hours each week for about 20 – 30 dollars. Also, remember that your teacher should be the first tutor that you get. You can go to their office hours or work with the TA. If you can't afford a tutor on your own, try to go in with a friend to pay for a tutor. You can at least get the person to help you get your homework done and then share the information with your friend. They can help you pay the cost. Financial setbacks can be overcome if you are creative about it.

Choose your major!

By now, you should be close to choosing a major. Remember: it's ok if you don't have a major by the start of your sophomore year, but most of your time should either be spent in a major or trying to find one. Don't be like those 10 gillion undeclared students who just wander around and wait for God to smack them upside the head with their major. It doesn't work like that. If you don't know where you are going, that is the quickest way to end up where you don't want to be. Don't screw yourself with indecision and make sure that you are always seeking direction.

If you have a set of majors that you are not sure about, choose at least one of them by the end of your sophomore year. If you want a double major, that's cool. Check to see that the classes fit together nicely. For example, a double major between computer science and social work doesn't usually fit too well, while a double major in computer science and electrical engineering might require a lot of the same classes and save you time.

If you are choosing a major, make sure that you think carefully about what the career involves at every stage. For example, if someone says "Top Accountants can earn over $250,000 per year", you have to also find out what regular accountants make, since you are probably not going to make that much as soon as you graduate. You also have to find out what accountants make who graduate from your school, since your school might be above or below the average. Next, find out what you are getting into. You may be in this field for a long time, so don't put yourself into one that you are eventually going to hate. Find a way to shadow someone in the field, and definitely get some experience, even if you have to work for free.

Find out what the job demand is in that field. Not just what it is right now, but what it is expected to be in the future. Don't go into a field that is dying, try to find one that is growing so that you know that you are going to still have a job 10 years from today. There are a lot of books that project what areas are going to gain jobs in the future, so try to check some of them out.

Find out what your school is good at. If your school has a nationally recognized engineering program, then maybe that is the major for you. But don't choose that major just because your school is good at it. You have to enjoy working in that field.

Talk to your professors about your thoughts, and maybe they can guide you into areas that you might find interesting. When I was in college, talking to my teachers taught me about fields that I knew nothing about. In fact, I never knew anything about the job that I have today until I met a nice black professor who took me under his wing. There are a lot of ways to make money doing what you love, you just have to find out what's out there.

Switching majors

If you decide to switch majors, be sure to think it through. You should not feel bad for thinking about switching majors, since students do it all the time. In fact, most students switch their major at least once while they are in college, and many switch 2 or 3 times. That is nothing to be ashamed of. What you have to watch out for is *why* you are switching your major. Some students switch majors for all the wrong reasons: they can't decide what they want to do, they took a really hard class and got traumatized, they are a little bored with their current major, so they want to try something else, etc. Those are some bad reasons to switch majors. There are a lot of ex-engineering students who were so stomped by their first Calc class that they decided to go find a major that was as far away from math as possible. They would end up doing sociology or philosophy only because they decided that they were afraid of math and hated it. The point is that if you change your major, don't do it for emotional reasons or because you are afraid. Do it because you really want to be in the field you are switching to.

If you decide to switch majors, start by asking yourself if it is because you think that your current major is too hard, or if you just really think that something else is for you. Think carefully about the consequences of your actions. Switching means that you are probably going to extend your time in college. Try to keep that from happening by finding a major that will accept the classes you have already taken. Also, make sure that you know what the program requirements are for the new major. You may find that the new requirements are harder than the old ones, or that the class you are trying to get away from is required in the new area also. Check to find out if you are going to even be ALLOWED to choose that major. If your GPA is hurting, some departments won't even let you choose their major in the first place. Just do your homework before you move forward with anything.

Stay on the straight and narrow path

Now, you're all up in the mix. You're no longer a green freshman, you're an experienced vet. You're probably taking the tougher classes of your major, and you are starting to get more and more focused in your learning process. A lot of the classes that you take during your sophomore and junior years are what they call "weed-out classes". That means that these are the classes that are designed to get people to quit and do something else. Some of these classes can beat you so bad that you wonder how you got past Kindergarten. But the key is to remember that when you are at your best, nothing can stop you. This is the time to buckle down.

You have to explain to yourself very clearly: "No matter how good or bad things are going, dropping out of school is NOT an option". That means that you are there to stay, and you are not going to fall for any of the traps that others have fallen into. Most people that drop out of college and never finish don't PLAN for things to go that way. They make one little decision after another and suddenly, their ability to finish school is completely gone. It reminds me of a trip to the beach that I took with my family when I was 14 years old. I got into a little raft and set sail into the cold water. I inched out and inched out, not worrying about how far I was getting from the shore. Before I knew it, the beach was no longer close by, and I was just this little black dot way out in the ocean. Getting back was scary because now the water was cold and deep, and I couldn't even swim!

The lesson of that story is that when you inch through life, you have to think about where every step is taking you. You want to make sure that you stay focused, and keep your hands on the shore. You are there to graduate with some paper (a diploma) in your hands, and you are not going to let anything keep you from getting there. DO NOT DROP OUT OF SCHOOL FOR ANY PERIOD OF TIME FOR ANY REASON AND TRY TO KEEP A FULL COURSE LOAD AT ALL TIMES. That is how you make sure that you are continuing to move forward, never backwards or staying still.

Get your work experience!

If you are planning on getting a job after college, then you had better make sure that you get some work experience to go with it. Work experience is ABSOLUTELY CRITICAL to being prepared for the job market when you graduate. Some schools are good about helping you get the experience that you need, and some honestly just don't give a damn.

If your school gives a damn…..

If your school cares if you get a job or not, then they probably have a career center in place. This is a "middleman" for the companies that decide to come and interview at the school, where they can find students to fill their positions. They usually have a list of companies that are going to come through, along with a list of the jobs that these companies are trying to fill. You sign up for the interviews, show up in your Sunday best and nail the job from there.

Get to the career center early in the year. If you want to land a job or internship for the summer, then you need to get started in the fall. You also have to make sure that you go to any sessions the center has on interviewing skills, job searching and writing a resume. How you present yourself to potential employers is very important. You have to make sure that you are together and that you are well-prepared.

Another thing a school that gives a damn might do is hold a job fair right on campus. They will invite companies in and you can give them your contact information. Show up dressed as nicely as you can, and then give them your professionally-done resume. Also, try to get their business cards, so that you can call them later if you haven't heard anything. Don't take that "don't call us, we'll call you" reply. You have to be aggressive to land these positions.

If your school doesn't give a damn.....

If your school is not all that interested in helping you find a good internship, don't worry about it, you can do it on your own. It's just going to take some work. Remember: the main thing that you are looking for is EXPERIENCE. It doesn't have to be anything special and you don't have to get paid. You also don't have to work full-time. The important thing is that you find some way to get a meaningful job on your resume so that you can show the world that you've done something while you were in school.

With that said, you should try every resource you have to get a job. There are programs out there like INROADS (www.inroads.org) that are specifically designed to help minority students get jobs. Also, there are web resources out there, like Monster.com that have jobs listed. You could possibly apply for some of these jobs to see if you can work for the summer with these companies. Also, there are usually career fairs that you can find on the

Internet that may be held at places close to your university. It is usually worth the trip.

If worse comes to worse, then just remember what I said in the beginning: It's all about the experience. Volunteer to work for a company in your community if you need to. Just make sure that you get something out of it. They are probably going to be happy to have you around if you are asking to do things for free. But you can also get ahead by making sure that you pick a company with a strong reputation that is recognized nation-wide. Just being able to associate your name with that company can mean a lot when you search for jobs later. Also, since you are volunteering, that means that you get to pick your hours. You also get to choose what you do and do not want to do. It can be nice, especially if that means you are going to have something on your resume to show for your work.

Coops

In some fields, they ask you to do a coop, which is short for "Cooperative Learning". Usually, these jobs are for students in Engineering, where work experience is extremely important. In cooperative learning, you basically spend time off campus at a company working for them just like you're actually in the real world. This can be a good chance to get good experience, and also a chance to be a "savage for the cabbage". You make solid money on these jobs, and it gives you a break from school.

The downside of these positions is that they take you away from school, which can take you away from your focus if you are not careful. Money has a way of making people cross-eyed. Also, most of the students who coop take a little longer to graduate than others. If you don't watch your butt, this extra time can be much longer than you expect it to be.

The way to make sure that your Coop doesn't turn into a lifetime thing is to always have a plan. You may want to consider getting a Coop in the same town as your university so that you can stay in school at the same time. That way, you can kill two birds with one stone. Or, you could also make sure that you enroll in classes wherever you end up working. If you do that, check to be sure that your credits are going to transfer without a problem. Summer school is another option that students use to shorten the amount of time till graduation. Some students just work and don't go to school at all, which is fine also. The important thing is to keep your mind on track and always have a plan.

Now, you may be ready to pledge

There are a lot of folks who go down the fraternity and sorority route while they are in college. Pledging can be whatever you make of it. It can be your most wonderful dream or it can be your worst nightmare. I have seen students pledge and go on to do great things and to become great people. I have also seen people die. Death is not something that you want or deserve when you head off to college. It's certainly not what your parents want for you either.

First, you need to make sure that you don't forget what you came to school for in the first place. Some students go to college and practically major in pledging. That is the dumbest thing I've ever seen in my life! They spend all their time with their frat or sorority and even skip lots of classes for organization functions. If they were to put that same energy into their school work, they would be straight "A" students. It's not that hanging with your friends is not a cool thing to do, it's that you don't want that kind of activity to take over your entire collegiate existence.

You are in college to learn and get an education, not to pledge. So, that means that if you have any serious GPA issues, then you need to wait and try to join the grad chapter (the grad chapter is when you pledge AFTER you graduate). Pledging takes time, money and usually involves a lot of late nights, which isn't exactly going to make you ripe and fresh the next morning. A good rule of thumb is to expect that your GPA is probably going to drop a bit when you pledge. Don't take all your tough classes when you pledge, and you might even want to take a reduced course load. The worst thing in the world would be for you to have your GPA hit the skids and to not be crossed because you couldn't put the time into it. If your GPA is already struggling, then you don't need to pledge right away. That is like buying a new house when you are already two dollars away from bankruptcy.

Be ready to chunk out some "dolluhs" if you pledge. The cost of pledging can range from a couple hundred bucks to more than $1,000. If you don't have the money, you might need to save beforehand to make this happen. I don't recommend using rent money for this kind of thing, unless your new sorority sisters are going to give you a place to live for free. If the money is too much for you, then don't do it. Also, make sure that you are prepared for the other expenses that might crop up as a result of pledging, like paying for the shirts, jackets, canes, pimp hats or whatever the group likes for you to have.

Beware of Hazing

"Hazing" is a term that is used to describe an abusive form of passage that is sometimes used by organizations to make its members prove that they are worthy of joining the organization. It is also banned on nearly every college campus in the nation. Some organizations still take part in hazing for one reason or another. But this is a very dangerous type of initiation, and you need to stay away from it. If you try to join a group and you find that you are being excessively abused in some way, do not remain quiet about it. Take your story to the academic administrators or the Dean of Students IMMEDIATELY.

I had a friend who was hazed when I was in college. For some reason, he let the guys he was pledging with use his tongue for an ashtray, putting cigarettes out on his lips.

He also let them beat him until he was nearly unconscious and had to be taken to the hospital. After that, they still didn't let him join the fraternity. It was his need to be accepted by others that led him to let others beat on him in that way. Do not allow a desire to be accepted cause you to let others abuse you. You deserve better than that.

The final thing I want to mention is that if you choose to pledge, make sure that you have a strong impact on your organization. Most fraternities and sororities mention community service as one of their primary goals. However, there are some chapters that are much better at throwing parties, stepping, barking, and squealing than they are at helping the community. These organizations are powerful collections of educated people that can do a lot of good in the world with the right amount of effort. If you join one of these groups, make sure that the power is used for good, not wasted on parties and squealing. If you are smart about pledging, it can be a wonderful experience. If you are stupid about it, then it's going to really, really suck. That's as plain as it gets.

The Senior Year: Two inches from the throne

Almost there!

Congratulations! You have finally reached your last year of college. You should be extremely, extremely proud of yourself, since the majority of Americans never reach this point. You are an inch away from making some of your greatest dreams come true. You will soon see a world of opportunity open up for you. You will soon have the chance to tell other people what to do, rather than having to sit there quietly while they jump all over your nerves.

Graduating from college is one of the most powerful feelings that a person can have. You are definitely on your way. The thing is that being on your way doesn't mean that you are there yet. You have to make sure that you keep your eye on the prize and get what you came for. I don't care how smart you are.....98% of a college degree isn't worth very much, only 100% of a degree is going to get you anything. Don't find yourself looking like those 30-something year old fools who say "I am only 2 classes short of my bachelors degree." That is the DUMBEST thing I've ever heard! Why in the world a person would do 3.8 years worth of college work and then stop right at the end is beyond me. My guess is that most of those folks worked hard for 98% of the way and then let themselves get distracted toward the end. Those last second distractions can take you way off course. Don't let this happen to you.

Watch out for Senioritis

Senioritis is something that happens when students get to their senior year and start to get lazier than a pig in a pizza parlor. There is something that just shuts off, and the ability of the person to go to class, do their homework or prepare for tests is just gone. I think that part of their brain falls out of their ear. It happened to me, and my brain is still sitting on the sidewalk somewhere in Kentucky. All through college, my GPA was smoking like a cigarette in a house fire. I was rolling with a 3.9 grade point average…pimpin territory for sure. Well, during my senior year, when my brain fell out of my head, my stuff dropped like a brick with hemorrhoids. I am not sure what my GPA was during that last semester, and it probably wasn't that terrible compared to most. But I do know that it was MUCH WORSE than what I usually got. If I were not such a good student, I could have kept myself from graduating.

Don't let yourself lose sight of the things that you normally do. Also, do not put your career and your academic life in jeopardy by making the wrong decisions during your last year of college. This is when you have to really start preparing for your future, no question about that.

Think about your future

Right now, your mind should be in "future-mode". That means that you are thinking to yourself "Where do I want to be next year? What about the year after that? Five years from today? What about ten?" You have to have a long-range plan. Your plan should be long range because if it is not, you can end up making decisions today that will keep you from being able to make certain decisions later. If you take some dead end job just for the heck of it and skip out on graduate school, then you may find yourself stuck in a low-paid job that you hate, where going back to school to get more education is nearly impossible.

One thing you don't want to be is an "Idunno". An "Idunno" (also known as an "I-O-No") is someone who has no idea what they are going to do with their lives. When you ask them what they are going to be doing next year, they say "Idunno". I am not making fun of those people who are not sure what they are going to do, but the thing is that if you are in that category, you should be spending a lot of time trying to figure out what you are going to do. You should be asking questions, checking library references, going to the Internet, anything you can to try and figure out what in the heck you are going to do with your life. Those who have no mission or purpose in their lives are usually not the ones who are going to be the highest achievers. How can you outrun everyone else if you have no clue which direction you want to run in?

Close all your loose ends, both academic and non-academic

College graduation has more loose ends than a dude with 14 baby-mamas. There are all kinds of people you have to settle with, offices that you have to deal with, places that require you to turn in this and do that, etc. It's kind of a mess, but nothing for you to be afraid of. If you meet the situation head on and handle your business, then you are going to have a good experience during your final year of college.

Make sure that you have taken all those little classes that your department requires for you to graduate. Sit down with a counselor during the summer before your senior year and ask them "Exactly what else do I need to do to get my degree?" Don't take their word for everything, and make sure that you do your own research. You should already be strongly familiar with your program and know exactly what you have to do to get out of there.

You should also not lengthen your time at the university for any reason. There are a lot of folks who say things like "Well, I want to get that third major, or that second Bachelors degree, so I am going to stay another year." This is not the best idea in the world, mainly because after the first Bachelors degree, no one cares if you have another one. Your mama might be proud to put the extra paper on the wall, but that's where it stops. Also, second and third majors are not as big of a deal as some people might think. It's a lot like having an extra Big Mac after you already ate the whole value meal. The extra food is a waste of money, and an extra year in college just to get another major is pretty much a waste of time. When you are 40, nobody really cares how many majors you had in college. I had 3 majors and got 2 bachelors degrees, but it only gives me a good story to tell at parties.

A better way to spend that time would be to graduate and hop into graduate school. That extra year toward a Masters degree or PhD can be extremely beneficial to you. There are even some programs that have one-year Masters programs, and a person with a Masters and Bachelors is going to have much better job prospects than a person with a Bachelors degree with two majors.

Talkin bout the money – little and big financial considerations that you have to account for during your senior year

The funny thing about getting out of any kind of academic program is that it all ends up becoming sort of like a videogame. If you've done everything you have to do to beat the game, and you are strong enough to finally kill the big ol monster at the end, there is always a bunch of crap that flies at you to try to kill you right before you are done. That's when the monster becomes a super monster and a bunch of other little monsters pop out of nowhere, and all hell breaks loose on you. You spend as much energy doing that last 10% of the game as you spent during the previous 50%.

Finishing school is sort of like that too. The senior year is where everything is reconciled. You have to be settled up with your university in every way, and they are definitely gonna do all that they can to get your money as you walk out the door. Why shouldn't they? This is their last chance to make money off your butt for the rest of your life. Also, they have something that you desperately need and have invested in (your degree). They know that you are willing to do almost anything to get that piece of paper out of their hands.

That's all right though. If you are focused and keep the game tight, you will surely emerge victorious. You just have to keep your eye on the prize and make sure that you know all the rules. One of the financial issues that pop up are your student loans that you may have used to get through school. Most of the time, the financial aid office wants to do what they call an "Exit Interview", where they talk to you about your loans, let you know how much money you owe and find out where you are going to be for the next few years so they can hunt you down and jack you for your paycheck if they have to.

Make sure that you don't blow this one off. You are about to begin your financial future, and the last thing that you want over your head is a bunch of bad credit. If you don't tell them where you are, they are going to send letters to the place that they *think* you are, and even though you are not going to be there, they are going to assume that you are just ignoring them. Don't do that, it's not a good idea. You are going to be forced to deal with the situation at some point, and when you finally do, it's going to be pretty darn messy. I have friends who ignored their exit interview and student loans and were never able to go to graduate school because the university would not release their transcripts. A lot of jobs require your transcripts before you can get certified or hired. If you owe the school money, they are not going to release anything to you, ever again. You might think that you will never need to go back and get anything from them, but you will be surprised. You also would be surprised how all the interest, penalties, fees, and creepy-crawly costs can turn that little $400 baby into a $1700 behemoth. It took me years to learn that lesson (wait: did I just tell on myself?).

Another financial issue that pops up during graduation are those little costs here and there that you have to pay to get out of there: cap and gown, class ring, graduation fee, pre-graduation get-you-before-you-get-out fee, the funky-fee, the dirty sock -fee, the stanky-bugar-and-pig-feet fee, the list goes on and on. Just joking. Only about two of those fees are real (the stanky-bugar and dirty sock fee), but there are a lot of others that come up out of nowhere and smack you right upside the head. If you are not ready for all these costs, then the senior year can be a pain in the butt.

Try to put yourself into a position where you can cover these costs and still be ok. You may want to get a part-time job, or ask to borrow money from family members. Also, you should have a few hundred dollars saved up so that you can pay for things when they surprise you. For example, interviewing for jobs or applying to graduate school costs money, and you also have all the normal costs of school, like food and textbooks.

The last thing that you want to remember about senior year finances is to pay back ANYTHING AND EVERYTHING you owe the school before you leave: library fees, late fees, registration fees, phone bills, parking tickets, whatever. Make sure that you owe them NOTHING when your last semester comes around. If you owe them money, they are going to make your life a living hell by not allowing you to get the things that you need to graduate. Take it from someone who learned all this first hand. What is also funny is that sometimes, you can owe money for quite a while before they tell you anything. You might have some outstanding parking tickets or a university phone bill that you forgot about, but it might come into play to keep you from graduating.

A good way to find out what you owe is to simply call the place that you pay tuition and ask them if there is anything outstanding under your name. This office might be called the bursar's office, the fees and accounts office, or something like that. We can just call them "the money people". So, call the money people and ask them if you owe anything. Do this at the start of your last semester so that you can make sure you are good to go on graduation.

Learn the rules of engagement

Graduation usually has a bunch of fine print and little rules that no one knows about. Some schools are good about telling you everything you need to know, some are not. Protect yourself by learning everything that you need to know in order to ensure that you can get out of that place. There are typically a ton of deadlines that are very early in the semester for those who want to get out by the end of the semester. Do not miss those deadlines, for they can keep you in school longer than you want to be. You should also find out about the necessary paperwork in advance so that you can have it turned in on time.

Hunting for a job

Obviously, when you leave college, you have to have a plan for the future. Don't think of graduation as the end of anything. Think of it as the beginning and the time for you to look forward to the rest of your life and your career. You may consider going right to work after college. Although I recommend going to graduate school, I can say that sometimes, going right to work is ok too. But the thing is that going right to work means that you have to be prepared. You want to have a job waiting for you when you graduate. You do NOT want to end up selling shoes or working in a grocery store with a college diploma stuck up your butt. If you plan and prepare, you can find yourself walking right into a solid gig. If you don't plan and prepare, you are going to end up in a hole of disgruntlement, as you flip burgers angrily and snarl at the customer who told you to clean her baby's milkshake off the floor.

Keep the big picture in mind when you go out there and start working. Think about where you want to be in 10 years, and whether your current job fits into this picture. Also, try to figure out if additional education and training are necessary for you to reach your goals. Don't get yourself trapped.

To get ready for the job market, you should begin searching during the fall semester of your senior year. That is when the hiring sprees are taking place at most schools.

Your school may not have a lot of companies coming through and interviewing, but do all that you can to be first in line to get those interviews that do come by. You can do this by getting in good with your school's placement office.

The good thing about the placement office is that they also have seminars on resume writing and interviewing skills. Go to all of them and participate fully. Learn everything about everything when it comes to interviewing and impressing potential employers with what they want to hear. The things that you think work during interviews may not be what they are looking for, and it might even make you look a little silly and immature. For example, there are certain types of clothing that they consider too liberal, or certain things that you don't want to say during an interview. Learn all of that.

Keep your resume tight. Update it about once every 3 months, and keep adding to it: organizations that you've joined, additional work experience you've attained or any awards you have received. Keep it updated so that you can be ready for any opportunity that might emerge.

Get some business cards for yourself. It might seem a little silly now, but it will serve you well in the long run. This will help you stand out from your peers and make you look more impressive to those who are checking you out. You might also want to get a website together that describes you and your professional ambitions. It should be somewhat professionally done and not have anything silly on it (i.e. links to naked women or sloppy grammar). This is yet another way that people can find out about you.

If your school's career center doesn't have a lot of options, then consider going to local career fairs. That is another good place to get your resume circulated. There are also job search sites all over the Internet, like www.monster.com, and a few others. They can be helpful when it comes to finding employment.

Consider starting your own business

One thing about minorities is that we are not always very quick to consider starting our own company. Yes, that is tough to do, but as they say, "Necessity is the mother of invention." Sometimes, we find ourselves without any type of financial support: there are no jobs, and there is no one that we can turn to for help if we need it. If you find yourself in that situation, then starting a company may be right for you.

If you do think about starting your own business, start off small. Remember: all you have to do is make enough money to pay your rent, your bills and a few other things, at least in the beginning. After you reach that goal, you can start aiming for more. So, we may be talking about something as small as $2,000 per month in the beginning. Finding a way to make that money may be as simple as buying something in one place and selling it in another. For example, if you have friends who love makeup and jewelry, maybe you can buy them cheap and sell them to your friends. All people you know represent a potential market if you have the right product.

If you decide to start a company and get incorporated, then make sure that you read a book on this process and go into it with your eyes open. Also, set a list of goals, and make sure you are clear on exactly what it is that you want to accomplish. You don't have to start a major corporation to be financially self-sufficient.

Be careful about dead end careers

When you do go job hunting, be smart. Don't just take any position because it seems nice right now. You can sometimes end up in a job that is a dead end for you, with no salary growth, no prospects for the future, and no chances for promotion. Try to watch out for these things when interviewing with companies and researching the positions you are applying for. A good way to think about this would be to factor in future chances for promotion when considering a job. So, if there are two jobs, and the one that has great promotion possibilities is paying a little less, you may want to pass up the money now for a chance to have more money in the future. Also, you may have to take one job today in order to break into another job later. For example, if you have to take a low-paying job as an office assistant in order to get a higher position in the music industry, it may be worth the gamble for you.

There are times when students can't get jobs in the areas in which their education is focused. That is nothing to worry about. Bad things happen sometimes, but you can't allow a temporary problem to keep you permanently out of the field that you believe you were meant to go into. In fact, a big chunk of students end up in the same boat as you do. The economy changes all the time, and so do certain industries. If you can't get into your field right away, then continue to wait and try sending resumes to the companies you would like to work for. Until then, keep the job that you have, and gain experience.

Go get it!

The main thing about the senior year is that this is a year for planning, thinking and preparing for the future. You want to move forward with a strong determination and focus that is going to carry you to the doorstep of your goals and dreams. Before you begin a long journey, you must have a map and you must also have a tank of gas. That tank of gas is your spiritual energy and motivation to succeed. Fill your tank up, and if it runs out, find a way to fill it back up again. If you are focused and learn the terrain, you can do just about anything.

What do you do with the summers?

There are some silly and old-fashioned stereotypes that people hold onto when it comes to their image of what a college student is supposed to do during the summer. Some people think that you are supposed to go to your parents' house, maybe get a job in a grocery store and pick your nose till school starts in the fall. That is one of the DUMBEST things you can do with your time.

Time is money, and the summers are a valuable chance for you to do things that are going to make life easier in the long run. Also, if you don't do good things with your summers to prepare yourself for the competition, you may find yourself left behind by your peers when it comes time to get a job.

The TOP PRIORITY for yourself during the summer should be to find an internship that will give you some valuable work experience to drop on your resume. This work experience doesn't guarantee you a job, but not having the experience will surely guarantee that you WON'T have a job. Getting a good internship after your freshman year is a bit tough. That is when you should consider doing something else, like going to summer school and volunteering for a company. All you want is the chance to associate your name with a strong company, and that can mean a lot for you in the long-run.

There are programs such as INROADS (www.inroads.com - mentioned earlier in the book) that help minority students get internships. You also want to check with your career center to try to find something. Start looking in the fall, since these jobs are usually gone by the spring. But if you don't have something by spring, that doesn't mean that you shouldn't keep trying. The summers should be planned well in advance, not at the last minute. Make your arrangements and never let yourself get caught in the group of students that have no idea what they are going to be doing for the summer.

If you can't find an internship that is suitable, then at least go to summer school. Try to go to school at the same university that you attend during the fall and spring, not at the community college at home or some other place. Transferring your credits back will be a pain. Also, if you are going to school in your hometown, there may be distractions that throw you off track.

Going to summer school is a great option because it can help you get that much closer to graduation. Those tough classes that you might have been afraid to take during the year are not going to seem so scary, since summer school can sometimes be easier than the regular school year. Also, you can get that double or triple major you might have wanted. Summer school is just flat out fun, believe it or not. I had a lot of fun in summer school, and I am still not sure why. I guess it was because I was kicking it with my friends, meeting girls and building my future, all at the same time.

Another great option for the summer are study abroad programs. Many universities have opportunities for you to leave the country for at least 4 – 6 weeks and take classes in another culture. These can be great experiences, and they also have a wonderful and powerful effect on your resume. One professor friend of mine said "When you have worked or gone to school overseas, potential employers don't look at you the same as they would have if you had not. They see a certain type of sophistication on your resume that makes you more attractive to them." I recommend going overseas, since American students usually don't get a chance to see what the rest of the world has to offer. You won't regret it.

If you can't find anything else to do during the summer that is going to build your future, then at least get a summer job. Try to find something that you can add to your resume, and that will also help you pay for school. This way, you are not only making money during the summer, but you are also creating opportunities for yourself in the future. Wasting your time with some goofy job that you could have gotten in high school only gives you a tiny paycheck today and does nothing for your future.

If you have to go home, remember that things have changed

If you are going to go home for the summer, be careful. There is something strange about going home during college, like you're walking back in time or something. You are a little different from the environment that you came from, and the people seem to have changed in odd ways. You are going to have friends from high school who aren't doing the same stuff they used to do, and may be doing things on a worse level than before: the guy who used to be on the football team with you is now a drug dealer, the girl you used to kick it with has 2.5 baby-daddies, the lil homie that you were in home room with is now living with his mama, playing videogames all day.

These mentalities are poison. If you have friends that are doing negative things, and that is what you hang around all the time, eventually, you are going to be pulled in that same direction. People share spiritual energy through their mentalities, and these things are eventually going to affect you. It's like putting a bowl of hot soup in the freezer. Some of the ice in the freezer might melt, but eventually, the soup is going to be cold. If you have been away at college, working hard and becoming something better than you were before, you are like the hot soup. You are being heated up and filled with lots of motivation and positive energy that is going to guide you through your life. But when you get home, you are going to find a lot of friends who are like that ice in the freezer. They may not understand or appreciate what you are or what you've gone through, and they may have lifestyles that don't match your own. All friendships have a reason and a season, and what is sad is that some friendships are outgrown over time. Sticking around the same old people just because you grew up with them can be harmful and even deadly. I know many a person who is now six feet under, mainly because of who they were associated with.

When choosing who you want to be associated with on a regular basis, don't feel like you have to get rid of your old friends. Keep them if that is what you want to do, but respect yourself enough to let them know that you have changed, and that the negative stuff doesn't interest you. Make yourself a leader, not a follower. Also, try to find some friends who are doing the same things you are doing. In fact, don't pick people who are just like you, pick people who are what *you would like to become.*

Ins and outs of college (once you get in, how in the hell do you get out?)

I. Tips for the "Get out Quick" student (GOQ)

GOQ 1: draw the map and know the path

Once you get to college, you are probably going to find out what everyone else has known all along. It's fun! The thing is that you have to make absolutely sure that you don't let the fun take over your life and cause you to fail. You have to stay focused from the time you get there, and you should be sure to know what you have to do to get out. Here are some general things that every college student should know.

First, from the day you get to college, try to draw a map from where you are right then to where you want to be in 4 years. That means you have to sit down with an academic counselor and get their help in putting together a plan so that you can get done before you turn 40. This sounds simple, but a lot of students go through college without a single bonified clue of where they are going. They just sort of graduate on accident. I can tell you this right now: most good things in your life are not going to happen by accident. Most good things are planned. There is that old saying "You don't plan to fail, you fail to plan." That means that nobody *wants* bad things to happen to them, but they don't take precautions to make sure that only good things happen. I don't plan to die in a car wreck, I just fail to put on my seat belt. In that case, I haven't created the failure, but I was stupid enough to leave the door open for bad things to happen.

If you can't get an academic counselor to help you put together your program, just do it yourself. Every university has an ACADEMIC BULLETIN. This is a book that contains all the information about all the different majors, and what classes you have to take to graduate with that particular degree. Get a copy of one of these books *three months before you even set foot on that campus.* Read every nook and cranny of the section that describes your department and your major. If you haven't picked a major yet, then read everything about every major that you are thinking about picking. This book is important because you can make sure that nothing surprises you later on down the road. Also, most schools have plenty of on-line information about every single major they offer and what the requirements are. If you can't buy a book you can hold, go to the Internet and print out what they've got. It will pay off in the long run.

GOQ 2: Get those tough classes out of the way and don't procrastinate!

Another problem that some students run into when they are in college is that they keep avoiding certain classes that are tough to get into and find themselves stuck during their last year trying to get into that one class or two that is only offered every other semester, or is always full. These are the classes that you should get out of the way as early as possible! Also, don't back away from a class that you are afraid of. A lot of students end up having a fear of, say, an algebra class, and then they keep passing it up every single semester. They ultimately find out that the classes they have to take in their senior year all require them to have taken algebra already! If you haven't taken the first class that is required, you can't take the second. It's like trying to get to a star without going past the moon, or like trying to take the fifth bite of your dinner when you haven't even taken the first one. It's not possible. Procrastination is a bad thing, don't do it.

GOQ 3: Don't waste too much time on extra majors and degrees

The next thing that the *get out quick* student knows is that you don't waste an extra year of college trying to get a double or triple major, or that second Bachelors degree. Sometimes it's worth it, but most of the time, it's not. Most jobs or graduate schools don't care if you have a second or third major or if you have more than one degree. They only want to see that paper in your hand so that they know you went to college and finished.

GOQ 4: Summer school is your friend

The *get out quick* student also knows that summer school is a good way to knock out a lot of the requirements for graduation. Now, if you have a good internship lined up, then forget about going to summer school, at least not full-time (although it's not impossible if you are disciplined and focused). But if you've got the time, summer school is some good sheeyat! (Sheeyat would be slang for "shit". That is a translation for those who are not familiar with the way an excited brother with ADD (Attention Deficit Disorder) – such as myself- might want to communicate. Also, since it's not appropriate to write the word "shit" in a book like this, I am going to leave the word "shit" off these pages and not use it here- funny, huh?). Back to summer school. Basically, you can kill almost an entire semester of stuff during one summer, which leaves you plenty of time for error or just chillin during the regular school year.

Another good thing about summer school is that in some universities, it can be easier than regular school. You can take the same killer Advance Microcosmic

Poleyeuropeanitical Post-humous Bioclavature class during the summer and it is sometimes much easier than it is during the regular school year. I am not sure why the classes are sometimes easier during the summer. Maybe the professors are just more relaxed, or maybe it's because the professors are all on vacation and they are paying their assistants to teach the class. I have no idea. I only know that at a lot of schools, the best time to take the hardest classes on your schedule is during the summer.

GOQ 5: Don't waste your time taking unnecessary junk

The last thing that the *get out quick* student remembers is not to waste too much time taking unnecessary classes. I'm not trying to say that those extra classes are not good for you, because they are. Most colleges require what are called "electives", just so that you can take all that EXTRA CRAP. Also, college is pretty much full of EXTRA CRAP, since that is what the first two years are for. But there are two things you should remember about the EXTRA CRAP: It's definitely good for you. Knowing all that EXTRA CRAP gives you plenty of EXTRA CRAP to talk about during business meetings, and all that special OTHER CRAP that you are going to deal with in the future. I mean, if you never study anything except computers, then all you can talk about are computers. But think about it like this: most of the time, you are not selling computers to another computer expert/geek who only wants to talk about computers. You are going to be selling to some regular person who went to college, who is going to want to talk about EXTRA CRAP that has nothing to do with computers. That is what you have to be prepared for.

The second thing you need to know about the EXTRA CRAP is that it can waste your time and keep you in college for the rest of your life! Some students get to college and have no focus at all. They take whatever classes they are in the mood for that semester, and then they never ever graduate in a million years. You DO NOT want to be one of those people, unless you're rollin like the Rockafellars. That EXTRA CRAP can put you behind so far that you will be sittin in class right next to your great grand kids' baby-daddies.

If you want to make room for the EXTRA CRAP, then remember that this is what the electives are for. Universities make a lot of room for all the EXTRA CRAP that you can handle. Take a lot of EXTRA CRAP if you want to, but only take it when it is UNIVERSITY-SANCTIONED CRAP, which means that it is an ELECTIVE.

Academic Butt-whoopin 101 (AAW for those with uncensored minds!)

Handle your business

Ok, you are chillin in college, you have a plan, and you know where you are going. You are a soldier on a mission, ready to tear apart anything that gets between you and the BMW sedan you are going to buy in 6 years. You want to conquer this college thing and do whatever you can to make sure that you create the best life that you possibly can for yourself in the long run. What do you do next?

First, we should start in the classroom. There are two things you should know right now about Academic Butt Whoopin (I call it AAW, and those with enough imagination know what I am talking about!): First, you don't have to be a genius to do it. You have to just be a man or woman who knows what they want and is not afraid to step in there and take it. You have to be a person who does not let things get in the way of their goals, and one who conquers all obstacles that get in their way. You have to be a person who is not afraid to work, sacrifice, kick-scratch-bite-claw-stomp to get to the top of your dreams, no matter what ANYBODY IN THE WORLD HAS TO SAY. That is what it takes. As a college professor, I have seen a million and one stories about people who came to college thinking that they were going to dominate college just because they dominated high school, only to falter in the first semester. But I've also seen a lot of cases where people come to college on a No-Bull mission and blow everybody else out the water. You have to have a No-Bull mission. That is the first lesson of AAW.

The second lesson about AAW is that it pays off in the long run. You can find yourself in a great position that will pay off for the rest of your life if you subscribe to AAW early in your freshman year. You get the first pick on jobs that recruit on campus, you get chosen first for a lot of scholarships, you can get into any graduate school in the country, the list goes on and on. There are a lot of good things that come with AAW, so I recommend it completely to anybody who wants it.

107

AAW 1: Get a book on study skills and come up with a study plan

Now, lets start a conversation on how a person like you can go to college and dominate till ya pants fall off. The first thing I would do is to buy a book on studying and study skills. You've sort of already done that, since you are reading this page right now. But another book won't hurt, since I definitely don't know everything (a lot of people would say I don't know anything, but they can kiss my butt). Don't get anything too dull, just something that goes through some techniques you can use to help you study. Choose the one that is right for you, and don't think that every strategy you read about is going to work for you. Different things work for different people.

After you've learned some rules for good studying, develop a study plan that you like. Keep your mind open, since you may decide to change it as you learn better ways to do things, but try to stick with what you put together. Also, review your study rules every day to make sure that you keep these rules at the front of your brain. Remember: this is a day-to-day venture. Even the best of us have our off days. You should have a belief that even if you falter, you will get right back on track. Don't be afraid of failing or coming up short. If you are setting challenging goals, you will sometimes fail. The key is to make sure that if you are not reaching your goals, then you change your attack and get closer to those goals every time. Some goals take years to achieve, but you have to keep trying. If you never give up, then you will never fail.

AAW 2: Jam, don't cram

Make sure that you don't get fooled by the fact that a lot of college classes only have one test per month, with no homework. No homework might sound like a great thing, and it is. However, that doesn't mean that you don't have to study. You see, there may not be any homework, but that test at the end of the month is probably going to be a WHOPPER. This also means that more of your grade depends on these exams, so you don't want to blow it. The key is to spread your studying out. DO NOT CRAM. Cramming is a stupid habit that usually leads to bad results. I've seen a million and one students who've come to me over the years, swearing that they stayed up all night studying for my test, only to get an "F" on it. The reason that cramming doesn't work is because a) you are trying to get too much into your brain all at once. Your mind is going to forget most of the junk that you're trying to stuff into it, and b) you don't remember nearly as much when you are sleepy as you do when you are well rested. Cramming is silly, don't do it.

Another way to get on top of the studying game is to learn the right kind of cramming. Let's call it Jammin. See, cramming is not a bad thing if it's done in the right way. A smart student doesn't cram right before the next test, she crams right AFTER the previous one. Jammin means that as soon as the last test is over, you start reading the chapters for the next test. You read and read and read and read and read until your eyes fall out, just like you would if you were cramming. Then, you've got two legs up on the rest of the class. You know everything there is to know about the subject before the teacher even teaches it! You get to look smarter than everybody, since you know the answers and they don't. Teachers are impressed by that kind of thing, at least I am. Also, if you do not understand everything that you read in the book, you get to hear it a second and third time from the teacher. You are ready for any pop quizzes that come up, all that. Remember: Jam, don't cram.

AAW 3: Control your study environment

When you find yourself trying to get your work done, start by making sure that you set yourself up to succeed, not to fail. Studying in the dorm room is a good way to set your self up for failure. Dorm rooms are cramped, loud and full of all kinds of distractions. Even the roaches want to come up and have a conversation. You might be well intended, but if are planning to do most of your studying in the dorm room, you might as well go ahead and call your teacher and ask for your F in advance. The TV is there, the bed is there, the fridge is there, the Play Station is there, there is noise all over the place, and all your best homies are right down the hall. DON'T BE STUPID.

Also, studying in groups with friends is a dicey kinda thing to do too, since it's hard to study with a group of people without talking. You see, studying can sometimes be BORING. When something is BORING, that means that you are naturally going to want to do something else. You might want to talk about the game that was on last night, about the big-booty princess at the table next to you, or whatever. The LAST thing you want to be talking about is that thermo-nucleic-polydynamic-osmophoric compound in your chemistry book that is both confusing and really yucky to look at. Now, I'm not saying that studying in groups is always a bad thing. In fact, it can sometimes be a good thing. There may be people who are smarter than you who can teach you a few things. Also, you might be working on a project where you have to work in groups. Those situations can work, but you have to carefully choose who you work with. Don't work with somebody just because they're your homie. There's a time for friends and a time for work; sometimes friends and work don't mix. You might have a real good friend who may even be kind of smart, but if they can't keep their concentration or their mouth shut, then that is not the person for you to go studying with. Also, if YOU are the one who can't keep your mouth shut, then you need to stay by yourself.

The best way to study good and hard is to find a special place in the library that is well lit and really, really quiet. Then, go to that place and stay for a very long time every day of the week. It might be tough at first, but after you do it for a while, your butt will eventually stick to the seat. The way the brain works is that when you first start working, it's a little tough, but after you've done it for a while, you start to enjoy it more and more. The hours eventually go by like minutes. Working in groups can also be beneficial, as long as you work with people who are going to make you better. Sometimes, having a good study partner who is knowledgeable, focused and quiet can really help you. Make sure that anyone you roll with in the study room is one of those people.

AAW 5: Study tricks for the true academic pimp

I am going to talk about a few more study tricks that I've learned along the way. One thing that I learned had to do with how to manage my time. There is NOTHING wrong with going to parties, having fun, or doing all kinds of social stuff. The only thing you have to remember is the idea of BALANCE. That means, take care of your business before you go have fun. Most students who flunk out of college might have happened to go to a lot of parties, but the parties were not the reason they flunked out. They flunked out because they didn't take care of business first, almost like eating your vegetables before you eat dessert. Dessert doesn't make you unhealthy or fat, it's when you eat too much dessert with no vegetables or exercise that you get into trouble. BALANCE is one of the keys to success in college.

So, let's say that you want to go to the step show at 8 o'clock Saturday night. Then, what you could do is get up at 8 am…..no, wait, that's kinda early. If you want to get up that early, you can, but let's start with something easier to deal with: 10:30 am. I'll leave 8:30 am for the true Academic Pimps. Ok, then you have to brush the gold teeth, eat some cheerios and get your "hair did". Let's say that takes a couple of hours. Then, you decide that you want to keep your high GPA, so you plan to study. Well, how do you do it? DO NOT sit at the kitchen table and get to work. Take your butt right to the library and find that isolated spot I told you about and work from there. Remember: ANYTHING is better than trying to study in your dorm room: The library, at McDonald's, in the middle of the street, or even butt-naked in a cornfield. But whatever you do, DO NOT study in your dorm room!

So, let's say that you sit down in the cornfield (or the library, whatever you choose) at 12:30 pm. You can work till about 6:30 and cover 6 hours of studying on a Saturday afternoon and still get back in plenty of time for the step show. So, here you've had plenty of sleep, plenty of time to get ready, and plenty of time to have fun at the step show, and you've still cleared 6 hours of studying that day. You can do even more on Sunday, since there is a lot less to do that night. This 6 hours of work on a Saturday afternoon is more than most of your friends are going to get done the whole weekend, since they will probably spend the day wasting their time.

Time Management 101

One of the biggest keys to doing what you want to do is <u>managing your time</u>. You would be surprised to see how much time you have in a week if you really were to sit and think about it. What if I said to you that I expect you to study no less than 7 hours a day, 7 days a week (49 hours a week)? I am not saying that this is what you should do, I am just putting it out there. Would you think I was crazy if I said that this would not take up a lot of your time, and that you would still have plenty of time for parties? Let's see.

Every day is 24 hours long. There are 7 days in a week. That gives you 168 hours per week that you have in your Time Bank Account (TBA). Let's think of every hour as being worth one million dollars, so you're living it up like the rapper, P Diddy (If you don't like his music, you can call him P Doody). So you have $168M in your account. Let's say that you spend $8M every day on sleeping, adding up to $56M total for the week. That leaves you $112M in your TBA to do whatever you have to do. Let's also say that you spend $2M every day getting ready for school, eating, taking a shower, or whatever. That is $14M per week, leaving you with $98M. Let's then say that you are taking 5 college classes, with each class meeting 3 hours a week. That is another $15M that you have to give up. What's left? $83 million, or 83 hours

So, if I said that you should study 49 hours a week (which would probably be enough to get someone a very solid GPA), then you would still have a ton of time to go to parties, visit your girlfriend, whatever. To be exact, you would have 34 hours left, which is almost as much time as people spend on a full time job (actually, it is a little less than 5 hours a day, plenty of time to go to parties and watch BET). So, a person who manages their time intelligently can go to every single party, go to all kinds of movies and do whatever they want and still get a 4.0.

Don't believe me? Here it is in a chart for you to see:

MANAGING TIME AND HANDLIN YOUR BUSINESS		
Total hours in a week	24 hrs per day x 7 days per week	168
Sleep	8 hours per day x 7 days per week	-56
Washin ya ass	2 hours per day x 7 days per week	-14
Classes	3 hours per day x 5 days per week	-15
Studying	7 hours per day x 7 days per week	-49
Time to getcha freak on!		34

The key thing to remember is that TIME IS MONEY. You have to think of your time the same way that you think about the dollars in your pocket. I'm not saying that you can't waste some time, but you just have to make sure that you are aware of how much you have and what you are doing with it. A good way to start getting on the study tip is to keep a time sheet. On the sheet, you should list the date and the number of hours that you spend studying each day. You should only record high quality study hours, not the time that you spend chillin, going to eat, or talking to friends when you are SUPPOSED to be studying. I mean, the time that you are actually spending doing work. At the end of each day, you should look at that sheet and figure out how much work you are REALLY doing, rather than how much you THINK you are doing. You see, some people think that they are working hard, when really they are not. In their minds, they are studying 6 hours a day, when in reality, they are studying 2 hours a day and screwing around the rest. That's bull.

Another tip for good studying and time management is to always keep a book with you wherever you go. You don't have to have all your books, just keep a bag that has at least one book in it, a pad and something to write with. The thing is that you never know when you are going to be stuck in line at the grocery store, sitting in McDonald's waiting for your girlfriend to pick you up, or whatever. You would be surprised how much of our lives are wasted doing that kind of stuff. Also, get a good pair of earplugs to go with the book. Keep the earplugs with you at all times, so that you can easily filter out the noise of whatever place you are in.

Managing the trips home for the weekend

If you go home on the weekends, manage your time there too. Don't plan on spending all your time studying, since that would make for a terrible trip. But don't plan on just throwing away an entire 48 hours. Remember: time is money. But time is more valuable than money, because money can be replaced......TIME CANNOT. No matter how hard you work, you will never be 20 years old again. Make the most of your time.

If you have an exam coming up that week, I would be careful about leaving town. You probably need to be at school so that you can be fully prepared. But then again, if you've been jamming and not cramming, you will have the free time that you need to be able to go home. If you do not have an exam coming up, then going home is all right. But don't plan on wasting all your time, because you don't want to have a big pile of crap waiting for you when you get back. BALANCE IS THE KEY. Rather than wasting the entire 48 hours doing nothing and looking around for something to do, cut about 2 –3 hours out each morning for studying. That could be a time where you go to a quiet place and get done with your homework or studying to get ready for the next week. If you work on homework from 9 – 12 on both Saturday and Sunday, then you have from 12 noon onward to do whatever you want. 10 – 14 hours of "kickin-it time" is enough for anybody.

What I am telling you here about time management is not rocket science. It is just organized common sense. Just like with alcohol, food, or exercise, everything should be done with moderation. Going home and wasting the entire 48 hours and then having a ton of work waiting for you Sunday night is NOT moderation. Going to parties and drinking till you puke is NOT moderation. Working 24 hours a day, 7 days a week is NOT moderation. Keep balance in your life, and you will be in great shape.

Class room butt-kicking (CRAK)

(What do the letters "crak" stand for? Use your imagination!)

I use an acronym for Classroom Butt-Kicking, CRAK (hmmm, there is an "A" where the "B" should be. I wonder what that means?) This will make it easy for you to remember, since everybody has CRAK if they want to have it. If you are ever in doubt about how to dominate your classes, then always commit to your CRAK and you will be just fine! You can think about CRAK as cracking the door open to greatness. You can think of it as getting off the crack of your butt to make things happen. You can think of it as "fiending" for success like a crack head with $3 in his pocket. Whatever floats your boat. The bottom line is that you should think of these strategies as ways to clear your path and control your own destiny. Why should someone else control YOUR destiny? If someone else controls your destiny, wouldn't it be called "Their destiny" instead of yours?

CRAK 1: Always be front and center

Another way to get on top of your GPA is to do some damage in the classroom. The first thing you should remember when you go to the classroom is that where you sit makes a HUGE difference. It can affect what your teacher thinks about you and it can also affect how much information you absorb from the class you are taking. If you are a minority student at a predominantly white school, chances are that your professor is already going to notice you anyway. So, you might as well use it to your advantage. When you go to class, you should sit *very close to the front row, right in the middle*. This will make the professor take notice of you, and since you are going to be prepared for every class, he/she is going to be more likely to notice how prepared you are. Sitting in the back corner of the room might seem comfortable, but really, you're messing yourself up.

117

CRAK 2: Always be prepared for class

The second CRAK rule is that you should never go to class unprepared. There are two elements to classroom preparation: *pre-class preparation and post-class review.* Pre-class preparation means that you should read the chapter that is going to be covered BEFORE the teacher covers the material, not after. If you haven't read the material in advance, it may seem confusing and take some time to absorb. It's hard to ask questions when you are confused, since the information is rolling in at a fast clip and you are barely able to write it down, let alone absorb it. But if you've read the stuff before hand, then it is going to be your SECOND time seeing it. This means that instead of spending all your time panicking and writing, you can spend your time thinking and reflecting on what the teacher is talking about. You will also find it easier to come up with good questions to ask that will help you understand the material better. It won't be the first time that you've seen the stuff, so it will make more sense to you than everyone else.

Post-class review means that after every lecture, you should try to go over the notes that you just received. Try to do this as soon as possible after you have finished the day's class. The stuff will still be fresh in your brain, so you are more likely to remember it. You will find that a half hour of post-class review can make up for a lot of studying later on.

CRAK 3: Go see the teacher!

Next, make sure that you *always* go see your teacher during their office hours. Every professor has office hours every week, which is a time where students can ask questions. I have office hours, and the only time I get a lot of visits is when my students have an exam the next day. That is the WORST time to come see me, because I have too many people trying to see me already. The best time to go see your professor is right after the previous test, or during the time between exams. You should also go see them during exam week, just in case they are available.

Here are some reasons why I think that it's important to go see the teacher:

1) You can get specialized attention and help with your work. Tutors are expensive. But what most people don't realize is that you can get a lot of free tutoring from your professor if you go see them.

2) The teacher is more likely to think you are working hard if they see your face. That is stupid, but true. Most teachers end up thinking that the hardest working students are the ones in their office saying "Whew! I just read that chapter 8,000 times and I also did this and did that and did that….." For some reason, teachers fall for that crap, so you have to know the game too.

3) Teachers sometimes let the little secrets for the exams slip out during their office hours. A lot of times, when you are in the teacher's face right before the test, they might tell you some things about the test that other students don't get to hear. For example, you might say "Professor Watkins, I was looking over this stuff in section 3 of chapter 5 and….." Now, while I may not say anything, there may be other times that I might say "Well, don't worry too much about the stuff in that section, it's not going to be on the test." A lot of professors would much rather tell you that something isn't going to be covered on the test than to spend 20 minutes discussing concepts that don't matter.

4) The number of visits can make a big difference at grade time. Many times, if a student is on the edge between one grade or the next, the number of visits that the student has made to the

teacher's office can push that person over the hump. If the professor knows you as a person and not just a name on a piece of paper, they are usually much more sympathetic when assigning final grades. But the key is that they have to know you as a hard working student. Most professors are not going to reward or forgive laziness.

5) Getting to know your professors on a personal level can be very helpful when it is time to come back and get letters of recommendation. They remember you and know that you were a good student, even if it was a couple of years back. You see, it might mean something to you that you earned an "A" in Dr. So-in-so's class, but you have to remember: that person has hundreds of students every year, and there is NO WAY IN THE WORLD that they are going to remember every single one of them. You have to find ways to differentiate yourself, so that later on, when you come back for a letter of recommendation, they won't have to write something stupid like "I had Billy Bob in my class 3 years ago. I guess he is smart because he got an "A" in my class". That kind of letter doesn't impress graduate schools or potential employers.

I recommend going to see your teacher 1-2 times per week. Just make regular rounds and see all of them. Consider yourself to be a doctor making house calls. The more they see your face, the easier they are going to be on you in the long run.

CRAK 4: DO NOT miss class

Missing class is a bad habit to get into. It may seem like you don't have to be there, but before you know it, you've missed a few pop quizzes, fallen behind in the lectures, dropped a couple of homework assignments, or missed out when the teacher changed the date of the test. Don't let that happen to you! The best way to avoid these problems is to understand that even if you don't think that going to class helps you very much, you should be there anyway.

A lot of teachers like to punish those who miss class by giving pop quizzes on the days that they know most people are going to miss. Some teachers simply lower the grade of those students who are not there. They may not list this on the syllabus, but that could be what they are doing. If you haven't been in class, there is NO WAY you are going to get any sympathy if your final grade is not what you need it to be. Attending class is kind of like visiting your teacher during office hours. Even if you are studying hard, they are going to assume that you are being lazy if you are not in class every day. So, by doing all of your studying at home and not showing your face, you are putting yourself in a very risky position. When you are a minority, they are most likely going to notice that you are gone. At white schools people of color stand out like a cockroach in vanilla ice cream.

CRAK 5: Remember: Quality, not speed

The last part of being a true academic pimp is to make sure that you remember that overloading yourself with classes may not be the best thing to do. Sometimes, we can get in a major rush to graduate, and find ourselves really digging to get as many classes in as we possibly can. College is about QUALITY, not speed. If you graduate from college in 4 or 5 years with a high GPA, that is much more impressive to an employer than if you graduated quickly with a GPA that was in the toilet.

When I taught math a few years ago, I met a student who was 17 years old and finishing college. Obviously, he was a genius, since he graduated from high school at the age of 14 or something like that. However, because he worked so hard to get done with college so fast, his GPA was crap. Also, he was going to a very mediocre state university, and he didn't do so hot in my class. He was clearly gifted, considering that he was 4 years younger than everybody else in the class. That doesn't matter when the grades are given out. If he had, say, waited to go to college at 18 like everybody else, then he would have been that much smarter than the rest of the pack, and instead of going to an average school, he could have gone to Harvard or Yale. His GPA would have been higher, and he probably would have gotten a few more dates with girls (I mean, honestly, how many 15 and 16 year old dudes do *YOU* know who can get dates on a college campus?).

Most of us are not in the same category as this guy that I am talking about. But a lot of students get it in their heads that they are going to take a ton of classes every semester so that they can graduate a semester or two early. I am not saying that you shouldn't try to graduate early if you can, but you have to be smart about it. Each semester, you should take a full, healthy course load, but only take as many classes as you can comfortably kick butt in. That is how you get that high GPA, and that is how you pave a nice road that you can travel for the rest of your life.

How to ace your exams

I can't guarantee that what I tell you will help you ace all of your exams, but I can guarantee that it will help. Obviously, the tests are very important in college. They are more important than they were in high school because there is usually less homework to outweigh the tests when your grade is calculated. This is not something to be afraid of, it's just requires a change in the way you approach your courses.

The weeks before the exam

You should always have a carefully drawn up calendar of all the major tests, projects and quizzes that you have for the entire semester. Put everything for every class on the same calendar so that you can see how all these things relate to one another. You may find that you have 3 exams within a two-day period, or two exams and a quiz on the same day. You need to be prepared for that, and waiting till the last minute to get prepared is going to beat you into the ground and set you up for a lot of stress and failure.

Keep two calendars: a standard planner, maybe something that you even keep on the computer, and a big calendar that you can put on your desk or on your wall. That way, the stuff is all up in your face long before the test day is on your lap. Make this calendar at the beginning of the semester, right when you get your syllabus in hand. Don't delay on this, it's very important. In order to conquer something that is coming at you, you have to know when it is coming.

Do your cramming early, not late

Another thing that you have to do is start cramming early. Right after the previous test, go ahead and figure out what you need to learn for the next test (remember "Jamming", not "cramming"). Knowing that you have to understand 4 chapters over the next month is much less intimidating than knowing that you have to learn those same 4 chapters two days before the exam. Go ahead and start reading the material, and get ahead in your class so that when the test day arrives, you are ready to go. You can understand things a lot better when you have been reading them all along than when you are trying to learn them all at the very end.

Try to get copies of the old tests and talk to the professor

There are a lot of lazy professors out there who have no problem giving the same test over and over again. Students eventually catch onto this and start studying the old exams to get ready for the next one. If you know that old exams are circulating out there somewhere, find them and study them. You have to do this to make sure that you are on even keel with the students who do have access to the old tests.

Also, go talk to the professor and TA several times before the exam. You would be surprised what information you can get out of them by talking with them. Usually, they will at least give you hints on what you can expect from the test. They may also give you extra brownie points because they see you working hard everyday. It is worth it.

Getting ready for the exam

Getting prepared for a college test can be a bit stressful. However, it is more stressful to be unprepared, since you have to deal with the pain of taking a test on stuff that you don't understand, and you also have to deal with the crappy grade that you get afterward. So, think of this stress as your chance to get rid of stress later on, and maybe even create some good feelings when you get your test back.

If you are smart, you will know that being ready means that you have to begin preparation as much as one month ahead of time. Waiting until the last minute is the best way to ensure that bad things are going to happen. If you are confident and do what you have to do, then you are going to be in great shape.

Get the right mental and emotional attitude

Attitude is everything. A bad attitude can take the best situation and make it into the worst. A good attitude can take the worst situation and make it into the best. Be sure that when you are getting ready for your exams, you tell yourself "I will succeed, as long as I prepare properly." Don't do stupid things. Don't try to get ready for the test the day before you take it. Don't try to come see the teacher the day of the exam and expect to receive help. Don't miss a stack of classes and then expect to be caught up with everyone else. If you have the right attitude and do what you are supposed to do, then good things are going to happen.

Clear out your schedule

If you have some big exams coming up, make sure that you have cleared enough time for yourself to study. If you are an athlete, make your coaches aware that you have this test coming up and are going to need some extra time to prepare. If you have a job, check your schedule, and take a few days off. Don't put anything on your calendar for the week before and the week during the time that you have the exam. It's like making a beautiful piece of art: you can't paint the thing if the canvass is cluttered up. You need a clean slate to create a masterpiece.

Go to all the review sessions

Many instructors and Teaching Assistants are going to hold review sessions for every exam. This is a time when you can go see them and get extra help for the test. You should take full advantage of these sessions, since your well-prepared classmates are going to do the same. Come prepared to ask a lot of questions, and don't leave the room until you are clear on what they are telling you. But you have to help them out by making sure that you've done your reading in advance. If you are not equipped to understand what they are telling you, then everyone is going to be very frustrated.

If your teacher has offered you the right to make appointments (rather than going to set office hours), then make one. This will give you the chance to have some one-on-one time during exam week. Come prepared with lots of questions, they do not want anyone to waste their time. These individuals are incredibly busy.

Your final prep

Your final prep for a given exam should not be stress-ridden. You should already have done the hard part, keeping up with everything as you went along. The homework assignments and reading should put you in a position where you only have to fine-tune the things that you already know in order to do well on the test. This should NOT be the time where you are learning the material for the first time! Think about it: you have been given almost two months worth of stuff, and you are learning it all in one week? That doesn't add up. How can you expect to do well under those conditions? College exams are not designed for you to learn everything in one week. That is why we give you 3 or 4 weeks to get ready.

A lot of college students like to play "the catch up game". That is where the student lets things get way ahead of them, and they then try to get caught up before the test. Sometimes this works, most of the time, it doesn't. This approach is way too risky and you are setting yourself up to be seriously screwed. If you want to have an advantage over the other students, get out of this game. Play the "stay ahead" game instead. That is where you get ahead and make sure you stay there until the next exam. You will be head and shoulders above everyone else, and this element of maturity will take you a long way. Winners are hungry to stay on top, and losers are only concerned with staying off the bottom. You are a winner, if you choose to be one.

The last few days before the exam, you should be going over all the critical topics. If your teacher has given you a review sheet, then go through the material on the sheet. If he/she has given you hints and clues during class, go through those first. Go through the class notes carefully, and make sure that you understand those. If there are problems you are going to have to solve, be sure to practice the problems that your teacher has considered important. Also, if there are old tests, go through those also. You want to fully pre-empt everything that might be on the exam.

Most college classes can be broken into at most 3 components: the reading, any problems you might have to solve or things you have to write, and class notes. You have to attend class to get the notes, the reading should have been done outside of class, and problems (if any) should have been done in the homework assignments given by your teacher. Make sure that you hit all areas of a class, and are not strong in just one or two areas. I have had many students over the years who only study the class notes, and then get body slammed when I give a test that asks questions that are right out of the book. Beware of that age-old tactic and do whatever the professor thinks you need to do to deserve an "A" in the course.

The day before the test

The day before the test is not some ultra-bionic, super-duper cramfest. A cramfest is nothing but an opportunity to put yourself in the insane asylum. Don't put that kind of pressure on yourself. Some people end up drinking eight gallons of coffee, taking No-Doze and looking like dopehead zombies on the way back to the cemetery. Don't be one of these people! You should have already done everything you need in order to do well on the test, and this is a day for rest, focus and going through the notes casually to make sure that you've hit all the major points.

Another bad bad bad idea is to get up a few hours before the test to study. If you have a morning test, your night should be for resting. Fatigue makes you forget things, and you don't want to forget whatever it is that you have learned. A well-rested person who remembers 90% of what they've studied is better than a sleep-deprived person who can only remember 50%. The only time you might want to consider studying the hours before the test is if you've put yourself really far behind, and you've also had some sleep the night before. If you find yourself in that situation, deal with it as best you can. But you should never put yourself in that situation again.

Find out where the test is being held. Teachers will sometimes hold exams in larger rooms so that they can accommodate all the students. The location of the test may change, and the last thing you want to do is show up to the wrong place. You may even want to find a buddy to go to the test site with so that the two of you can exchange information and help one another out.

The morning of…..

The morning of the test, make sure that you get up on time. You should have at least two alarm clocks (preferably 3, since they are cheap), and at least one that doesn't plug into the wall. Life is always going to give you excuses to fail, and the last thing your teacher gives a crap about is that your electricity went out and caused you to oversleep. I mentioned this in an earlier section of the book.

Don't eat too much that morning, but eat enough that you won't be hungry. A banana, a bowl of cereal or whatever will do. Stay away from heavy things, like pancakes, since that will put you to sleep and make you feel like you are 8 months pregnant. Also, stay away from stimulants like coffee, caffeine pills, etc. It will only make you nervous.

Make sure (you should actually do this the night before) you have all the stuff you need to take the test: paper, pens, pencils, calculators, whatever. The goal is to take care of everything in advance, so that the ONLY thing you have to think about is the test.

Plan to get to the test 15 – 20 minutes early. You want to be able to get a good seat, and get comfortable with the environment before you start the exam. There is something about being relaxed and comfortable in our surroundings that makes us perform better on exams. Find a seat near the front of the room so that you can ask questions easily. Make especially sure that you are not sitting next to someone who might cheat or make you look bad by asking you questions during the test. You don't need that kind of drama in your life.

When you begin the test

First of all, always keep a positive attitude. Remember that attitude is everything. Just be confident that your preparation is going to guide you. If you are relaxed enough, the knowledge will just flow from your brain like an old lady with diarrhea. Also, make sure that you ask the teacher any clarifying questions before you start the exam, as well as during the exam. You must be clear on every little detail.

Before you begin the test, look it over and figure out how much work you have to do in the time that is allotted. If there are problems or questions that require quick attention, hit them early. You should hit the questions that have the most points the fastest. The worst feeling in the world is to spend all your time on questions that don't mean anything, and then have to rush through the ones that are most valuable. Before you begin, take a deep breath and relax yourself. If you are religious, say a short prayer. Whatever it takes to get comfortable, that is what you need to do.

Use all the time you have available, be neat and check your work

Try to use all the time that you are allotted to complete the test or quiz. If you are given an hour but the test only takes 30 minutes, you should spend another 30 minutes going through your answers and making sure that you did everything right. It is a terrible feeling to lose test points over something stupid. You may want to hop right up and leave when you are done, but you may regret this decision later on.

If you don't think you know the answer to a question, make sure that you spend a lot of time thinking about it. NEVER LEAVE THE ANSWER BLANK. If a teacher gives partial credit on questions, leaving the answer blank gives them no leeway to give you anything for your work. That is a good way to give your self a terrible score. Rushing, in general, is not good on important exams. You would be amazed at how much insight we can gain on things by just thinking about them for a while. When I was a Masters student in mathematics, I learned the art of thinking carefully. We would get some problems to do at the beginning of the week, and I would have no clue what the answer was at the time that I received the problem. However, after mulling over things for the entire week, the answer would come to me. So, thinking through things is a good way to go.

Be neat on your work. You must remember that your professor has to go over a ton of tests just like yours. They are going to be tired and irritable when reading through a bunch of essays, short answers and multiple-choice questions. You want it to be as easy as possible for them to figure out what you know and what you are trying to say. Imagine if you go to a website to buy a product. If you find a web page that is sloppy, the links don't work, it takes a long time to download and you can't find what you are looking for, how are you going to feel? Are you more likely to buy the product? No! Well, that is the way the teacher feels then they are grading your test. The silliest thing in the world is when a student comes back with their test after it's been graded and says "My answer was here, on the back of the page, at the bottom, next to all this scribble, but you didn't give me credit for it." If the teacher misses it, it's partly your fault for not putting the answer in clear sight and circled in bold ink so that the teacher can see what you are trying to say. Also, the work should be organized so that they can follow what you are doing and give you all the partial credit that you deserve.

When it's over

When the test is done, it's done. Turn the thing in and go on with your life. Your grade is what it is, and worrying about it is only going to make you more stressed out. Find something fun and relaxing to do, like sleeping or going to see a movie. The test will be there for you when you get back.

When you get the exam back from the teacher, make sure that you go over your questions and answers to find out what you did wrong. Also, try to get a copy of the solutions so that you will be ready for the final exam. Schedule a meeting with your instructor so that they can give you their insights on what you need to do in order to make your grade even better on the next exam. They will be impressed that you are concerned and working hard to do better.

You also want to check for mistakes. Professors are human, and they can screw up too. You might be able to dig out some partial credit. Just be respectful in the way that you bring up the errors. Don't bring your issues up in class, since this can really tick the professor off something terrible.

Finally, start thinking about the next test. This is the best time for you to reflect on what you want to do in the future, since you are fresh with emotion from the score you just got back. Hopefully, you are excited and enthusiastic about future exams because your last performance was great. You may also be burning mad because you didn't do what you needed to do. If you didn't do well, it's because you need to approach the exam differently. The worst statement in the world is to say "I did everything I needed to do, and I still got an F". Making that statement, you are throwing in the towel and giving up on yourself. You are also placing the blame and responsibility on someone else for your shortcomings. This is not the way to go through life. You must take responsibility for everything that happens to you, even if someone else had something to do with it. If you do find yourself in an embarrassing situation, just pick your face up off the floor and come back charging harder.

This is the time to start jamming, not cramming. Find out what your next exam is going to cover, and start reading that stuff NOW! Make it a point that you are going to be so far ahead of the class and on top of things at such an amazing level, that you are going to blow them out of the water. That is the attitude you want to have, and that is the attitude of an academic champion.

How to handle a dispute with a prof

It's sad to say this, but there are times when the wonderful, loving, caring relationship between the student and the professor gets a little messy. This is when the professor does something that doesn't make sense to you, or maybe isn't fair. It can also be a time when there is just a breakdown of understanding between each of you that needs to be resolved.

These are tough situations to judge, because there may be times when YOU are the one that is wrong. You may get a "C" when you thought you should have gotten a B-minus, or maybe your grade for a given test was in the toilet.

The first thing you should do is self-reflect. Ask yourself if you did what you needed to do in order to get the grade that you think you deserved. One of the important aspects of maturity is learning to take responsibility for the things that happen to us. It is human nature to take responsibility for the good things, but we do not always want to take responsibility for the bad things. Don't get yourself caught up in that situation. If you got a bad grade, or even put yourself into a position to get a bad grade because you did not work as hard as you could have, you have no one to blame but yourself. Do not hold the teacher responsible if you played a strong role in the grade that you received. This is part of growing up, and the last thing you want to do is spend your life as someone who is constantly blaming the world for your disappointments.

There are times when THE PROFESSOR is actually the one that is responsible for the problems that have been encountered. This is when you may have to go after their butts. But don't go crazy right away; be civil and professional as you approach the situation. Remember, you catch more flies with honey than vinegar, but if the fly won't take the honey, you may have to break the honey bottle upside the fly's head.

134

Types of disputes you can have with a professor

There are some serious issues you can have with professors, and some that are not so serious. Racism, sexism, sexual or other types of harassment are not to be tolerated from anyone for any reason. Most professors and teaching assistants are too professional to do something that stupid. They are going to treat you with at least the baseline amount of respect. But sometimes, someone may do something that is out of line. If this kind of thing happens, you must immediately alert someone who can help you handle the situation. If you are still in the professor's class when you report the incident, then you may want to make the report anonymously or wait until the semester is over.

Most of the time, professor disputes involve grades: the student got a grade they didn't think they deserved or the student was punished for missing a test or quiz. Most of these situations can be avoided if you keep your stuff tight in the first place. Don't miss a lot of classes, don't let yourself fall behind in your work, and don't go into your exams unprepared. If you are not proficient in the way you do things, then no one is going to believe you when you try to complain to outside authorities. The student who has consistently made bad grades all semester and missed a ton of classes is not going to be respected when something wrong really happens to them. The same thing would happen if you were a consistent criminal and charged with a crime you did not commit. How many people would believe you then? It's not fair, but that's just life.

The professional way to handle things if you are wronged on an exam

It is amazing how many students out there do not know their rights. For some reason, a lot of people think that professors are all-powerful and can't be touched. It is true that some professors have a lot of power, but everyone can be touched if you hit the right spot. So, when you find yourself in a dispute with a professor, you just have to find his/her "spot" so that you can get what you want. Now, this doesn't mean that you attack straight up with everything you've got, it means that you carefully assess the situation, put together a battle plan, and then execute your plan to precision.

The first thing you should do is make sure that you know what the students' rights and responsibilities are. Every school has a list, and it is probably somewhere on the Internet. Calling the admissions office is also a good way to get a copy of the list. This list (or some other like it) will probably tell you something about how to handle disputes with professors.

Next, you have to think clearly about what it is that happened to you and why you were wronged. You have to know EXACTLY where the strength lies in your argument, since most professors do not like to make corrections on exams. If they were to give in to everyone who complained about something, they would go crazy. Go over your exam (or whatever it is) carefully to figure out what the professor did wrong and why they should fix it.

Do not bring your problem up during class! Professors are human too, and they can feel bombarded by students if the entire class ends up complaining at the same time. You may address a legitimate grip, and the next thing you know, everybody in class has something to say. The natural human tendency in this situation is to shut down and defend. You don't want the teacher to get into defensive mode, because you will never get what you came for. The best time to talk to the professor about a grade or exam is in private and in person.

The big disappointment - Tactics of the stoic professor

What I am telling you here does not apply to all professors. Many of them are decent individuals and really work hard to take care of the students. But there are some who are already thinking way ahead of you. They know that you will be coming before you even get there.

Let's pretend that you've got a dispute about a final grade. You went into the final exam knowing that you have a strong "B" average, and only a final exam grade purely from the depths of hell could bring your "B" into the "C" range. You feel good about the final exam, go take the sucker, and come home expecting to see your "B" when you check your grades on-line. You even told your Mama that you are going to have a "B", and you know that your GPA can be safely calculated under the assumption that you got a "B" in this class.

You get on-line to check your grade, just to make completely sure that you got the "B" that you are completely sure that you got. But nope. You see that big, ugly curly thing called a "C" in its place! What! You are boiling with anger. Your stomach is turning like you just ate an old rusty burrito with extra hot sauce. The pain is every bit as horrible as the first time you got dumped by the cute little girl in second grade. You want to cry, but the desire to kill keeps the tears from flowing out of your face. What in the world are you going to do?

The first thing to do is assess the situation. The feeling that I just described has happened to nearly every college graduate in the history of the world. There are always those times when you think that you are on top of things, and then you find out that you are not. It's just a part of life. You have to figure out what happened, where you thought you were before, and how you went from where you thought you were to the place where you actually were in the end. It is a tough process, but you can figure it out if you try.

You should first try to call or email the teacher. Be respectful, and don't immediately jump into a fight with them. Just tell them politely that you would like to see your final exam, and you would like to know how you got a "C" instead of the "B" that you thought you deserved. It could have been a mistake, and at the very least, you would like to find out what happened. This is strictly for gathering information, not for picking a fight.

Go through your exam carefully

After you've gotten a copy of your final exam, go through it and analyze it carefully. If they don't want to give it up, keep chasing the professor until you get the chance to see your test. See where you lost points, and then recalculate your final grade with all the information that you can get from your other exams and quizzes, etc. You should keep all of your assignments through the year, in case you need them as evidence to support a change in your final grade. The way the final grade is calculated should be clearly stated on the syllabus, and if it is not, then you have a right to ask your professor to explain it to you. After calculating your final grade, go through your exam and see if they made any mistakes in the grading. I'm not kidding. Professors, when going through over 100 exams, can sometimes forget to grade an entire question and cause the student to lose 20% of their points. They will almost always make a mistake on *someone's test*. Make sure that you are not that student.

After that, look at the subjective questions and see if there is any room for argument that you could have gotten more points. If you have to look at a friend's exam to compare answers, do that. This gives you extra latitude to argue when you go talk to the professor.

If you feel that you were wronged in some way

If you feel that you have been wronged in some way, try to set up a meeting with the professor. Now, let me tell you this: Sometimes, getting these meetings can be tough. Most professors are very busy people, so meeting with a student from the previous semester (that they now think is in their past) is not always at the top of their priority list. You may call, email, or drop by, and never catch up with this person. Sometimes, this is just coincidence, but other times, it's not such a coincidence. I have seen professors who tell their students "I am going to be in Europe, so I can't meet with you for another year" just to make sure that no one bothers them. They may say this because they are banking on the fact that you don't know what your rights are. It is your RIGHT to dispute your grade and get answers from your professor. They MUST give you a reply and deal with you at some point, in some way. So, DO NOT TAKE "No" FOR AN ANSWER.

If you are sending emails and making phone calls to the professor and can't find the person, then go to their secretary and find out where they are. If that doesn't work, then go to the department chair and let them know that you can't get in touch with the professor, and that they are not replying to your emails. This will get their attention, since they don't want to look bad to their colleagues. I don't recommend doing this right away, since you want to give them a few days to reply to you. But a courteous email reply shouldn't take longer than 2 – 3 days.

Remember that the department chair is "homies" with most of the professors. So, you may think that you are talking to a person who is independent of what is going on, but you are probably not. You are talking with someone who is more likely to side with another teacher than with you. Think about it: they have to work with this person forever, but you are going to be gone next year. So, why would they ruin their relationship with their good friend to make you happy? That is a sad statement, but it's true.

The professor hierarchy

It is always important to know who you are dealing with. All professors are not created equal, and there are different categories you should be aware of. The differences in professor ranking can impact how you approach them and how they respond to you. Think of it like the NBA. If someone is the star of the team and they get into trouble for doing something wrong, they are not going to catch a lot of heat. But someone that rides the bench that gets in trouble is going to be pushed right out of there. This is true not only in athletics, but in any professional discipline.

First, there are Instructors, Adjuncts, and PhD students. These people are on the very bottom of the totem pole. Many of them don't have their PhD yet, so they are not even called "doctor". They are probably the easiest to influence and the ones who are most concerned with looking bad to their colleagues. Their job performance usually depends a great deal on how well their students are satisfied, which means that they are going to listen to you if you have a complaint.

Next, there are Assistant Professors, who just got their PhDs within the last 5 or 6 years. These are the lower level professors and they also tend to worry about looking bad to their co-workers. So, if they are not replying to your emails, make sure that you let someone know after a couple of days (after you've sent at least two emails and given them 2 –3 days to reply). Unlike the Adjuncts and Instructors, their job performance is not completely based on how well they teach, but you can still have some impact if you talk to the right people.

The second and third levels of professor are the Associate Professor and the Full Professor. These are people who have tenure. "Tenure" means that the professor has been given a lifetime job with the university, and the person can't be fired unless they do something really crazy or stupid. These are the tougher professors to get to, because they have "homies" everywhere. Chances are that the Department Chair has worked with this person for years, and they may be very good friends. So, be careful about what you say to the chair, because it will probably go right back to the person that you are worried about.

If you decide to talk with the chair, that person should give you some kind of reply and will make sure that the professor gets in touch with you. If/when that time happens, make sure that you are prepared to sit down with the professor and have a meeting. Make your points firmly, but respectfully. Try to squeak out whatever grade you can, as long as you feel justified in doing so. Remember that the professor may be a little annoyed by your presence, and they have no interest in going through the trouble of changing your grade without a good reason (since there is some paperwork they have to do and they are already under a lot of pressure as it is), so make sure that you back up your points and don't take "No" for an answer when you are trying to get a meeting with your prof. The squeaky wheel gets the oil, and if you squeak enough, they are going to pay attention to you.

Here is a personal story about something that happened to me when I was an undergraduate. I had an Accounting Professor who said some things to me that were flat out racist. I was so angry about what she said that I went to the Dean of the Business School to discuss my concerns. I asked him to promise me that the conversation would be completely secret, and that he would not even mention to the professor that I came to see him. He made the bold promise that everything between us would be kept confidential, so I felt comfortable telling him everything that was on my mind.

Do you know what the dean did? He turned RIGHT AROUND and not only told the woman that I came to see him, but he also told her EVERYTHING I said! It turned out that while I thought they didn't know each other very

141

well, they had actually been friends for over 25 years. So, I was screwed from the beginning. Take a lesson from my mistake: these people are *hardly* independent from one another.

If you have to get a little "geto"

Most campuses have someone called an "Academic Ombudsman" or something similar. This is a person or people who are responsible (supposedly) for representing the rights of students and protecting/defending them. This is your "ace in the hole" in case your needs aren't being addressed by the department at hand. If the chair is not being responsive to your needs and helping you to resolve your situation, then you are going to have to go to war with them to get them to listen to you. It's sad that you have to go this far, but sometimes it happens that way.

You have to make sure that SOMEONE listens to you. Going to the Ombudsman is a great way to bring attention to your cause. This means that the department your professor is in will receive calls from people that they may not want to hear from. They will then have to arrange meetings that they do not have time for, and do things they do not want to do. If you are persistent enough, they may make a compromise with you just to get you out of their face. If that is what you can get, then take it and go on with your life.

General Academic stuff that you don't want to forget

About Academic counselors

In case you don't know, you are probably going to go through some form of academic counseling when you head off to college. The counseling basically comes in the form of someone from the university sitting down with you at the start of every semester and helping you to get on the right path and stay there. They go through the classes that you've already taken, and look at the classes you want to take. They make recommendations for you that you may or may not be forced to follow. If you are not pushed toward counseling, then get some. However, like anything else, you have to understand that counselors are as different as the days of the week. There are some counselors who really really really really care about you and want to see you succeed. They go out of their way to make sure that your life is laid out before you, and they will even consider counseling you in things that have nothing to do with school. These people are rare birds, and if you find one, you should do all you can to keep that person involved in your life for as long as you possibly can.

Then, on the other extreme, there are those counselors who just don't give a damn. They don't care if you graduate. They don't care if you die. They don't care about anything other than passing "the student cattle" through their office so that they can get their paycheck. They will tell you whatever you need to hear, as long as you will hurry up and get the hell out of their office.

Sometimes you can figure out the kind of person you are dealing with, but sometimes you can't. But you should not be concerned about how much your counselor cares about you or your education anyway, that job is up to Y-O-U. Also, you should remember that there is an advantage to having a good counselor or a bad counselor, the same way it is sometimes good to have your mother around, and sometimes it's not so good. Having your mother around might mean that you are going to have somebody cooking for you, buying you things and looking after you. But not having her around means that you have more freedom to do what you want, and you don't have somebody who is all up in ya business. So, whether or not you want to have a guide to tell you what to do depends on the situation.

Be prepared and learn to think for yourself

When you go see your counselor, you should already be prepared. You should already know everything there is to know about your program, and exactly what you want to do. NEVER let this person be the one who gives you all the information and completely determines your path. If you give someone else that much control over your life and they screw you, you can only blame yourself. If the counselor wants to show guidance, then accept the guidance. Listen to what they have to say, use that person as another avenue of valuable information that you can add to the arsenal that you've already created. NEVER make that person your only source of information.

When you go see your counselor during the second semester of your sophomore year, you should already have a major in mind. Many counselors have a ready-made plan for their "Lost students". "Lost students" are the ones who don't know what their major is going to be. Since most sophomores have already taken most of their elective and general classes, the only thing for counselors to do with lost students is to put them into even more electives and general classes. This wastes your time and it wastes a lot of money. It is not wise to be lost and then trust someone to tell you where you need to go. Remember: an idol life is the devil's playground.

Don't let your counselor pick your major for you, pick one yourself or just allow them to make suggestions. This is especially true for athletes, who usually have a ton of academic counselors, most of whom only care about the football or basketball team. Athletes, particularly minority athletes, are the people who need to be most focused and have the greatest understanding of where they want to go in life. If you don't, then the counselor will waste your time and only give you the easiest route possible. That is not good for you in the long run, I assure you.

NEVER let the counselor put limits on you and what you are capable of achieving. Sometimes, people see what we are right now, and they use that limited information to decide what we are going to be capable of for the rest of our lives. That's a stupid way to think about things. For example, if I can't read today, does that mean that I can't ever be a lawyer? No! It means that I need to learn to read first, and then I can do something else. We can sometimes be judged that way by others. If you have a weakness, you have to understand that it is going to take some hard work to get rid of the weakness (low grades, bad study habits, etc.). But NEVER let anybody, including your counselor or even your own parents, tell you that you can't accomplish certain goals with your life just because you have a weakness right now. No matter how smart a person might be, we all started out not knowing how to read or write. It only takes practice to get where you want to go.

I recall going to see my academic counselor during my sophomore year. He was a professor of Finance (just like I am today), an old white dude. He looked at my transcript and said "You have good grades, what do you want to do with yourself?" I told him that I wanted to graduate with honors and then go to graduate school at Harvard one day. He said "Well, you're probably not smart enough to go to Harvard, maybe you should pick a school that's easier for you. I mean, you *could* get into Harvard because you're black, but do you really want to do that?"

What I didn't understand that day was why he would say that to me, even though I had a 3.9 grade point average. What evidence in the world did he have to say that I wasn't smart enough to go to Harvard? I had classmates who went to Harvard, so why not me? What was saddest was that I listened to that man, and I never had the chance to go to

Harvard because I DIDN'T EVEN APPLY. I eventually went on to get my PhD at a better school than he could have ever gotten into, and I earn more money today than he has ever made in his life.

Do not ever make the same mistake that I did. Don't let anyone steal your dreams away from you, no one has that right. You can fly with the eagles if you believe you are an eagle. But you can never be an eagle if you've allowed the world to convince you that you are a duck.

The other thing to remember is that YOU are the only person who knows what is best for you and what is going to make you happy. If you are going to make a mistake or a bad decision, at least make it because you thought about it carefully, did your research and then did what YOU wanted to do, not what someone else told you to do. Ten years from now, if your life has turns out horrible because you did something that someone else told you to do, they are not going to be anywhere around to accept the blame, and they probably won't care. All they are going to say is "Sorry I told you to do that. You shouldn't have listened to me!" Now, that doesn't mean that you shouldn't listen to other people. You should take all the advice you can from people who love you and you can trust. Listen to your parents, listen to good friends, listen to counselors, and listen to older people. But don't let *anyone* make the decision for you, because it is your life not theirs.

Think about how the president of the United States makes decisions: does he make decisions alone? No. But does anyone else make the decision? No. What does he do? He listens to his trusted advisors and experts and lets all of them speak their piece. Then, he tells them to get out of the room so that he can gather all the information he's gotten and make the decision himself. That is what a wise person does when they are making a decision: they listen to everyone, but give the authority to no one. You must be like a wise King or Queen when you make the decisions for your own life. Your life is your kingdom, and you are the ruler!

A final trick to getting good advice is to get more than one counselor. You don't have to have formal counselors. Counselors can be professors from your classes or in your major, older students who have gone through your program, administrators, etc. Find ways to get good advice from different people, and ask many of them all the same questions. They are going to have different points of view because not everybody has the same experience. For example, if I were to ask 10 people "What's it like going to The University of Minnesota". There are going to be some who majored in biology, some that majored in business, some that dropped out, some who had good grades, some who had bad grades, some who had great social lives, some who were book worms, some who were in frats, etc. By talking to all these different people and getting their answer to the same question, you can look for consistency in responses, and you can also see the issue from every angle. If they all say that U. Minnesota was a great school with lots of fun things to do, then you can say to yourself "Hey, 10 people said it was a great school, so I am going to go." But remember: the final decision must be up to you.

Academic problems and how to get rid of them

As much as I really hope that your college experience is going to be perfect, there's a good chance that problems are gonna come up. That's just life. You have to remember that everything worthwhile is going to be a pain in the butt to go out and get. There is a REASON that most Americans do not have college degrees. So, to get into that exclusive group of college graduates, you are going to have to watch out for the land mines that trip other people up.

Prevention is the key

The first thing to remember is that an ounce of prevention is worth a pound of cure. Working hard from the jump is a good way to make sure that you never have to even read this section of my book. When you start college or start your next semester, make sure that you are geared up and ready to go. The only way to have serious academic problems is usually by being a lazy butt. Don't be lazy and you will at least have decent enough grades to get yourself through without too many major problems.

Never give up!!!!

The second thing to learn is that you should always keep a positive attitude. Never get down on yourself, no matter what. If you defeat yourself in your mind, then you are already losing the battle. Quitting is the absolute worst thing for you to do, and it is the only way you can GUARANTEE that you will fail.

Even if it takes you 11 years to finish college, you are still ahead of 75% of the population, since most people don't even have college degrees. Both of my parents graduated from college near their 30th birthdays, but they get to keep their college degrees with them for the rest of their lives. When you are 40 years old with a good job, making good money, no one is going to care how long it took you to graduate from college and most people won't care if you had good grades or not.

Academic Bankruptcy

Some schools have some type of "academic bankruptcy". This is sort of when you get the school to erase your transcript and let you start from scratch. Different schools have different rules for this procedure, and it may be called something other than what it is called here. But the description should be similar at most universities. This is one way to wipe the slate clean and to get on with your life.

Academic bankruptcy tends to be a double-edged sword: you lose the bad stuff, but you also lose the good stuff too. So, that means whatever credits you've earned toward your degree are now gone forever. There is no chance for you to get them back. You are ineligible for many academic awards you would have received if your new GPA happens to be very good. Also, you are going to have to pay to retake these classes again, unless you have a good financial aid package. It is like blowing up a building and starting the whole project over again. So, it's not something to be taken lightly.

I don't recommend going this route if you are past your sophomore year. You would lose way too much stuff, and you don't want to have to start all over again. However, I do recommend this strategy if you are still early in your college career and need a fresh start.

Does your school have repeat options?

Another possibility might be repeat options. This is when your school gives you the chance to retake some of the classes that you didn't do so well in and improve the grade on your transcript. Again, your school may not call them repeat options, but they probably have something like this that you can use. The university I obtained my undergraduate degree from allowed students to retake up to 3 classes, and have the original 3 grades erased from their grade point average. The old grade stayed on your transcript, but the new grade was the only one that went into your final GPA calculation.

The impact that a repeat option can have on your GPA is amazing. Here is an example: Let's say that you are a sophomore with a 2.5 GPA and you've got a D on your transcript that you want to get rid of. By changing that D to an A, your GPA could jump from 2.5 to as high as 2.7 or 2.8, depending on the school you go to and how many credit hours the class is for. If you do that 3 different times, then that could raise your GPA from 2.5 to 3.1, making a big difference.

The key to repeat options is this: First, you should pick classes to repeat that you didn't do too well in. It is better to repeat a class that you got a D or F in than one where you got a B. That is because there is a greater impact on your GPA from turning a D into an A than turning a B into an A. You are gaining because you are not only getting rid of a negative grade, you are also gaining a positive grade. It's like trading the worst player on your basketball team for the best player in the league, creating a double-whammy effect.

Second, you should pick a class that you know you can do well in the second time. For example, an English literature class is not usually the kind of class you want to repeat, since the grade is typically up to the professor's discretion. They read your work, and then *they* decide if you deserve a good grade. Math is less subjective most of the time…. a right answer is a right answer, no matter who writes it. Another reason that math is a good class to repeat is because you are going to be better at the class the second time than you were the first time around. If you take Calculus I your freshman year, and then take Calculus II your sophomore year, going back and taking Calc I again would be a piece of cake.

Third, you should choose a class with a lot of credit hours. That is because a high credit hour class has a greater impact on your GPA than a low credit hour class. That doesn't mean that you should pick a high credit hour class without thinking about the grade you are changing (i.e. whether it's a D or a B). But if you have two classes with the same grade that you know you can do better in the second time, choose the one with the most credit hours.

The next thing to think about is whether the class you repeat is in your major. Sometimes, the grade point average that you have within your major is very important when you are looking for a job. If you have a class in your major that you messed up in, you might want to repeat that class, just so that you can say that your GPA in your major is pretty high. Then, when you write your resume, you can focus on the GPA in your major, rather than your overall GPA. That is another tactic that a lot of students use to cover up bad grades that they might have earned early in their college career. For example, if your overall GPA is 2.7, but your GPA in your major is 3.2, you can simply put the 3.2 on your resume, stating that this is the GPA in your major. Many employers will only pay attention to that GPA anyway.

Find a tutor and work on your study skills

The next thing you might want to try is to find a tutor. Now, the thing about tutors is that they usually cost money. However, there are ways around this. First, going to see your teacher or teaching assistant is a good way to get free tutoring without paying a dime. You can only get this for about 2 hours per week, but make sure that you at least get your two free hours before paying any money to anyone. Also, these are the best people to get help from, since the teacher understands the class better than nearly any tutor you could possibly have.

You may want to also improve your study skills. Sometimes we think that we are working hard and doing the right things, but really, we are not. There are a lot of books out there on how to manage your time and how to study. You should buy one of them. Reading this book right now is a good start. However, I am not the only person in the world with an opinion. There are other books out there that can help you. Some of these books may come in audio form, and some may come on CD Rom. There might also be study skills classes that your school offers for students who are having problems. They are usually free, and you just have to do a little digging to find out what is available.

What you should definitely NOT do

One thing that you DO NOT want to do is take time off from school. Drop your course load if you have to, but don't think that spending a semester away from school to "find yourself" is going to make you a better student when you come back. You can find yourself during Christmas Holidays, over the summer, and when you decide to visit your parents for the weekend. Leaving school for any amount of time is not a good idea because the longer you are away from school, the easier it is to stay away. Getting away from school means that you no longer have classes to worry about, and you get the chance to just kick it for a while and chill. This lifestyle can get tempting, and you can get addicted to it. But believe me, it's bad news. I have a million friends who had a little trouble in school during their first or second year, and then went home "temporarily", only to end up staying there forever. After going home, life sort of just hopped on their backs. They found a boyfriend or girlfriend, maybe had a baby, got an apartment and new job, and before you know it, that one semester off turned into 10 years. Don't make that same mistake. There are millions of people who graduate from college, but there are millions more who have dropped out with one or two years under their belt. Getting TO college is a good first step, but it's getting THROUGH college that counts.

Cheating

I am going to say this quickly and only one time: Cheating is the absolute dumbest, most retarded and idiotic thing that you can do while you are in college. DO NOT DO IT. That is all that there is to say about it. I have no idea why students choose to cheat. Wait a second, I think I have some idea why: People cheat on tests and projects because they didn't prepare the way they should have and are in serious trouble going into the exam. They are worried about getting a failing grade, so they bend a few rules to try to get a passing grade.

I can't begin to state all the reasons that cheating is dumb. I'll start by saying that it's just not worth it. Cheating can end up getting you expelled from school. Getting expelled from a university will put a scar on your record that rivals that of most sex offenders! No school is going to want to come near you, and you are going to have a hard time getting into any reasonable graduate school or undergraduate institution. There are also going to be a lot of jobs that you no longer have access to as well.

I had a friend who wanted to get into law school so badly that she decided to cheat on her exams to make sure that she could get the 4.0 GPA that she needed in order to be admitted. She got caught eventually and ended up getting kicked out of school during the last semester of her senior year. So, she went from being a candidate for the top law schools in the country to being a college dropout. That is a long way to fall, especially over a few stupid points on an exam.

If you are not ready for a test, just take the hit for it. Cheating is probably not going to improve your score very much, and you also do not want to risk your future over something stupid. In the long run, that one bad grade you get is not going to be important anymore. But being caught cheating will haunt your record forever.

Going to graduate school?

I recommend graduate school to almost anyone. If you want to reach the highest levels in your field, either financially or in terms of status, you should have as much training in your field as you can possibly get. Now, that doesn't mean you should always go for a PhD, since that can take a long time (although the rewards are usually worth it). Most of the time though, some type of graduate school is a good long-term investment.

There are basically three components to applying for graduate school: the letters of recommendation, your transcripts, and your score on standardized tests. These are the things that can make or break you as you try to get into the program of your choice.

Your application process should start during the fall semester of your junior year. That is when you have to start getting ready to take the standardized tests so that you can get the score that you need for admission. The test you take will vary depending on the field that you enter into: Law students take the Law School Admissions Test (LSAT), Medical students take the Medical College Admissions Test (MCAT), Business students take the Graduate Management Admissions Test (GMAT), and students in Arts and Sciences take the Graduate Record Examination (GRE). Those are the big four, but there are a lot of other specialized tests for fields that lie outside of the ones that I've mentioned so far.

None of these tests are easy, but there is no such thing as getting a failing or passing grade. The score that you get is used as part of the criteria to determine whether or not the school you apply to is going to admit you. These scores can really make or break you. The tests are standardized, meaning that it's not based upon a class or things that you should already know. Most of it is based upon things that measure your ability to think problems through.

Make sure that you prepare in advance! The dumbest thing you could do when taking one of these exams is to go into the test cold-turkey. A lot of students get good scores on these tests not because they are smart, but because they know the test and know what to expect. You should make sure that you are in that category. You should spend several months preparing for the tests before you take them, and you should go through as many practice tests as you can get your hands on.

The bookstore usually has a large number of books that will prepare you for the tests that you have to take. The books are not expensive, and can be as low as $15 apiece. But the information the books contain is extremely valuable. If you really have access to a decent amount of money, there are professional courses out there that prepare you to take the test. The classes are expensive, but I recommend them if you can afford them. Also, even if you can't afford them easily, it is worth saving your money to pay for these classes, or even getting an extra student loan. The score you get on these tests can make the difference between getting into Harvard with a full ride, and having to pay your way to Stank Butt University.

Even though you won't be applying to graduate school until the beginning of your senior year, you still have to make sure that you have a test score on record by the middle or end of your Junior year. This will be one less thing for you to worry about as you scramble to get ready for graduate school during your senior year. Also, in the event that your scores are not what you want them to be, you get to take the test over again and still have plenty of time. But if you take the tests too late, you are going to have some trouble.

Component II: Letters of recommendation

Letters of recommendation are also an important component of graduate school admissions. This really matters if you are applying to schools that are tough to get into. One really bad letter can screw up the process for you in a heart-beat. A good letter or two can open a lot of doors, especially if they are written by influential people.

There are things that you can do to make sure that your letters of recommendation are on point when you apply to graduate school. First, you have to understand the nature of the college professor. They are not as smart as you think, and they are probably busier than you think. Also, you have to realize that when you take their class, you are one of several hundred students who come into and out of their life. So, unless you do something just insanely out of the ordinary, they are probably not going to remember you 3 years later when you come back asking them to write you a letter.

So, you have to help the professor out a little bit. You may already have the advantage of being a minority at a white university. That alone makes you stand out. If you happen to be an exceptional student (because you've applied some of the stuff we've talked about in this book), then that is even more power to you. But you also have to do more to make sure that they remember you FOR LIFE!

Things you can do to help your professor remember you

Having your professor remember you personally can have a nice payoff when you need a letter of recommendation. First, they would write the letter with personal emotion. When people become emotionally involved, they are going to go out of their way to be nice and help you in any way they can. If they are writing a letter for a student they barely remember, they are going to write it from a very detached perspective. You can't blame them, because they don't know you! How would you feel supporting someone that you know almost nothing about? The second benefit to having the professor remember you is that they are going to have an easier time coming up with things to say about you if they know who you are.

One way to make sure that they remember you is to not let yourself be just another face in the crowd. Go see your professors on a regular basis so that you both know one another on a personal level. After the class is over, continue to call that person or stop by and visit, at least once every semester. That way, you stand out in their mind from the other 600 students that they might have had during the past 2-3 years. Consider even taking the professor to lunch. They will be impressed and flattered that you want to spend time with them, and they will probably even pay for the food!

When you ask the professor for a letter of recommendation, be sure to give them a reminder of how you did in their class so that they know you were a good student. Also, give them a nice, professional copy of your resume so they know that you are active outside of the classroom also. The more good material you give them to write about you, the better.

Other things you should know

There are some other things that you have to think about when dealing with professors. First, you have to know that not all professors are created equal. Just like basketball players, there are some who roll with the biggest ballers, and then there are those who wobble along at the end of the bench. It's not that the lower-level professors are not smart, they are. It's just that some people have more clout than others.

Students have a hard time knowing this when they are in school. If you take a class, all that matters to you is how good of a teacher someone is, not whether or not they have some kind of national reputation. But this DOES matter to the professors who are going to be thinking about letting you into their graduate program. So, it helps your chances if you spend some time asking around the department to see which professors are the big ballers in their profession. Usually other professors know and secretaries know also. If you happen to take a class from this person, and they write you a great letter, that can carry a lot of weight.

Stay on top of those absent-minded professors!

The next thing you should remember is to stay on them! Professors are smart, but they are also very busy, and some can be downright forgetful. When you go to the professor and ask for a letter of recommendation, you should make sure that they follow through on what they say they are going to do. It's very easy for a professor to leave someone's letter sitting on their desk for 8 months. Then, by the time the letter is done and turned in, the admissions deadline has passed.

Give them about 6 weeks to finish the letter (this is another reason that it's important that you apply early, in case there are some problems). Then, after 6 weeks, start contacting them every 10 days or so to see if they've done it yet. Send them email, make phone calls or go see them, whatever it takes to get them to reply to you. NEVER leave your success or failure in the hands of another person. Most people are not going to be as concerned about your success as you are.

You can also help yourself by making it as easy as possible for the professor to get that letter done for you. Don't just hand them a form and say "Here, do this." Give them stamped, addressed envelopes so that they can easily put the letter into the envelope and mail it away when they are done. The easier you make it for them to do what you need, the more likely you are to get what you asked for.

Does your professor really like you or just pretend?

Make sure that the professor likes you before you ask them to write you a letter! This may sound silly, but I've had some students ask me for letters of recommendation who were either really bad students or didn't rub me the right way for one reason or another. I never hammered these students in their letters just because I didn't like them, but I was amazed that they thought that I liked them well enough to want to write them a letter of recommendation. The person who writes a letter for you should be the person who thinks *the most highly* of you, not someone who kinda thinks you're all right. Before you ask for a letter of recommendation, you should ask the professor how comfortable they would feel writing you a letter at all. Even if the professor does not give you the whole "up and up", they might at least give you some clues about whether or not they are going to write a good letter. A really good question to ask is "If you wrote a letter of recommendation for me, what would you be able to say that would support my admission to a graduate school?"

If you have a professor who is writing bad things about you (sometimes that happens), being able to see the letter in advance can give you a chance to "stop the bleeding" and find other professors who can write you good letters to other schools. I have seen it happen where a student thinks that a professor is writing good letters, but really he is not. Bad letters can be a major problem when you are getting rejections and have no idea why.

There is a section on most graduate school applications where the student must check a box that gives up their right to see the letter that the professor has written for them. Some professors will not write a letter if the student does not check the box and give up their right. However, some professors don't care if you check it or not. Not checking the box means that you can look at the letter later to find out what the professor is saying about you. This is another good way to protect your self from a bad situation. But the best approach overall is to check with the professor in advance to determine if they would be interested in writing a good letter.

Graduate school, in some ways, is actually *easier* than college. First, most Masters degree programs are less than 2 years, while college is 4 years. Second, you don't have to spend the first 2 years taking a bunch of stuff that doesn't interest you, like you did in college. In graduate school, your program allows you to spend all your time immersed in your own discipline. This can make things fun, or at least interesting. You learn to take your game to a higher level and learn your field unlike ever before.

The job prospects are much better also. If you are working for a company and you only have a bachelor's degree, they can treat you how they want, say what they want and do what they want to you. They do all that because they know that you have no place else to go. Additional education gives you more leverage and ability to negotiate with employers. The unemployment rate is usually much lower for people with Masters degrees, and they also make between $500,000 and $1 Million more in their lifetimes than people with just a bachelors degree.

Things to take care of before heading to graduate school

If you are planning to go to graduate school, you should have taken care of a few things during your Junior year. If you haven't done these things yet, that doesn't mean that you can't go to graduate school, it only means that you have to seriously get moving. The fall semester of your senior year is when you should be applying to a lot of schools for the next fall. You should put aside plenty of time to get applications done and have everything in place for the following year. There are a lot of schools out there looking for high quality minority students. But if you don't apply to very many places, then you will never get to see what scholarships are out there with your name on them. Here are some things that you can do during your senior year to make sure that you are ready for graduate school.

Start applying as early as possible

The earliest you can start applying to graduate school is usually the end of the summer before your last year in college. You should spend much of the summer trying to get things together so that as soon as those apps are ready, you are too. The earlier you start, the greater are your chances of being admitted and receiving financial aid. Also, this reduces your stress in the long run.

The first thing you should do is line up all the profs that you want to write letters for you. Talk to them individually and ask them if it is ok. Then, come by later with all the materials. Try to give them everything at once, since giving them a bunch of different things at different times increases the chances that they are going to lose something or forget to mail it in (see my earlier discussion on graduate school preparation). Make a list of how many letters each school needs, and then write down the names of the professors who are writing letters for each particular school. This will help you keep up with things.

Next, you need to order all the transcripts that go with your letters. Find out if they need to be mailed by the university or by you. Order a copy of the transcript for yourself so that you can see what the schools are going to see. You also should be aware of your GPA at all times.

Make sure your test scores and apps are in order

If you need to retake some of the standardized tests, then do that also. Sometimes, the first time around, we can screw up the tests. That is O.K. The thing is that you have to figure out what you did wrong the first time and then fix it. Test scores are EXTREMELY important when trying to get into graduate school. This is what the schools use to determine which students are really smart, and which ones just have a high GPA because they majored in Synthetic Ankle-Scratching at "Really Bad" University. Yes, these tests are also known to be a little biased against minorities, but that should not be an excuse for you. If you are prepared, this can be your chance to shine.

Also, put your applications together early, making a list of all the schools that you are going to apply to. Many places will want you to write essays and fill in a lot of personal information. Go ahead and get all that done in a systematic fashion. You might want to make yourself an assignment to get two apps done per week until you've done all 12, 16, or however many you are going to cover. Treat the application process like you would an extra class. That means you should not do it in the fringes of your time, or only when you feel like it. It means that you should force yourself to sit down on a regular basis so that you can reach your goals.

Find a way to get the money, no matter what

The graduate school application process is not cheap. It can be downright expensive, just like pledging a fraternity or sorority. The difference is that this is a fraternity that will almost definitely give you your money back over the long run. So, this is a good investment for you, and something that you need to make happen by any means necessary. You should spare no expense, borrow, beg and crawl to pay for application fees, transcripts, or whatever else you are going to need.

The best way to get the money for all this is to start saving during your Junior year. If you haven't done that, then you can try getting an extra student loan to pay for the transcripts and all the application fees. It is worth it, since this is the best investment you could ever possibly make. Another option is to borrow money from family, or to get a job to pay for things. A small paycheck of $200 per week can cover a lot of application fees. In fact, that is how I paid my fees when I was in college.

How do you pick the graduate school that is right for you?

Let's say that your application process has gone very well, and you are on your way to the top. How do you decide which school is right for you? How do you even decide which schools to apply to in the first place?

Well, your professors are a great resource for figuring out which schools are the best in your field. Find a professor that you trust and get them to help you in your search for the right school. But don't just listen to one opinion, try to get a bunch of inputs. There are professors all over the U.S. who would love to hear from you and give you their opinion. I am probably one of them. I recommend sending emails to people asking them what they think about the places you are interested in applying to. If they don't reply to your email, then forget about them and move to the next person.

When you are admitted to a graduate school, visit the place before you commit. Some places may be willing to fly you in so that you can see the campus. If they aren't willing to pay, then maybe you can drive or get there yourself. But you have to also remember that the school that is willing to fly you in is probably the one that wants you the most.

Next, you can check some of the publicized rankings, like the ones in US News and World Report, Business Week, etc. Every year, they have rankings of the top law schools, medical schools, business schools, etc. This will give you some idea of which schools are the strongest and what areas they are strong in. Don't pay *too much* attention to these rankings, since your pick has to be a school that is best for you. A place that wants you and is willing to fund you can be better than a more highly ranked school that doesn't help you at all. Also, be careful about paying attention to what a school says about itself. Every school you talk to is going to try to convince you that they are the Harvard that nobody heard about. After you listen for a while, it starts to sound pretty convincing. Don't fall for the hype.

Sometimes, it's best to wait

Sometimes it's best to wait when it comes to graduate school. That means, maybe spending a year or two working first, and then going back. That is a good idea in some cases, like when getting a Master of Business Administration (MBA). In these programs, they are more likely to admit you if you have good work experience with a good company, rather than if you have a high GPA and no experience at all.

For most other fields, it's not usually the best idea to wait before going to graduate school. The education train is one where you have a hard time getting back on it if you decide to jump off. Once you leave school, all the little elements of life start to creep up on you: Bills, marriage, kids, laziness, etc. You then find that picking up a book and reading all night is not as easy as it used to be, and also finding the money to go back to school is a lot tougher. There is probably never going to be as much money available for you to go to graduate school as there is right after you finish undergrad. That's the truth.

If you do decide to go to work before heading to graduate school, there are some things that you should think about. First, try to find a job with a company that will pay for you to go to school or one that provides some kind of incentive for you to go. This means that you are working for a company that values education and is willing to put its money where its mouth is. But beware of the program before you sign up. Find out if you have to pay first and then get your money back or if they pay for you in advance. Also, find out what types of classes they are willing to cover for you. Some companies are even willing to let you leave the company for 2 years to get a masters degree. This kind of offer can be beneficial if there are no good schools in your area. Speaking of which, all masters degrees are NOT created equal. You should check to see if there are good schools in the city in which you are going to be working, so that you don't have to get your degree just anywhere. If you are good enough to go to a good school, don't let a dumb job cause you to go to bad one.

After graduation, don't let your financial and personal life swing out of control. If you stack up on a car payment, house note, credit card bills, and all that, then you are not going to be able or willing to head back to graduate school when the time is right. So, your desire to spend money today might mean that you can't make more money in the future. Also, getting married, having kids and all that is ok, but you have to realize that every personal decision you make could be closing another window of opportunity for you. There is nothing wrong with getting married before the age of 25, but there is nothing wrong with getting married at 30 either. In fact, when you hit your 30s, you've had a chance to do most of the educational things that you would like to do with yourself. You also have had a chance to experience a bit of life. I have seen so many friends with a lot of potential throw all that away just so they could get married young. If you are really meant to be with a person forever, then they should be willing to wait another 3 or 4 years to marry you. If they can't give up 3 years to wait for you, what makes you think they were meant to spend the rest of their life with you anyway?

If you want to make sure that you are always flexible enough to go back to school to finish up your education, here are some things that you can do:

1) Keep going to school – always keep your foot in the door so that you are still used to being on a campus and studying. Also, you are maintaining and creating contacts with professors that can help you get into programs when you are ready to go back full-time. Your motto should be that you are going to continue to go to school at least part time until you have finished the highest degree that you ever plan to earn.

2) Keep money to the side so that you can apply for things when you are ready – the application process is always expensive, so don't let money be an obstacle. Also, you should save so that if you have to go back to school full-time, you've got some money available to support yourself for a while.

3) Study for the standardized tests – when you go back to school, you are going to be expected to produce test scores again. Even if you already took the tests in undergrad, it definitely helps you to retake them

again later. You will probably be smarter then than you are right now.

4) Don't bury yourself under a financial mud pile – don't buy an expensive house just yet, and if you get a car, make it one that you can afford to pay for while you are in graduate school. It would not be a good idea to put your self under a ton of debt.

Social stuff

Balance is the key

Like you probably already know, there is a lot more going on in college than just studying. The best thing about college is that there is a whole world of stuff out there for you to do and learn. Many of your most memorable lessons are going to be social ones, so I recommend fully participating in the social side of things when you head off to college. If you are already sociable, keep at it. Just remember that the key is BALANCE. You have to make sure that you don't do too much of anything: you shouldn't study 100% of the time, and you shouldn't have fun 100% of the time. Life is a mixed bag, and you should make sure that your bag has plenty of mix in it.

Let's go down the list of some of the social stuff that goes on in college, and how you can prepare to deal with it.

Frats and sororities

As you might already know, Greek life is a big thing on college campuses. Being "Greek" means that you have pledged one of the Greek fraternities or sororities. "Pledging" means that you have gone through the rituals necessary to join the organization, and they feel that you have completed the requirements necessary to be a part of the group. A big bunch of college students are "Greek", and if you go across the campus, you would probably see a stack of Kappas, Alphas, AKAs, and Deltas, along with a bunch of white fraternities and sororities as well. That stuff is cool, and if it's your thing, then go for it.

There are some things that you should watch out for when it comes to Frats and Sororities. There is the good side of being Greek, like having a pile of instant homies, some visibility on campus, you get to be part of a group that you are with for the rest of your life, and you get the chance to get involved in community service. There is also the bad part of pledging. Like the fact that you may not want to hang around with the new-found homies that you just got. Some of them may pound on your nerves like 50-pound barbells. Then, there is the fact that pledging is expensive, time-consuming and can destroy your grades. I have seen a lot of students jack up their GPAs for life by pledging at the wrong time or giving too much time to the process. Different organizations require different amounts of your time before they will let you join. Some of them want you at their every beck and call, and some of them just want you to do things for them every now and then. But pledging is usually a pretty difficult process.

"Hazing" is when members of the organization do something abusive to make you prove your loyalty to the group before they allow you to join. They might beat you up, paddle you, make you put your head in the toilet, or something crazy like that. It is usually designed to be painful and humiliating (at worst), and sometimes to teach lessons about loyalty and trust (at best). Hazing used to be prevalent on college campuses, but it is now banned on nearly every campus in the United States. However, there are some places where hazing is done underground. DO NOT EVER allow anyone to haze you. If you find out that hazing is going on in your organization, then anonymously go to the academic administrators and let them know what is happening. You may actually save someone's life. I had a friend who died after being hazed. He is no longer breathing because he wanted to be part of a group. It's not worth it.

Another thing about pledging is that you shouldn't do it if you don't want to. If you decide to join a frat or sorority, make sure that you do it for the right reasons. Some girls might try to make you think that you won't get any "play" if you're not Greek, or you may be led think that you will have more friends. Well, anybody who is your friend just because you're in a frat or sorority was never your friend in the first place. Don't feel that you are not going to be accepted by others if you don't pledge. If you are a good, confident person, people will want to be your friend whether you are in a frat or not. If a girl or guy is decent for you to be with, they are not going to decide to date you just because you are in a frat or sorority. That is not what friendship and love are all about.

Think about when and how you pledge

The next thing you should know about pledging is that if you decide to do it, you have to be responsible. You have to understand that this process is going to take a lot of your time, probably 6 weeks or more. You also have to remember that you are a student first, and in the frat or sorority second. You DID NOT come to college just to pledge! I can't tell you how many fools I've met who either stayed in college an extra year just so that they could pledge, or dropped out of school and became "Professional Q-Dogs" or AKAs (I'm not just picking on these two groups, it can happen in all of them). You have to be responsible and focused and realize that you need to handle the important business first, and everything else second.

DO NOT pledge during your freshman year under any circumstances! Even if you think that you can handle it, pledging during your freshman year is a big mistake. I have seen friends ruin themselves for life by pledging too early in their academic career. The fraternity is not going to go anywhere if you wait till the next year to pledge. If they want you now, they will want you later. Take your time, get used to college first, and then pledge.

Second, once you decide that you want to pledge, choose your organization carefully. Make sure that you mix well with the personalities of the people that you are going to be hanging around. Do they make you a better person or do they make you worse? Are they a lot like you? Are they like the kind of person you want to be? For example, if you want to be a better student, and you see that every other person in a certain frat or sorority has good grades, then maybe hanging with those people is going to make you into a better student. Do they do community service, or just have a bunch of parties? Then again, you may want to have a bunch of parties. It all depends.

171

Next, you should be careful to manage your time during the semester that you are pledging. You should probably not pledge during your "advanced super-duper brain buster" semester. If you find out that your study time is being cut into because of pledging, then let your organization know what's up. If they don't want to cut you any slack, then you don't need to be a part of that organization. I can guarantee that the homies who are keeping you from getting your work done are not gonna be around when you're 40 years old without a job because you never graduated from college.

Peer pressure

Another thing about pledging is that you are suddenly going to have a long list of new "friends". The same as in life, some of these so-called "friends" may try to use you and they are also going to use the fact that you are in the same organization as an excuse to dog you. This is especially true if you happen to have some loot in your pocket, or a nice car. Be cool with your friends, but don't let them abuse you. If you don't like the fools that are coming to your crib, then tell em to get the hell out! The thing is that a fake friend has no value at all. If people are "frontin and fakin", then get rid of em.

Also, there is the peer pressure side of things. Whenever we join a group, there is always going to be peer pressure from people who want us to do things that might not be too good for us. They might try to get us to drink, to go around having sex with anything that moves, to drive fast or to just do foolish stuff. Don't fall victim to all that. Remember, you are an adult now, and YOU are responsible for your own life, not anybody else. If you get arrested, you are the one who has to spend the night in that jail cell. Here is where it can get tough. You have to have confidence in yourself, and you have to care enough about yourself to say no whenever people ask you to do things that you don't want to do. That's all there is to it. I have had friends who went to college, got caught up in peer pressure, and 10 years later, they were hooked on drugs, dying of AIDs, or have a criminal record, all for the sake of doing things with "their boys". Don't be stupid. Make the right decisions with your life.

Don't forget the grad chapter

Some people who don't want to deal with the toils of pledging in undergrad consider pledging the grad chapter. This is simply when a person has already graduated from college when they join the organization. In most cases, the grad chapter pledging process is not as time-consuming, since they understand that you are busy. It is still expensive in most cases, especially since they know that you have a lot more money to spend than when you were in college.

The cost of pledging grad chapter is that there are some Greeks who don't consider you to be a real member. Some of the old school types think that if you didn't go through the crap they went through in undergrad, you are somehow unworthy of being Greek. Personally, I wouldn't listen to them. Most people will accept you as part of the group, especially if you are working to make a valuable contribution.

An additional benefit of pledging grad chapter is that the people you kick it with are more likely to be mature, professional individuals. At the very least, you can get the chance to run with these kinds of people rather than being stuck with just the people who happen to be on your campus. You have most of your education behind you, so you've got time to get engaged in certain activities.

Boyfriends and girlfriends

The opposite sex is one of the things that makes college so exciting. Never in your life are you ever going to be in a place that has so many thousands of people who are the same age as you. If you are a dude, there will be fine women left and right every day, on your way to class, in the hallway, etc. If you are a girl, you are going to see guys everywhere. Women usually outnumber men, I am not sure why. Everyone should consider going to college, regardless of sex.

Finding a future wife or husband is never as easy as it is in college. When you get out into the real world, a lot of people have to go places like church or clubs to find a date. The pickings get real slim later on. But you should not think that college is ONLY for finding somebody to date and marry. There are a lot of dudes who like hanging on campus for the girls, and there are a lot of girls who don't care about getting their BS degree as much as they care about their M-R-S degree (so they can be called "Mrs." after they find someone to marry).

You should not make stupid decisions just because of some girl or dude that you meet in college. People are usually interested in only taking care of themselves, so you have to make sure that you don't let that guy pressure you into sex when you are not ready, or let that cute little girl pressure you into finding ways to get a better car. As much as I wish that I could tell you that you are probably going to marry the guy or girl that you meet in college, there is a good chance that you won't. So, I would be really careful about betting your life on someone that you may or may not know in the future. If they are meant to be with you for good, then they will be around years later. That is when you can start making those heavy decisions.

Let life happen to you slowly

One big mistake that a lot of young people make is that they are in a rush for everything. They are in a rush to get married, in a rush to have kids, in a rush to move in with someone else, just in a damn rush to do everything. That's stupid. Why? Because it's all going to happen at some point! I'm telling you the truth. It all happens eventually, and when it does, you are probably going to get sick of it.

I have a ton of friends who got married in college or right after college, and they are now sitting in divorce court, or in their 2nd or third marriage before the age of 30. I am not saying that marriage can't be a beautiful thing, but it is most beautiful if it's done with the right person, at the right time. Most of the problems in marriage have nothing to do with love. They have more to do with money, time, frustration, and somebody just flat out getting on your nerves. There can be plenty of love in the equation, but if you are not ready for marriage, then it's not going to feel like love at all.

You can think about children in the same way. You can have kids at the age of 25, 30 or 35...why have them when you are 19? There is so much more life out there to enjoy, and once you have kids, a lot of that is going to be closed off to you. Kids are fun and loveable, but they can be very frustrating and make you want to choke their little butts. On top of that, they are very, very expensive. You will be a much better parent if you have the educational and financial resources to get them what they need. Don't rush into parenthood, since you will enjoy it that much more if you've experienced life first and are mature and financially settled. Marriage and kids aren't going to go anywhere, and your future family is going to appreciate the fact that you got your ducks in a row while you were young.

Living together with that "special someone"

Living with someone of the opposite sex when you are in school is a pretty bad idea. I'm not talking about roommates. I'm talking about living with that dude or that girl you've got the hots for. Your parents are probably going to kill you first of all. And if that's not bad enough, you've also got to deal with the reality that living with

175

somebody is probably not what you think it is. First of all, that person is gonna be all up in ya butt crack 24-7. If you get pissed off at them and tell them to go home, they're just gonna go into the next room, because they ARE home. You will run into them on the way to the shower and in the kitchen. You're going to have to deal with cleaning up their messes and with their friends coming over. You are going to have to open the cabinet and see that they ate up all your favorite food. You are going to have to share the remote control with them. When they get sick, they puke on YOUR bedspread. When they snore, they are going to keep YOU awake.

What makes this even worse is the fact that the rules of breaking up change completely when you are living together. Normally, if you get mad at the person you are dating, you can say "Get lost", and you never have to look at them again. You can break up that day. But if you live together, you have a whole list of things to think about. First of all, you can't kick them out right away, since they live there too. If they are paying half of the rent, the landlord ain't gonna give a DAMN what happened when they come looking for their money. If you have everything in your name, then that other person can just move out and leave you with the rent. Then, you have all the other bills that you have to worry about. You could be living with "Nikki-No-credit", and after putting everything in your name, you find yourself stuck paying for a bunch of stuff that you are legally responsible for. This can ruin your credit for a very long time.

On top of all that, the big breakup means that you get to spend time fighting over who bought the couch or who owns the blender, this is in addition to all the bitterness that is already there because you are breaking up. There is a greater chance of somebody getting pregnant if you are living together, since the bootie is right there for you to get it whenever you want. Sometimes people end up getting careless and not using condoms, which is a very very bad idea. It's a mess, a big ol mess. I'm not saying that you can't live with someone one day or get married, I'm just saying that you might want to avoid the unnecessary stress.

Don't sign for a DAMN thing

One of the biggest mistakes that people make when it comes to their boyfriend or girlfriend in college has to do with money. It's easy to think that because you are in love with someone, that it's OK for you to pay "yo boo's" tuition, buy her books, or pay money to get his car fixed. If you've got it like that, then that's fine. Also, there is nothing wrong with being a generous person. However, you should think carefully before doing too much for other people, because it can lead to nasty consequences.

No matter what you do NEVER CO-SIGN OR PUT ANYTHING IN YOUR NAME THAT BELONGS TO ANOTHER PERSON. The thing about relationships is that the closer someone is to us now, the more ability they have to hurt us if things turn sour. If you put your name on a lease, a car payment, or whatever, then you are now LEGALLY tied to the person you are signing for. I can't tell you how many times I've seen people do that kind of thing out of love, and spend a lot of time afterward trying to fix the serious problems they've created for themselves. It's just not worth it. That person who loves you so much today can be your worst enemy later if things don't go right.

Also, letting someone else drive your car is not a good idea. You have to remember that nobody is going to respect your property the way that you do. Even if they are your "boo", there is just something about human nature that makes people say "Hey, if I wreck this car, it's gonna be bad. But it's gonna be worse for her than it is for me." You see, everything is fine at first. They promise that they are gonna take care of the ride that ya mama got you, they are gonna put gas in your car, they are gonna drive slower than my great grandmother without her

177

medication.....gonna gonna gonna. But how they treat your stuff in reality might be a whole different story. Also, they swear to you that they are only going to need to borrow your car just this once, but never again. Then, the evolution begins: The one time borrowing of the car turns into two times, then another and another, till they are driving your car more than you are. They even pick up the keys without asking sometimes. You dare not "check him" on the issue, because then he starts with the whiny guilt trip about how you don't trust him, you're being selfish, stingy etc. You have opened a CAN-OF-WORMS!

Then, there is THAT DAY: the day when they come home and tell you that your car has been in a collision, making it look worse Michael Jackson after his 148th nose job. It's stacked up in somebody's junkyard, looking like some kind of weird abstract painting. Of course he is not without remorse: He is sorry, really sorry. He swears that he is gonna repay you for everything, even though he ain't got no insurance. But he swears that he is gonna give you $5,000 within a year, even though he ain't got no job. You quietly wonder where he is going to get the money, but you don't dare question his commitment and loyalty. After all.....he LOOOOVEE YOU GURHLLL!!!

Then, you wait. And wait. And wait. No money is coming, so you start to ask him about it. That is when the amnesia sets in. He doesn't ever bring the money up during conversations, and if you bring it up, it's as if you are just begging for a fight. He snaps at you, then tells you that you are stressing him out and being a butt hole for constantly bothering him about money. But you are only asking him to do what he said that he was going to do in the first place. Let's just hope that you don't break up before he finishes paying you back (if he ever started). Then getting your money back is gonna be as easy as getting Tiger Woods to do gangsta rap.

The example above doesn't just apply to men, since women can do you just as wrong. I'm not saying that you shouldn't trust other people or be a nice person. I am also not saying that you shouldn't help out a friend in a bind. I am just saying that you should understand the consequences of your decisions, and realize that when you loan something to somebody, you are giving them control over something that is valuable to you. You are also opening a great big can of worms that you might wish you had never opened in the first place. Worms come out of the can quite easily, but it's a BEEYATCH to get them back in.

Other financial "No-No"s

Other absolute no-nos are lending someone else your credit card, your cell phone or your calling card. When the company sends the bill, they don't want to hear your sob story about how your girlfriend ran up the cell phone bill calling the man she was seeing behind your back.

Another big mistake that a lot of people make is to think that somebody else is going to take care of you. Just because "yo boo" says that he is going to be a doctor one day and swears that he is going to pay you and your mother's bills for the next 100 years doesn't mean that you shouldn't try to get an education on your own. There are a lot of women (this usually happens to women, but it can happen to men also) who end up stuck because they listened to the promises of some guy that never turned into reality. Don't make yourself into one of those people.

Watch out for more of the tricks

There are a lot of tricks to the dating game in college. Not tricks that you should play on other people, just tricks that some others are going to play on you. One of them is the freshman bait trick. When girls arrive on campus, there is usually a long line of dudes waiting for the "freshman bait". They will come up to you, talk a good game and tell you whatever lie they can tell to get you in the bed with them. Sex is not something that you should do if you are not ready or interested in doing it. Yes, it is a natural part of life, but if you do it the wrong way, it can be hurtful or even deadly.

When you meet someone who seems interested in you, take your time to get to know that person. They might claim to really like you and to be trust worthy, but time reveals all things. I'm not talking about a few hours or a few days, I'm talking about a few *months*. If he really likes you and wants to be with you, he is going to be willing to wait for you.

For the fellas, there are some other things that challenge our dating situation in college. Some guys are just a little shyer than others, and it always seems like the brother with the big mouth is the one that gets all the play. The nice guys are the ones that women say they want, but that doesn't seem to be the ones that they pick. The other thing is that a lot of women tend to like older guys, so getting a date during that freshman year can be tough. What else? The dudes with the cars and the money get the play too, so since cars and money are not the easiest thing to get while you are in college, then you will probably come up short in that area, at least for your freshman year. Yep, the freshman year is the toughest year for a man to get the hook up.

But there is hope. You see, the older people get, the more sense they start to have. That girl you liked back in the day eventually figures out that the baller with the nice car might not be the best guy for her, and maybe the smart guy with a future is the one she should prefer to be with. Hope DOES lie on the horizon, so be proud of who you are and good things will usually happen.

Whether you are a boy or a girl, the main thing to remember is that you always want to keep bettering yourself. No one worth anything wants to spend their life with somebody who doesn't want to do anything with their self. Even if you are single and having a hard time finding the person that works for you, keep working to improve yourself so that you will be ready when you meet that special person God has in store for you. If you find that person in college, you may want to be nice to them, since the right person is a rare gem of infinite value.

Two more things to remember

One final thing to remember when it comes to dealing with the opposite sex is to not be afraid. Don't spend your time worrying about what is going to happen if you try to holla at that dude or girl that you like. Life is too short to be afraid. If you don't take that chance to say something to that person right when you feel it, you are going to spend the rest of your life wondering what would have happened if you had opened your mouth. The worst thing they can say is "no", and usually they are going to be flattered that you thought so highly of them. If they are a butt-hole about it, then that is their problem. Also, that means that this person wasn't right for you anyway.

Being told "no" doesn't mean that there is something wrong with you. You can think of it with this analogy. Let's say you go to a car dealership and there is a black Mercedes and a white Mercedes on the lot. Someone may come along who only likes the color white. They may pass up the black Mercedes, but that doesn't mean that the black Mercedes is an ugly car! At worst, it means that the black Mercedes will sell just as good as the white one when the right customer comes along. So, think of yourself as the black Mercedes, and all you have to do is find the right customer. Some girls only like guys who are over 6 feet tall, and some dudes only like girls with long hair. So, if someone turns you down, that just means you don't fit their particular wish list, which may or may not make sense.

Another important thing to remember is that there is nothing more valuable in the world than to have someone who likes you, respects you and cares about you. You may want to go for the cutest girl in the dorm, the dude with the nicest car, or the girl with the biggest bootie, but you have to remember that it is important to choose someone who cares about you and is happy to be with you. The *worst* thing in the world is to be in a relationship with someone who feels that you should be *honored* that they are even spending time with you. You may be honored to have that fine-ass girl or dude on your arm, but if the relationship is not evenly balanced, they may end up treating you like a Hershey streak in the bottom of an old man's drawz. Also, they are going to have you on a short leash: if you mess up, you're gone. If you disagree with them, you're gone. If you don't give them what they want, you're gone. That is not the way to live, and eventually, the whole situation is going to make you feel trapped.

The big break ups and how to deal with them

It might seem strange that we are talking about relationships in this book. No, my name is not Oprah, and I'm not a relationship therapist. However, I have been there, done that, and your relationships with the opposite sex are going to play a prominent part of your college experience and the stack of memories that you walk away with after you graduate. Almost everyone who went to college can tell a story about a time when they got dumped or went through a terrible break up. They might also be able to tell you about how the emotional stress of the breakup threw their GPA in the toilet, and how their mama and friends were calling every other day to check on them because they were so worried. Of course, they were dumped by some fool who they thought they would be with forever. But then, she finds out that Joe Blow was dippin and pimpin all over the campus, or he finds out that Jane Doe decided that she was interested in the dude that sits next to her in biology class. This kind of thing happens.

The thing about these big break ups is that many people screw themselves and their grades when they go through this kind of thing. Suddenly, the relationship is more important than anything, and getting Shaquida back into your arms is the only thing that can make you breath again. You are so sad that you stop studying for 3 weeks, and you just let the grades go into the toilet. I can't tell you how many times I've heard this story, and there is a chance that this may happen to you. If you go through something like this and cannot discipline yourself properly, you can end up destroying your grade point average and ruining your academic record for years to come.

If this misfortune does pop up on you, you have to remember that this is the time where you really have to be strong. You have to realize that these problems are only temporary, and that they will eventually go away. The thing is that it doesn't feel that way at the moment. You feel like somebody just ripped your heart out through your butt, and you just want to go jump off somebody's bridge. The fact is that your mind is just a little bit sick, and since you are not used to this feeling, it's going to take some self-therapy to get over it all.

When I was in college, my big breakup came during the last semester of my senior year. It was terrible. I was sick all the time, I couldn't concentrate on studying, and all I could think about was this stupid girl that I thought that I was in love with. I spent more time calling her, sending her flowers and wondering who she was going out with than I spent doing anything else. I should have realized that she wasn't the person for me, and that I needed to forget about her ugly butt anyway. Because I spent so much time thinking about this girl, I didn't have very good grades that semester. She is long gone, but that bad semester is still on my transcript.

Here are some things that can help you get through the big break up.

An ounce of prevention is worth a pound of cure

A lot of people end up begging and crying for someone to come back to them because they messed up in the first place. They might have been cheating, beating, deceiting or just plain old mistreating. You can get a long way in your relationships by just knowing how to treat people from the very beginning.

The biggest mistake that a lot of people make is thinking that kindness is a weakness. Rather than appreciate the fact that someone is good to them and there for them, they think that this is their cue to act any old kind of way. Someone being nice to you doesn't mean that they are asking you to treat them bad. You might think that you are getting over now and that they are wrapped around your finger, but it won't last for long. If you meet someone who happens to think highly enough of you to treat you kindly, you should treat them kindly in return. But if they are treating you poorly, you need to roll on.

Also, with college relationships, there is usually what some call a "power structure". Some of the psychologists who study college students find that in most relationships, there is one person who calls most of the shots. The girl might know that the guy better do what she says or he's gonna get dumped, or a guy might know that a girl is so scared of him leaving that she will do anything to keep him. What they also find is that most of the time, *the power structure changes back and forth.* You might be calling the shots at first, but then something changes, and suddenly, they are calling the shots. Then, all the dirt you've done comes back to bite you in the butt. It just happens like that.

The point I am making with this story is that even if you are the one with the most power in your relationship, you have to remember that it probably won't always be that way. You will find out that they still remember EVERY SINGLE THING THAT YOU'VE DONE. If you've dogged that girl for the past 2 years, when she has a bunch of dating options, she is going to put you at the end of the list. This can be painful if it's someone that you care about. So, remember that the person you think is a lamb can suddenly turn into a lion and you won't even know what hit you.

184

Remember that time and space heals all wounds – stay clear of the person you are trying to break up with

The next thing you have to remember is that everything goes away with time. What happens during the love process is that when you meet someone you like, there are a bunch of chemicals that invade your brain, and you kind of become addicted, like a crack head. That is why people act so stupid when they first fall in love....they're always smiling, all starry-eyed, like a puppy with a bowl full of Scooby snacks. Then, after a while your brain gets hooked on these chemicals. That's why people start "trippin" when they break up. They are going through withdrawal, as if they are on drugs. Actually, they *are* on drugs, but these are natural drugs that the body produces, not the kind that you buy from "Pookie nem" on the street corner.

The thing about the withdrawal from any drug, whether it's natural or artificial is that a) it takes time, and b) the effects are only going to disappear if you stay away from the drug. The person you are trippin over is the drug, and the best way to get over them is to stay away completely. You will find that if you are away from that person for a while, you will eventually be over them and wonder why you were freaked out over them in the first place. The best time to get past a relationship is during the summer or Christmas break, since you can go home and not see them for a long time. By the time you come back, you should be much better.

Finding some business of your own

There is an old saying "Rather than gettin all up in somebody else's business, you should go out and get some business of ya own." When we spend our time managing our own lives, we usually spend less time being worried about somebody else's life and what they are doing. If you go through a break up, don't sit around by yourself, wondering what that other person is doing or when they are going to call. It will drive you nuts. It's the funniest thing in the world. When you've got something to keep you busy, then it's not so difficult to wait for someone to call. If you are out all day with your friends, you will have a bunch of calls on your answering machine when you come home. But if you are sitting next to the phone all day, it will seem like no one is calling. Also, you are going to drive your ex crazy anyway if they think that you are just sitting there waiting for them to call you. For some reason, people become less interested if they think you are not a challenge for them.

So, if you find yourself in the middle of a tough breakup, find things to do and perhaps someone else to go out with. Don't jump into another relationship, since rebounds are unfair to the other party involved. Spend time with friends, family, schoolwork, anything that will keep your mind off that other person. The *worst* thing to do is to sit around with nothing to do. You are only making things worse for yourself.

Violence and arguing have no place in or out of a relationship

Sometimes, you can end up in one of those highly volatile relationships, with more drama than Jerry Springer. All that fighting, screaming, crying, yelling and even

186

hitting is just a waste of time and flat out stupid. Disagreements happen, especially during break ups. There are the times when you want to go and scratch his car and flatten his tires, and there may be times when you want to go bust out her dorm room window. It's natural to feel the urge for violence, but indulging this urge can cause you a lifetime of trouble.

If you ever find yourself in a situation where you want to get physically violent with another person, get out of that situation IMMEDIATELY. Domestic violence is taken very seriously in this country, and in some states, the police are OBLIGATED to take at least one person to jail during a domestic violence call. Jail is not fun and the legal system can be very expensive. You are going to be REALLY HOT if you end up there over some stupid stuff. Being a minority doesn't help, since they love to lock us up every chance they get. If you see the situation escalating, find a way to get yourself out of it right away. Even if it means completely letting go of the situation and walking away without saying another word. Whatever it takes to keep yourself out of trouble, you should do it.

Remember your friends and family

When you are in a relationship, don't let a person monopolize your life. So many kids in college make the mistake of letting that newfound love take up all their time. They do every single thing with that person, ignoring their friends completely. They make that person the center of their universe. It is O.K. to be into somebody, but if you let them control 100% of your free time, then you are going to have an empty life if they decide to leave. Also, friendship is more valuable than nearly anything else you have. A boyfriend or girlfriend can be temporary, but a good friend will last you for the rest of your life if you play your cards right. Friends are not nearly as judgmental as mates can be, they don't usually get jealous, and they are down for us, no matter what. A girlfriend or boyfriend might hop up and leave if they find somebody better. A good friend won't do that. Also, our good friends and family care about us no matter what we look like, what we do for a living, or what kind of car we drive. That is not always true in a relationship.

It's not right to ignore your friends when things are good in your relationship, and then pop up on their doorstep when things are bad. They're going to look at you like "Where in the hell you been?" They may be resentful of the fact that you are basically using them to help yourself get through the tough times, since they think you are going to disappear once you find someone else to date. You should also be there for your friends when they are going through tough times. They need you the same way you need them.

Family is another place where you can get true blue, unconditional love. That is the only place where you are going to have people who really care about you, no matter what. Even if you were to go off and kill 100 innocent people, your Mama will still send you a fruit basket for Christmas. That's true love! If you are lucky, they've loved you from the time you were born and will continue to love you until you die. A lot of people make the mistake of getting into big fights with their loved ones over a boyfriend or girlfriend. Sometimes it's their fault, and sometimes it's your fault. Who is at fault is not nearly as important as it is to make sure that you remember and understand the importance of your relationship with your family. The thing is that this person you are dating is probably not going to last forever in your life. There is a chance that this person will become your husband or wife, but the fact is that your mother IS DEFINITELY going to be a family member forever. So, make sure that if you get into it with your family over the person that you are dating, you know what you are doing. When this person is long gone, they are not going to give a DAMN about the severed relationships between you and your family.

Try to be nice and learn something from the breakup

Sometimes, if a person hurts us, we want to hurt them back. That is human nature. However, spending your time thinking about how to hurt someone else is not good for you as a person. If that person has disappointed you, or done something that is downright dirty, getting revenge on them is not going to change anything. The best thing you can do for yourself is to have dignity in the situation and move on with your life.

While breakups are tough, you can learn from this experience and know what to do and what not to do in the future. A lot of people spend all their time making the same mistakes over and over again. You don't want to be one of those people. Think about the situation and what went wrong, accept some of your own blame, and then try to figure out what you are going to look for the next time around. Our most painful experiences can be transferred into valuable lessons, but only if we spend time learning from our mistakes. So, that time between relationships is a great chance for you to learn a lot about yourself, and about people in general.

The other side of the coin

The interesting thing about relationships is that we all get to spend some time on both sides of the table. Sometimes we are the one getting dumped (or dumped on), and other times we are the ones doing the dumping. The thing is that when you are the one doing the dumping, you have to make sure that you do it the right way, not in a way that is mean to other people. Also, you have to learn how to get rid of people that are not good for you to be with.

If you find yourself in a relationship that is not right for you and are trying to get out, here are some ways you might want to deal with that situation:

189

Be nice and considerate

Sometimes it's hard, but you have to remember that what goes around comes around. If you are going to drop the bomb on somebody, drop it as politely as you can. Don't just stop calling them, disappear, or make them find out about you dating somebody else. Treat them in the same way that you would like to be treated if you were in their situation. It's funny how people can act when they are the one in the dominant position. All of a sudden, that person who was so sweet and humble becomes an inconsiderate jerk. Don't be a jerk.

Be firm and don't be a sucker

Sometimes, people can use our kindness against us. If you tell them that you are going to leave, they freak out like it's the end of the world. They cry in front of you, beg you to come back and sometimes act down right looney. While you should be considerate of their feelings, don't let their emotional temper tantrum keep you from doing what you have to do. Many of these emotional reactions are nothing more than what scientists call "defense mechanisms". That is something that an animal (yes, humans are animals too) does to protect itself. When a person is crying in front of you and laying guilt trips all over the place, they are doing nothing more than applying a defense mechanism to try to get you to do what they want you to do.

What is funny though is that same person who is boo-hoo-hooin all over the place might have been the one who was trying to dog you last week. But this time, they promise you the world and swear that they are never going to do that thing again. Believe me, they probably are going to do it again, and if you let them back in after hurting you, you should expect to get hurt again in the future. Also, they may harbor resentment for the fact that you threatened to leave them in the first place. Like the old saying goes "Don't pull the gun out if you're afraid to use it." That could be translated as "Don't threaten to leave unless you're really prepared to possibly go." When things are going rough for people, they get humble. But when things are going good, some can get arrogant and mean toward others. If things are going good for you, do not get arrogant and inconsiderate, and don't fall for the act if someone else has decided to be humble. They may be humble now, but the ill will they harbor after your threat may come back to haunt you in nasty ways.

Sex and stuff

Ok, now is the time for us to talk about sex, which I think is one of the more popular extracurricular activities for college students. I am not one who is going to pretend that sex is taboo and something that we shouldn't talk about. It's as natural as taking a bath, farting or eating dinner, and it's something that you should spend your time thinking about so that you can make the right decisions.

I arrived to college as a freshly minted non-virgin. I had sex for the first time during my senior year of high school, and I thought it was the best thing since McDonald's French fries. I also found out the hard way that not being careful can make you pregnant, or at least make your girlfriend get that way. So, I also arrived on campus as a freshly-minted father. My daughter was born during Christmas break of my Freshman year. I went home for the break and spent the entire time in the hospital while her mother was in labor. I can't tell you how scared I was! I didn't even tell my poor parents that the baby was coming until a week before she was born. So, one minute my parents were regular, run of the mill 36 year olds, the next minute, they were grandparents. It's funny how your whole life can change during one episode of The Cosby Show.

Having a child young wasn't the end of the world for me. In fact, it made me more focused on achieving my goals, since I then knew that I had someone depending on me. But it did make life more complicated down the road, with child support payments and a little bit of baby-mama drama. So, although I love my child more than barbeque chicken, I don't recommend having a child too early. I do recommend being smart about the decisions that you make, because many of them are going to stay with you forever.

Virginity and abstinence

Some people come to campus as virgins or expect to abstain from sex until marriage. I didn't make this decision, but I applaud those who do. It's not that I think it's wrong to have sex before you get married, but sex can definitely make things complicated for you. People who keep their "stuff" in their pants don't have to worry about running back and forth to the clinic getting AIDS ((A)quired (I)mmune (D)efficiency (S)yndrome) tests. Also, you are saving some of your best experiences for later, when you are going to hopefully be with someone who really cares about you. You can't beat that with a bamboo stick.

The thing is that the rest of the world sometimes puts pressure on virgins and those who abstain. Even I didn't abstain myself, but I sometimes wish that I had. Virgins are told that they are being old fashioned, or just missing out on a lot. Or they might be dating somebody who says that they aren't willing to wait for them to have sex. That can make a person feel bad about their decision. But I say that if abstinence is the choice that you have made, stick with it, and be proud of it. People may make fun of you for it, but deep down, they respect your discipline and persistence. There are many times when I wish I had waited myself.

Don't be dippin all around campus

One mistake that a lot of people make when it comes to campus and sex is they start to think that their sex organs are to be put into action at every available opportunity. They act like kids in a candy store, taking all the "pootang" and "wee-wee" they can get. Or, they jump from relationship to relationship, having sex with one person after another, thinking that it's ok. Sorry, it's not.

If you do the math, you would realize that when you have sex with, say, 7 people in a year, you are also having sex with all the people that they had sex with, and all the people that those people had sex with. So, if you calculate all the people that you are exposed to, that could be 7x7x7

194

= 343. That's worse than a big ol nasty orgy, even if you are using a condom. But that is also assuming that those 7 people only had sex with 7 others. There are some people who pride themselves on the fact that they've had sex with 40 or 50 people during the past year. If that is you, you need to think twice about your sexual habits.

Sex can be a good thing, just like ice cream or going to the movies. But there is also such a thing as too much ice cream, and you don't want to go to the movies every single day. If you decide to have sex outside of marriage, make sure that the experience is meaningful and that you are with someone who not only loves you, but has PROVEN that they love you. How can they prove it? There are a lot of ways. For example, they can prove it by waiting. If a brother is telling you that he needs the bootie by next Tuesday, then he probably has more interest in your vagina than you. Or if a girl says that she needs to have it on the first date, then she probably goes the first date route on a regular basis.

The reason that I am spending this time to warn you about "dipping" is because venereal diseases are ALL OVER college campuses, including your own. AIDS does not have a cure, but I am willing to bet that a lot of your classmates are HIV positive. If you get pregnant, then that guy may or may not decide to be around to help with the life consequences of having a child early. If you get someone pregnant, child support is a "beeyatch". Remember these things as you engage in sexual activity. Sex is like driving a car.....it can take you to another level, but it can be deadly if done irresponsibly.

Protecting yourself

If you do find yourself sexually active, then make sure that you get an AIDS test every 6 months. Also, if you find yourself experiencing symptoms of venereal disease, take your butt to the doctor. Also, NEVER EVER EVER have sex without a condom. Yes, sex without a condom feels better than winning the lottery four times in a row. But it is S-T-U-P-I-D. I don't care how long you've been with that person, how much you trust that person, and how sure you are that they aren't cheating on you. It only takes one slip up to ruin your life forever. The person that you think is so honest and faithful probably has some secrets that they have never shared with you. Even if you've been with them for 2 years, you have little idea of what they came into the relationship with. I don't care if you have sex before you get married, but you shouldn't take the condom off till you are married, and even then, only do it if you are 100% sure that the person you are with is healthy and honest. Remember that dishonest and deceptive people are very good at making themselves look like something else.

Watch out for date rape

As much as I hate having to talk about it, there are also those on campuses who want to do things to hurt other people. The worst thing is that the bad people in the world don't wear a sign on their heads saying "I'm bad" (Like the Michael Jackson video). They disguise themselves as good people so that you think that you are safe. Then, as soon as you let your defenses down, they take advantage of you. What is worse is that the influence of drugs and alcohol can sometimes make good people do bad things.

Date rape is an extremely common occurrence on college campuses. It happens all the time, and usually between people who think that they know one another. I have known victims of date rape, and I have known some who have been accused. All of them were pretty normal people, and you never would have guessed that they were involved in something so terrible, either as a victim or perpetrator.

If you find yourself on a date with a man, even one that you think you know, make sure that you understand the risks before you find yourself alone with that person.

When you are alone, there may not be anyone around to hear your screams. So, make sure that you either stay in a public place or are extremely careful about being alone with anyone. Also, don't let that person make you a drink without your being present, since there are things that people can put in your drink to make you incoherent and vulnerable.

If you go out on dates with a man, bring enough money to get yourself home in case you need it. In general, bringing your own money on a date is a good idea no matter what, since some people think that you owe them something just because they've spent money on you. Rape can be related to power, and you don't want to give that person a feeling of power that is not necessary. Having your own money is a good backup, just in case that person starts trippin.

Date rape advice for the fellas

The first thing I would say to the fellas is to make sure that you understand the seriousness of having sex with someone without their permission. There are long prison sentences for people who do that kind of thing. Going to jail is no joke, not to mention the fact that you are hurting another human being. Be careful about what you do with alcohol, since many date rape situations have alcohol somewhere in the background.

Second of all, you should definitely stay away from dudes who are into that kind of thing. If you see your boys getting out of hand and doing something that they shouldn't be doing, get the hell away from there. Especially when you are black, being associated with the wrong people at the wrong time can get you in almost as much trouble as if you actually did it yourself. The police have no way of clearly differentiating between who was actually involved in the incident, and who was just in the room doing nothing. So, unless someone is willing to go out of their way to exonerate you, there is a good chance that you are going to go to jail with the perpetrators. The honest truth is that when "the stuff hits the fan", people are only interested in saving their own butts; your butt is a distant second! If you see other men doing something to a woman that they are not supposed to be doing, report the incident immediately.

Be careful about the women that you roll with, since some of them can be a little shady. There are a lot of men who have gone to prison on a false rape conviction that came from a lie that somebody told. Most rape is real and actually happened, but there is some that comes from vindictive women who want to hurt a man for some reason. So, if you get into a sexual situation with a woman, make sure that she is a good woman that you know and trust. If you go around hopping in bed with anything with a pulse, it will eventually catch up with you.

Last piece of advice: If you are in bed, getting hot and heavy with a woman, she may change her mind in the middle of whatever you are doing, have done, or are about to do. It is *absolutely critical* that you respect her right to say "no" to sex. A lot of men carry this stupid idea that women say no when they really mean yes. That's bull. There may be dumb women who play that stupid game, but that's not a game that you should play, because your life is on the line. If a woman tells you "no", take it as "no", even if she really means "yes". If she really means "yes", then she will eventually come out and say "yes". That is what mature women do.

Pregnancy, babies, etc.

We all make mistakes

Sometimes we make mistakes. Things just don't work out the way that we planned for them to. As I mentioned earlier, I arrived on my college campus with a daughter because of decisions that I had made during my senior year of high school. So, this kind of thing can happen to the best of us. Hundreds of thousands of young women throughout the country find themselves staring down at the wrong color on the pregnancy test dipstick. This is, without question, one of the most frightening experiences in the world for a young woman in college. She has to deal with the fact that there is now a young life inside of her and the fear that her parents are going to want to hang her from the ceiling when she comes home and gives them the news.

Prevention

How do you deal with this kind of thing? First, as I said before, an ounce of prevention is worth a pound of cure. Never take the condom off so that you significantly reduce the chances of this happening to you in the first place. Also, birth control pills can be another back up. Some women don't like to use them, some do. This is up to you. Keeping your "stuff" in your pants for a while is a good back up also (this goes for girls and guys both). The last good back up is to be careful about who you have sex with. Are they a responsible person, or just someone who's going to let the condom slip off? Are they going to take care of their responsibility in the event that pregnancy does occur? Does this fool already have a bunch of kids that he's not taking care of? If so, then he is probably not going to take care of yours either. Letting some irresponsible idiot have sex with you is like letting a drunk person drive your car with YOU AND YOUR KIDS IN IT. You are putting your life in that person's hands. The other thing to remember is that if you have a baby with this person, the other parent may be a part of your life FOREVER. That means that if they are trifling and you don't know anything about them when you lie down together, you could be tied with an idiot for life.

Try to stay cool

If you do find yourself pregnant, the first thing you have to do is remain as calm as you can. No, this is not the end of the world, even if your father said that it is. Your parents threaten and try to scare you to make sure that you are too afraid to ever make this mistake. Some kids think that their parents are going to stop loving them or caring about them if they get pregnant. For most parents, this is not the case. They are not going to kill you, and you should remember that a lot of women have gone through this same experience before you. Don't do anything drastic, and don't feel that you are alone in this process. But don't get me wrong...in some ways, you are in "deep doo-doo"! So, you are going to have to dig yourself out.

The first thing you can do is get with the fool who made you pregnant. Even if the man is someone that you are not involved with anymore, this is his responsibility too. If he is a real man, he will respond like one. He may have access to resources that can help you deal with the problem effectively. Sometimes things don't work out that way. If they do not, then you may have to take a less pleasant and more aggressive approach to get him to acknowledge his responsibility.

Next, I would try to talk with friends, since they can be helpful in this time of need. If they are good friends, they are not going to judge you, and they might have some good ideas on how to deal with the situation. Don't go through this alone. Talking to your parents is also a good thing. You may be afraid to tell them, but they love you and they would probably surprise you by offering to help rather than treating you badly because of your mistake. There may be some anger at first, but they would rather know what is going on than to be kept in the dark.

If you don't feel that you can talk to your parents about the situation, then talk with a counselor at Planned Parenthood (a place that counsels people on pregnancy issues), which is usually right near every major college campus. They will describe all the options that you have available, and at least make sure that you are healthy. If your family does not come across as helpful in the situation, then Planned Parenthood may be the best option available.

Dealing with the pregnancy itself

I am not here to tell you if abortion is right or wrong, since it is not my right to tell you what to do. There are benefits and consequences to whatever action you choose. Having a child is not the worst thing in the world, since you would have this little person around who is going to love you forever. Although I was afraid when my daughter was born, I am now glad that we didn't decide to get an abortion. Most parents that I've known who once thought about getting an abortion are now happy that they chose not to do it. There are some who would argue to the end of time that abortion is all right, and there are just as many who would argue that abortion is wrong. In the end, the decision is yours.

Whatever you decide to do, there are only two things that I can say that you should DEFINITELY do:
1) Think long and hard before you make any decision. Do not create permanent solutions to temporary problems. Having a child is something that you are going to have to deal with for the rest of your life, and having an abortion may cause you to spend the rest of your life thinking about the child you would have had.

2) Remember that abortion is not a simple form of repeat birth control. Multiple abortions can have terrible long-term health effects, and I recommend that if you get an abortion, try to keep from getting pregnant again until you are ready to actually give birth.

Getting support from that *&^(%$ who got you pregnant in the first place

As I mentioned earlier, you should not think that this is something that you have to go through alone. A lot of men get away with forgetting about the children that they create, and letting the woman take care of the child without any help whatsoever. Yes, the baby is in the woman's stomach, but it's someone else's responsibility also.

If the person does not want to help you in an amicable fashion, then don't give up and stay on their butt. Make sure that you take him to child support court, and that he helps to pay for the abortion if you choose to have one. He should also help to pay whatever medical bills you incur along the way. Don't let him off the hook.

If you are lucky enough to have a relationship that is working out, have him go to doctor visits and Lamaze classes with you. The father should participate fully in the child-bearing process and you should not be the only person who has to reduce their course load because the baby is coming. If you are not living in the same household, then consider joint custody if that is something that you can deal with. A lot of women think that they are the only ones who have to give up their freedom when they have children. Men should feel some of this too.

Do not feel ashamed of yourself

Sometimes, people make us feel ashamed of ourselves for the mistakes that we make in our lives. Single mothers are treated like dirty step children and not always given the respect they deserve. Rather than honor them for all they must endure, society seems to want to mistreat them because they do not have a man in the home. If someone tries to make you feel bad for what you've done, pay them no attention! Everybody makes mistakes, and although someone may try to make you feel like you are the scum of the earth for getting pregnant, I am sure that their own closet isn't completely clean either. Even your mother may have had her own "interesting" experiences when she was younger, so there is no one who has the right to judge you and make you feel bad just because you found yourself in a tough situation.

Some people might try to convince you that having a baby during college is just the end of the world. I can hear them now: "Guuerrllll, you had dat baaayyyybee. You ain't never gonna finish callige". The hecklers and haters say all this knowing full well that they've done their own share of messing up over the years. But that is the way some people can be. Having a child at an early age is not enough to keep you from accomplishing things for the rest of your life. If you do have a baby, then pick yourself up and put together a game plan for how you are going to deal with life as a student after that baby is born. Your child is depending on you, so that gives you even more reasons to be successful.

Do not consider dropping out of school, unless it's for a short amount of time, and you absolutely have to do it. The biggest mistake you can make is to let this "mistake" compound into another one. If you don't come back and finish school, you are hurting the future of both you and your child. There are ways to be a student and still have a child, and I've seen single and married mothers even get PhDs, law degrees or medical degrees while raising children. It's only a matter of persistence and self-determination. If you really want to accomplish your goals, you are going to be able to do that. Make sure that you graduate from *some kind of program,* and that you have a degree in *something.*

The financial side of things

When you are going to school with a child, financial aid is definitely your friend. The best thing about having a child is that you are now eligible for a lot of extra money from the government to go to school. Also, your university may have a day care that gives discount prices to students. Try to get enough financial aid that you don't have to work, even if you have to max out your student loans. Your child is going to benefit a great deal from the extra time that you can spend with him/her without working. The time that you spend studying would take enough time from the child, do not add to that missed time by working long hours on a low-paying job.

Manage your money carefully. Put together a disciplined savings and investment plan and make sure that your bills get paid on time. Don't get into the habit of trying to only live day-to-day; think about your long run future.

Think of life as a blank piece of paper

I was staying at a hotel in Kentucky once, and I happened to run into a guy who I went to college with. He was a cool white dude, and we sat together, talking about old times. It had been about 8 years since we both graduated from college, so I was curious to see how his life had gone. He said that right after college, he married the girl that he was going with at the time. A couple of years later, they were divorced, and he lost half of his financial assets. Then, two years after that, he got married again, divorced again. He was going through his second divorce as we were speaking. His life had not been fun. He was only 30 years old, and he was going through his second divorce. He wasn't able to see his own kids. He was being wiped out financially. I felt sorry for him.

You don't want your life to read like a sad Greek tragedy. Be smart. The thing you have to realize is that when you are young, your life is like a clean piece of paper. You are given "the ink pen called CHOICE" to write things on the paper. This is not a real ink pen of course, but it means that with every choice you make, you are creating a life for yourself, and you are doing things that you will one day look back on and regret or not regret. Every time you sleep with someone, every time you choose to go to school or not, if you decide to commit a crime, every decision you make, you are writing something on that slate of paper. When you are in your 30s, 40s and beyond, you will look back on the ink pen marks that you've made on your life, and see that some of the markings will be good ones, some of them will be bad. If you are 35 with a criminal record, that is a bad marking. If you are 35 with an MD, that would be a good one. Most of our lives have a lot of markings. The key is to make sure that the good ones outweigh the bad, and that you make good markings on the things that are most important.

You want to make sure that you write *something* on your page, because nobody wants their whole life to look like a blank piece of paper. But you have to be careful when you decide what to write on your page, since the ink doesn't erase very easily. Some people are stupid, they write just anything on the paper by making a series of very bad choices. When they are young, they say "Hey, I've got this nice, blank piece of paper, and it is still pretty blank, even if I write a few things on it." These people don't think about what they are writing on this page, or how it's going to look on the paper years from now, when they try to write something else. If you are going to try to be president of the United States one day, does it make sense for you to start smoking crack? Probably not. More seriously, if you want to have a happy life and a happy family that you can provide for when you are 40, does it make sense for you to drop out of school at the age of 18? I don't think so. That's just one example, but the idea is that you should think hard before you make decisions, and think your choices all the way through to the end. That is how you keep a sheet of paper that looks pretty good in the long run.

Drugs, alcohol, gambling and other collegiate vices

Turning up the bottle

Unless you've spent your life way up under a rock somewhere, you probably know that college is full of alcohol. Some people feel that college and liquor go together like sugar and Kool-aid. A lot of college students like to drink. Many of them drink way too much, and many of them have no idea why they drink in the first place. Some people drink to be cool, some drink to relax, some drink to make themselves feel more confident, some drink to get drunk, some just drink because everybody else is doing it. I've always thought that was kind of silly. Not that drinking is silly, but drinking for all the wrong reasons is definitely silly.

If you don't drink when you start college, don't start unless you have a good reason. Don't think that the only way you can have fun in college is to go to parties and get drunk. There are plenty of ways you can have a very good time in college that have nothing to do with alcohol. If you do decide to drink, make sure that you are responsible. First, you should understand that drinking before the age of 21 is illegal. Yes, the police will arrest you and yes, you can get a criminal record for drinking under age. So, I can't sit here and say that I believe you should drink. But if you do, don't go overboard. Here are some things that you should remember if you decide to turn up the bottle in college.

Don't catch yourself drinking around people you don't know

A lot of people think that because the dude or the girls that they meet seem pretty cool, that they can go out with them and get drunk without having anything to worry about. Just because you've been running with some dude for a month or so, that doesn't make him your boy. When a person drinks too much, they lose control. Being drunk makes you as vulnerable as a person can be, and a lot of young women get drunk only to wake up and find a strange penis inside their vagina. Yes, that was a vulgar way to say it, but reality can be vulgar and frightening if you are not careful. Don't let this happen to you. First, I would say that getting drunk at all is a bad idea. But in the event that you think you might end up getting drunk, make sure that you are around someone who is going to protect you in case something goes down. There is always a story on nearly every campus, every year, about somebody who dies of alcohol poisoning from drinking too much. There are many more stories about drunken rapes taking place during wild parties. Try not to make yourself the next victim, because there is always going to be one somewhere.

Watch out for the tricks and dump the DUI

If you find yourself at "the club" with a drink in your hand, be careful. There are a lot of shifty characters out there that use alcohol as a way to get over on women. One way is through the date rape drug, also known as Rohypnol. This is a drug that can be used by someone to make another person pass out. The drug is also known as "ruffies", "roche", "R-2", "rib" and "rope". No matter what it is called, it is dangerous. Someone can slip the drug into your drink, making you unconscious for a long period of time. If someone gets you into that position, you are pretty much open for whatever they want to do to you. PLEASE be careful when you are out, for you could spend the rest of your life trying to recover from the aftermath.

If you are woman who expects to be out drinking with a man, try to take a friend with you, along with her male friend. Bring along someone who doesn't drink so they can be the designated driver. The designated driver should not be someone who drank the least amount of alcohol, it should be someone who *drank no alcohol at all.* If you are on a date with someone, whether it's at the club, in a restaurant, or just chillin at their house, don't let them make a drink for you. Also, don't let the drink out of your sight, not for one second. If the drink leaves your sight, then get rid of that drink immediately.

Drinking and driving is not something that you should play with. No one PLANS to get in trouble for DUI or to kill anybody on the road, it just sort of happens. The way it usually occurs is that people don't do enough planning when they are sober to get ready for when they are not. If you see a friend trying to get behind the wheel after drinking too much, STOP THEM IN THEIR TRACKS, no matter what it takes. Even if they hate you forever, you still have an obligation to do the right thing. Don't let yourself, your loved ones or another person's loved ones get killed over something stupid.

Keep an eye on your drinking habits

One mistake that a lot of college students make is thinking that just because they are in college, they are not open to many of the problems that other people have in the real world. Getting an education does not mean that you can't go to jail, become an alcoholic, catch diseases, or whatever. If you drink too much, you will end up in Alcoholic's Anonymous just like everybody else. Don't let yourself get caught in that mental trap.

The funny thing about alcoholism is that you never know that it is creeping up on you. The same is true for any addiction, whether it's drugs, gambling or whatever. Most of the time, when you first start off drinking, it's not such a big deal. Then, it becomes every weekend, and then every other day. Before you know it, you can't stop, even though you always think that you can if you want to. If you find yourself drinking regularly in high amounts and frequency, go see one of the counselors on campus immediately.

Drugs and Gambling

Drugs and gambling are two things that I would tell you to stay away from completely. When it comes to drinking, most of society would say that if you are not already drinking, then you shouldn't start. But drinking is a lot like smoking: there are a lot of people who do it and many who think that it's ok. The choice is up to you, but life is a lot simpler if you stay away from alcohol altogether.

Most people would say that the use of illegal drugs and heavy gambling are not O.K., under any circumstances. Just like alcohol, they can lead to addictions, and they can also land your butt in jail. A lot of brothers think that smoking weed is OK. It's not. Marijuana is illegal first of all, and second of all, it takes away from your ability to accomplish your goals.

Gambling seems fun at first. If you like sports, it can be fun betting on sporting events with a "bookie" (the person who takes bets over the phone). You swear that you can predict the winners of every game, and you love the high of winning that extra 200 bucks when your team "beats the spread". However, it can get bad, and gambling debts can cause serious problems that you don't want to carry with you for the rest of your life. I saw a lot of friends ruin their lives in college, using drugs, alcohol and gambling as their weapons of choice. Don't be one of those people.

Dorms and Roommates

Dorm life: an experience that stays with you for a lifetime

When you first get to college, try to live in the dorm. It might seem fun and exciting to have the option of living off campus, but don't do it, at least not right away. Dorm life is the good life. You will never get the chance to live like that again. When you are 18, it's easy to come up with a ton of hair-brained reasons why living off campus might be better: maybe you think you can save money, you can live with parents, you can get a crib with your 88 best friends, etc. Some of those schemes might work, but everyone should at least experience dorm life for their first two years of college. Besides, you have the rest of your life to live off campus.

When you move onto campus, you should start by picking a roommate that you think you can get along with. That is a simple statement, but it is very hard to do. Most of the time, you have no idea who is going to be cool to live with and who is not. I would be very careful about living with a person that you are already friends with. You see, if you live with someone you don't know and you get into a fight, then that person may end up leaving your life forever. But that's not such a big deal, since you didn't know the person in the first place. But if your roommate is also your best friend, you are losing a lot more. You might know somebody on one level, but that doesn't mean that you know them in every way. For example, your girlfriend might know things about you that your parents don't know, or your sister might know some things that your boyfriend doesn't know. You may know your best friend like the back of your hand, but you probably don't know what it's like to *live with that person.* So, just remember that living with a friend is like going into business with a friend or dating a friend: you are being exposed to another side of them that you know nothing about. This can be very risky.

The best way to get along with your roommate is to *be respectful.* That means, being respectful of their time, their space, their stuff, their ears, eyes, whatever. You might love having your boys around at 3 in the morning, but your roommate may not. Since the property belongs to both of you, you have to share and be fair. If you have a girlfriend or boyfriend around all the time, you should remember that your roommate is not afforded the luxury of walking around in her "drawz" when your man is in the room. She may not say anything, but you are inconveniencing her if your man is there more than she is. You probably want to manage this kind of thing by sharing room time with your boyfriend or girlfriend: maybe they can come to your crib sometimes, and you can also go to theirs. It also helps to spend most of your boyfriend/girlfriend "alone time" when you know that your roommate is going to be gone. That way, you and your hottie can hang out and do whatever with no one to disturb you. Be extra sensitive when important things are going on, like final exams. It's not fair to ask someone else to leave when they need to get their rest.

Try to choose a roommate with a similar lifestyle

Try to pick a roommate that has a lifestyle similar to yours, even if they are not a minority like you. It is better to live with a well-mannered person of a different race than a crazy person who makes your life miserable. If you don't drink, don't get a roommate that does. If you smoke, try to find a roommate who does too. That helps you get along much better. Also, go to the drug store and buy a lot of pairs of earplugs in case you have to screen the noise that your roommate may be making when you want to study.

Learn your roommate's patterns. Figure out when they are going to be gone, if they go home a lot, whether they are a morning person or a night person. This can help you plan the things you want to do without getting interrupted. If they like to sleep late, then maybe you can get up and do your work early (but this is only if you have to study in the dorm room, which I don't recommend). If they like to go out on Friday nights, then maybe that's the time to invite your girlfriend/boyfriend over.

Another way you can help your roommate is to be gone sometimes yourself. Don't be one of those "up in the dorm room every single day no matter what" type people. That will make it unfair to your roommate if they want some privacy. Also, staying bunched up in a dorm room with another person all the time increases the chances of World War III breaking out.

Location, location, location

The next thing about choosing a dorm is to make sure that you get a dorm that is as close to your classes as possible. You also want to make sure you are near campus restaurants and/or grocery stores. You don't want to be trekking across campus in 10 feet of snow. So if you have to live away from campus, get yourself a crib that is close to the bus route. You should know when the buses are running, since you may be highly dependent upon them. If the bus isn't running, you might be stuck, and that would limit you in terms of what time your classes can end or whether or not you get to see your friends on the main campus.

Being near food is cool because everybody has to eat. The worst thing in the world is to be on a college campus at 2 am Sunday night "Hongree as hayell". Most dorm rooms only have space for small fridges which hold "a whole lotta nothing", and even then, the little fridge always seems to be empty when you are at your hungriest. So, live near the food, and try to live near a place where you can get food 7 days a week, 24 hours a day. Most campus restaurants are not open 24-7, so check to find the hours of the places that are close by. When you go to the grocery store, don't just stack up on junk food, or you'll end up looking like a

Chicago Bears offensive lineman about to have his first child.

Watch the tall, crowded dorms

You might want to stay away from the really tall, crowded dorms. For example, if your school has a statement in their brochure that says "We have the largest dorm in the history of all man-kind", that isn't necessarily something that you can look forward to. Getting up the elevator is "beeyatch", especially on moving day. A good trick might be to move into your dorm room late at night or early in the morning, before the crowds build up. Unfortunately, the freshmen get a little screwed and can only live in specific dorms (usually the worst ones), but if you are allowed to pick, try to find out where the best places are to live. You can find all this out with a little research, but it has to be real research, not just reading the school's manual. If you only read the university's manual, they are going to tell you that EVERY dorm is like the Crowne Plaza Hotel, with plush carpeting, room service, and your choice of a maid or butler. Then, their pictures of the rooms make you think you're moving into your own football stadium. But when you get there, you find that they got you all twisted up.....your room is too small for most prison inmates, hamsters or dead people.

The best way to find out where to live is to go on campus and ask some of the students. Ask more than one, so that you get a variety of opinions and information. Find out where the worst and best places are, and how you can get into those dorms. There might be a wait-list or something, but that's OK.

Moving off campus

First, I should say that I recommend NEVER moving off campus. Well, don't take that literally, since there are some folks who actually DO spend 10 or 12 years living on a college campus. What I mean is that if you are in college for 5 years or less, you shouldn't move. If you decide that you really want to move off campus during college, move after your junior year, no sooner. This will give you time to learn about college life and to get comfortable off campus. There is no reason for you to rush to get away from college, because the rest of your life, you are going to be able to live anywhere you want.

A lot of people think that moving off campus is going to save money. This can be true....sometimes. The mistake that people make is that they take a simple-minded approach. They say to themselves "I pay $600 a month to live on campus in this little-bity dorm, and I can pay $350 and get an apartment with Pookie nem" (translation for "Pookie nem": "Pookie and some of my other friends").

That logic can make sense under certain circumstances. But the things that people forget to factor in when they are making their decision to leave campus are: 1) hidden costs and 2) convenience. From "jump street", you should know that if you have a scholarship that covers room and board, your butt needs to stay right on campus till graduation. There are few exceptions to that rule. But if you happen to be paying for your own stuff, there are some things that you should think about:

First, the money that you are actually going to save is probably not as much as you expect it to be, and you may even end up spending MORE money by trying to live off campus. Think about it. On campus, you just have to worry about paying the cost of the dorm at the beginning of the semester, nothing else. If you live off campus, you are going to have rent, a utility bill, a cable bill, a heat or water bill, a phone bill, the cost of gas to drive back and forth to campus, plus the cost of bus passes or a parking pass when you come to school.

It will be harder to study when living off campus, since you have to drive all the way to campus every time you go to class. That doesn't even count all the time that you spend trying to find a parking spot. Parking is usually really difficult on most campuses. Also, universities are quick to make you pay money for parking passes, even the passes that give you crappy parking spots. When I was an undergrad, the students were given parking passes that only gave them the right to use the parking lot two miles away from campus! Then, we would have to catch a bus all the way to campus (wasting another 45 minutes, in the cold) before walking to class. So, you're talking about losing a lot of study time, party time and free time going back and forth to campus. Being in this situation is dangerous, because if you are away from campus and it is inconvenient for you to go to school, you may likely find yourself staying away from school more and more, to the point that you are missing more class than you should.

If you move off campus.....

I recommend that if you do move out of the dorm, don't move too far away from campus. It might seem cheaper to go live in that neighborhood on the other side of town, but you will regret that decision when you experience the pain of having to get up and drive all the way to school every day. What if your car breaks down? That means you are either going to have to miss a lot of class, ride the bus, or call your so-called "friends" to come and get you everyday for school. You will find out how strong your friendship is when they give you those 10,000 excuses for why their car ran out of gas right before you called. Don't rely on your friends, and don't put that pressure on them to do something that they may not have the time to do. The closer you are to a campus, the more likely you are to finish school. Remember: finishing school is the only goal; everything else is secondary.

I do recommend that if you move off campus, find a roommate that you can trust. Not just anybody, but someone you know is responsible and not going to stab you in the back. "So-in-so" might be your homie to the end, but you have to make sure that you know what you are getting into by deciding to live with that person. Also, there is a

219

sad fact in life that the closer you are to someone, the worse of an enemy they can become. That is because this person eventually knows all of your weaknesses, and they can take advantage of you. So, don't put yourself into a tough situation. There are a million and one stories out there about that roommate who moved out in the middle of the semester and left the other person with all the bills. Or, then there is the other story about the roommate who was nice enough to make $1,000 worth of long distance phone calls right before they moved. Then, you've got the real trifling brotha who has the nerve to charge up the phone bill, not pay his half of the rent and still stay in the crib! Choose your roommates very carefully.

Other aspects of a complete college life

There are a lot of things to do on a college campus. Many universities are like cities within themselves, with all kinds of things going on to keep you busy when you are not studying. As a young, educated student, the college campus is a place where you have the chance to make some serious change in the world. The student government association is a great place to start. Running for office on campus is not nearly as frightening as it may seem. You simply get a crew together that is going to help you, and then campaign like hell. The number of students who actually vote in these elections is very low, so getting the minority students on campus to come out and vote for you would seal most of the deal right there. If you are on a campus that is predominantly minority, you may want to get your fraternity or sorority to come out and support you, or the campus choir, if you are a member of such an organization. Campus political office is a great place for you to make a difference on campus and also work on your professionalism and public speaking skills. Additionally, you will have something extremely valuable to put on your resume. Participating in student government identifies you as a leader and team player, as someone that a company would love to have on their staff. You are also more likely to work your way into graduate school or law school. Most people don't go for student government positions because they don't think it's possible for them. You would be surprised at what can be accomplished if you put your mind to it.

I also recommend joining whatever minority student organization your campus has. If there is not one, then start one. This organization is extremely important for students working together to make change in the world. It also tends to be a place where students can go and feel comfortable. Consider yourself a leader of this group, participate and speak up at meetings. Many people in the world are looking for someone to follow. If you present yourself as a leader, then others will follow you.

Athletes, women of color and itsy-bitsy pepper spots

This is a section of the book for special segments of the minority student population. First, there are the athletes. Then, there are the women, who have special needs and should hear some things that I want to share with them. Finally, there are the pepper spots, like me: Minority students at predominantly white universities. I am not sure if the term "pepper spot" is accurate, since a speck of pepper in a parking lot full of salt might not feel as bad sometimes as being a minority student on an all-white campus. It can be a little lonely out there, and I hope to tell you some things that might make you feel better.

Athletes

The minority athlete: the most feared, intimidating species to walk the face of this country. The one who steps onto the field and makes opponents sweat with fear, and makes their stomachs turn to jello. The one who has the rest of the NFL taking steroids just to keep up with him. The one that has old college coaches scouring the projects looking for their next ticket to the Final Four. The group of men and women with untold power, yet no knowledge of how deep that power actually goes. The one who can change the world, but instead allows the world to change them.

Minority athletes run the fastest, jump the highest and throw the farthest. Physically, we are an amazing, dominant group of individuals, able to accomplish miracles. It doesn't matter if you're talking about Kobe Bryant on the basketball court, Alex Rodriquez on the baseball diamond, or Serena, Venus and Tiger at the country club. We are the "shiznit". That is our power. The question is, how can that power be used? Another important question is: how can these athletes make sure that their athletic prowess does not lead to their demise?

There are a ton and a half of stories about athletes who have gone to college and left with nothing. Some of them have played ball for the biggest ballers, and been the biggest star in the sky. But 10 years later, that person may be collecting garbage or getting arrested for smoking crack. Of course this is not the whole story. There are a lot of athletes who use college to their benefit and make sure that they get the education that was promised to them. Some of them also go on to the NBA or NFL and make millions. The story changes for each person, and it's up to you to decide how your story is going to end.

Remember: you are more than just a dumb jock

Unfortunately, there are a lot of athletes who are mushed through the system like stinky old dogs. They are just passed from one grade to the next without anyone, even their parents, monitoring their academic performance. Some student athletes get all of their self-respect and respect from others from what they do on the court or the field and not what they do anywhere else.

This is a dangerous position to be in because you are putting all of your eggs in one basket. I have taught at The University of Kentucky, Indiana University, Syracuse University and The Ohio State University. All of these schools have big time athletic programs, second to none. But, believe it or not, MOST of the athletes who played football or basketball for these schools DO NOT make it to the NBA or NFL. That is sad, but it's the truth. I have known guys who were high school All-Americans, and even athletes of the year for the entire U.S. who did not get a chance to play beyond their 4 years in college. Being good at sports in high school can make you feel that you are invincible. That no one can steal your game, and that you are going to be greater than the greatest at what you do. This might be true. You might go on and do great things. With hard work, anything is possible. But the thing that you don't want to do is put all of your energy into playing your sport and not focusing on getting your education. For most athletes, sports are temporary. The rest of your life is much, much longer. Without a good academic foundation, you are going to be lost. Even if you are not the best student in the world, don't worry about it. Whatever brain cells you use learning the plays in your coach's playbook can also be applied to passing your history test. Get that education and understand that you are NOT just a dumb jock.

Many big time universities don't make it easy to focus on academics. You get to the dormitory (which may be the one that is restricted to football players, or whatever sport you are in), and you see football posters on the wall, and everybody is talking about football all the time. Football, football, football. It is easy to get caught up in all that, and to dedicate your life to the sport that you play. Everybody likes to win, so you are going to want to win too. But you've got to make sure that you are thinking long term. When you get to college, most of the coaches are not focused on how well you are doing in class. That is not their job. Their job is to coach sports. It is your job to make sure that you are learning and getting the education that they promised you before you got there. So, be a winner on the field, but you also want to be a winner in life.

Sorry to tell you this, but…….

I hate to have to break this to you, but your coaches may not love you the way they say they do. If they say that they care about you, it's probably not that they care about YOU, it's that they care about SOMETHING THAT YOU CAN DO FOR THEM. They are not all bad people, but how can you *really* expect someone to care about you when they barely know you? The only people who love you forever without conditions are your mother, father and maybe your sisters and brothers, if you are lucky. The others people who truly love you are God and yourself. You have to love yourself. Loving yourself means that you should enter this situation with dignity and respect and not allow anyone to take advantage of you.

The NCAA is notoriously accused of taking advantage of its athletes. First of all, the athletes don't get financially compensated for their services. The two major revenue-generating sports for many schools are football and basketball. They generate literally billions of dollars for the NCAA every year. The coaches, administrators and college presidents get multi-million dollar salaries, money for their new yachts and campus libraries, all that. The players get damn near NOTHING. That clearly violates the American way, since slavery was outlawed a long time ago.

What they give you is your scholarship. Obviously, this is not a fair trade, since I am sure they would not give up their salaries for your scholarship. What is worse is that a lot of the schools don't even deliver on the scholarship that they promise. As soon as they find that you are injured or aren't panning out to be the player that they expected you to be, they are looking for any and every way they can get rid of you so they can free up that space. Watch your back.

How to watch your back when the hounds come a-callin

When the coaches come busting down your door, begging you to come to their school so that they can love you forever, remember that this situation is currently to your advantage. It's a little like marriage: your spouse is ALMOST NEVER as nice to you as they are when they are trying to get you to marry them. Once you sign on the dotted line, you don't have nearly as much negotiating power as you had before.

I.   Check the contract carefully

First, make sure that the loopholes on the letter that you sign with the school are all covered and airtight. You may even want to get a lawyer to take a look at the scholarship being offered to you. Find out what happens if you quit the team, are not performing on the field, get injured, etc. I know that you don't plan for these things to happen, but sometimes they do. You don't want to be in a situation where the coach could suddenly cut you from the team and take your scholarship money. Also, find out what happens if it takes you longer than 4 years to graduate and your eligibility runs out. You should prefer schools that give you at least 6 years to finish your degree, where the athletic department is always going to pay the tuition bill for you. If the school wants you bad enough, then they will make adjustments to get you there. If no school is willing to offer you the kind of deal that you need, at least make sure that you know what you are signing.

If you are offered the chance to get an academic scholarship rather than an athletic one, think carefully about this option. NCAA regulations don't allow athletes to work, so you are going to be broke. Also, when you take a scholarship from the athletic department, you are basically their slave. A lot of students start playing college sports and later find out that they don't enjoy the sport the way they used to. But the problem is that they are stuck, since the people paying for them to go to school are also running their sport. If you get the chance to get an academic scholarship and join the sports team as a "walk-on", that could be better than taking an athletic scholarship in the beginning. That way, you can do what you want and you don't owe anything to anybody.

II.   Get some advice from a vet

The best way to find out what a school has to offer is to talk to another minority who has been there before, preferably another athlete. Don't talk to someone that the coach tells you to talk to, since they are obviously going to find someone who says good things about the school. Find someone on your own. Also, talk to more than one person, so that you can get a variety of perspectives. Finally, make sure that you talk to at least one person over the age of 27 who also participated in the athletic program that you are looking to go into. This person can give you the big picture perspective and let you know how things work and what they look like in the long-run.

III.   Give the HBCUs some play

There used to be a time when sports teams at most HBCUs were about as talented as Porky Pig in the 100 meter dash. Racial integration led to many of the best black athletes heading to the white institutions that had the most money and TV exposure. But a lot of this has changed. There are quite a few HBCUs that are a hair away from being serious contenders in college sports. It never made sense to me that most of the best athletes are minorities, but the HBCUs can't get these players to their schools! It's not their fault however. Things are this way because white schools have dominated the television market, and tend to have all the money. Money talks.

If you hear an HBCU calling, you might want to give it some thought. There are some seriously good experiences that students can get from HBCUs. There are many who find that the teachers tend to care about you a lot more than they do at white schools, the students emerge with a great deal of confidence, racism is taken out of the picture for you (for the most part, although there are some other problems), and you get to go to class with a bunch of other people who look like you. That can be a very nice experience. So, when the HBCUs send you that recruitment letter, at least hear what they have to say. You may hear something that catches your interest.

IV. Think about why you choose the school

Some people pick a school simply based upon the quality of its athletic program. You have to be careful when you do this. There are some schools out there with big time sports teams where the university president barely knows how to read. You are going to have to live the rest of your life with the degree that you get from that university, so be sure that they at least have some decent connections that can help you get a job when you graduate. Pick a school that is good in your major, or that has a strong academic reputation to go with their athletic one.

The university should also have high graduation rates, since this is a reflection on their ability to get students through their academic program. DO NOT pick a school just because they are on national TV.

V.   Time management is the key

I recall a conversation I had with a friend who played football at a Division-I university. During a conversation once, he said to me "Boyce, I spend every single minute of every day being emotionally, physically and mentally drained." This was because he would get up early every morning to lift weights, then, he would go to class for a few hours. After that, he would have football practice in the afternoon, and then, as tired as he was after all that, he would have to go home and study. If I'd had a schedule like that, I doubt I would have had a high GPA. He could hardly even take a nap!

Since your time is limited, and you are already going to be required to miss a lot of class, make sure that you are careful with your time. Athletes have to be the most careful, precise, professional and mature students on the entire campus when it comes to time management. You should start every day with your own schedule to make sure that you have time to do the things you need to do, whether it be work or play. Not following a schedule can put you in a position to feel overwhelmed, as if there are not enough hours in the day for you to get by. That can lead to total chaos in your life, which breeds all kinds of stress. Time is money, and you should be careful where you invest it.

VI. You are a leader and role model, whether you like it or not

Minority athletes have the ability to change the world. In fact, great athletes like Muhammad Ali actually HAVE changed the world. His extraordinary courage and vision, in the face of tremendous hostility is what has led him to take his place on a thrown that covers every corner of the world and transcends all competitive sports. Minority athletes have visibility that is basically unprecedented, tremendous media access, and the eyeballs of the entire world on them while they are in the spotlight. That puts extra pressure on you because when you mess up, the whole world is going to find out about it.

Try to use this exposure to your advantage by making the right decisions in your life when it comes to alcohol and drugs, or illegal activities. You are in a position where a lot of things can go right for you, but a lot of things can also go wrong for you. How you use this opportunity is clearly up to you.

The colorful women of color

The plight of the minority woman in America can be especially toiling. They have to deal with the double-whammy of racism and sexism. Sometimes, other women of your same race treat you unkindly, and there are men of your own race who want to do mean things to you. But you have to remember that you are loved. The amazing strength and power of the ethnic woman goes back thousands of years, and you are the continuation of that legacy.

When it comes to attending college and making your way through, there are some unique issues that you should be aware of. I've seen so many young girls head off to college with high hopes and even higher GPAs, only to come back with a baby in their arms and their tail between their legs. You WILL NOT end up in that position.

Freshman meat

As creative and intelligent as men can be, they can sometimes use this intelligence to support the fact that a lot of men are just flat out sex hounds. Of course, this behavior is no different from other mammals on The Nature Channel, but it's still something to look out for. There are some men who measure themselves on the number of sexual conquests they can attain. This is a dangerous habit, and something that needs to change. Freshman girls are part of their "herd" that they use to obtain their conquests. Some of them will lie, be deceptive, or do whatever it takes to get you to get into bed with them. That is their goal. You have to watch out for this.

Some girls begin college after having been seriously controlled by their parents their entire lives. They see this freedom as the chance to do whatever they want, whenever they want, and to go wherever they want. That's all fine and good, but you have to be smart with this freedom. It's like getting a car for the first time; you don't just hop right in and start driving 90. You have to start off slow and get used to your newfound control and power.

You should also be careful about your decision to have sex with anyone, at least for a while. If you think you love the person, then at least give it some time before you think about getting into bed with the dude. Also, try to dig around and find out what kind of rep the brother has before you start getting busy with him. If he's had 10 girlfriends during the last semester, that probably means that you are going to be number 11, with number 12 coming next Tuesday. Of course he's going to say that you are the special one, the one that he wants to keep forever, but the fact is that even he probably doesn't know what he wants right now.

Making someone wait a while to have sex is a good thing for a lot of reasons. The main one is the fact that even if the dude runs off and disappears after you've done it, at least you know that you made him earn it a little bit. Men should also wait to have sex, but many of them don't think the same way that women do. If you don't want to be anybody's freshman meat, then make sure that you protect yourself. But if you don't mind being meat, then all bets are off. The key is that whatever you are looking for from your relationships, you have to make sure that you avoid taking steps that might keep you from getting it. I do recommend, however, that marriage is a good time to start doing all the crazy stuff, because at least then, you will know that you are with someone you can probably trust.

Be careful about the parties, till you know what's up

Don't just find yourself heading to college and going to every party that "your girls" invite you to. If you do, you'll find yourself at a club or house party with gunshots ringing out and folks running for cover. You don't know who is at these parties or what they are all about. You might be in the company of rapists, murderers, drug dealers or whatever. If you go out, try to make sure that you are out with a group of friends that you trust, and that you are together with them the entire time. That way, if something goes down, you'll be near friends who have your back.

Be careful about drinking too much, if you drink at all. You don't want to be in a vulnerable state in a situation that you are not familiar with. Alcohol, with a lack of protection is a recipe for major problems. Also, if you are out with a guy you don't know very well, make sure that you keep a plan to deal with this fool in case he starts trippin. That might mean keeping some mace in your purse, and at least having some money so that you can get home by yourself.

Pregnancy and all that

I am not here to tell you what you should think about abortion, condoms and premarital sex. I can only say that there are options in all situations, and you should be aware of what they are. I have an entire section on this topic in earlier parts of the book, but a quick recap never hurts. When it comes to premarital sex, always wear a condom. That means you keep the damn thing on, even if you have been dating this dude for 8 million years. There are a gang of brothers out there who have had girlfriends for years and cheated on them systematically. Don't make yourself into a person with another sob story to tell the world.

Also, make sure that the person that you have sex with is someone that you trust. If you don't know the person, you don't know if they are one of the idiots who will put a condom on the wrong way, or intentionally make the condom break while they are having sex with you. Not good for you, because you are the one who can get pregnant.

If you find yourself pregnant, go talk to someone who understands. If you can't talk to a family member, talk to some friends and perhaps an older person, like a counselor at Planned Parenthood. There is nothing to be ashamed of, and you have to deal with the situation in a responsible manner. If abortion is your choice, make sure you are aware of the risks and implications of that decision. If you choose to have the child, spend time understanding what you are getting into.

MAKE SURE THAT THE FATHER PAYS CHILD SUPPORT. I don't care how much you THINK you care about him. I don't care how proud you are. I don't care what kind of sob story he gives you. I don't care, I don't care, I don't care! For some reason, when a baby comes early, it is always the woman that gives up her future, not the man. Don't feel that you have to take care of that baby by yourself, since it took two of you to make it. If he doesn't pay, then have his butt sent to jail. Why shouldn't he go to jail for not taking care of his child? If you had a baby and weren't taking care of it, don't you think that the police would take YOU to jail?

Be careful about going out at night by yourself

Sorry to have to put it this way, but women should not travel by themselves across campus at night. Yes, men shouldn't either, but we can be goofy and don't listen to good advice. Also, men are a little better able to physically handle certain types of confrontation and less likely to be victims of rape. If you have some place to go late at night, do not think for one second that you are super woman and going to whip out a magic sword to kill anyone who dares to step up to you. You are mortal, and you can easily become the victim of horrible crimes. This happens all the time, all across the country, every single day, right on college campuses. Do not let this happen to you.

If you have to go to the library at night, try to find a partner to go with you, preferably 3 or 4 people. Also, bring weapons: mace, pepper spray, and even something else on your car keys to ensure that you can take out whatever fool tries to mess with you. Also, try to walk across the well-lit part of main campus, rather than the outskirts or dark areas. Be aware of whatever emergency system the school has: little phones that they have scattered across campus, or whatever they use to make sure that people can call police in the event that something happens to them.

Pepper spots: Non-white students at white universities

The life of a pepper spot can be a lonely one. You arrive on a campus that is covered with white folks. No one looks like you for miles, other than the nice people on the janitorial staff. They might even become your best friends, since they remind you of your mother, father and the people who helped you get there.

You sometimes have to deal with cops giving you funny looks for being on campus. You have to walk around campus and see all the great, big multi-million dollar white fraternity and sorority houses, lookin like the President of the United States decided to become roommates with P. Diddy. And then you see our frat houses: ex-abandoned buildings that couldn't hold 3 fat people at the same time.

It seems like the whole campus was just made for white people: all the students are white, the teachers are white, the administrators are white, the walls are white, and even the roaches have blue eyes and blonde hair. Every function you go to has maybe one other pepper spot on the other side of the room, but besides that, there is a sea.....no, an ocean....no, an entire universe of white people. This can be a somewhat intimidating environment.

It can be even worse in the South, where there are some places where people of color barely have animal status. You have to deal with the fact that a lot of people expect you to fail from the beginning. They see you as something inferior, as a man or woman who is *destined* to be second-class. This can not only be disheartening, but also downright freakin scary.

To hell with all that, this is your show

This experience is a great chance for you to see what the world is really like. It is also a chance for you to use the pressure of an experience to make you stronger for the long run. You are the next step of a long line of amazing people, who overcame the most unbelievable odds in order to succeed and achieve at the highest levels. Go into this situation with confidence, and with your head held high, knowing that you are MEANT to succeed. This is your opportunity to prove everyone wrong. This is your chance to shine, because everything great that you do is going to be noticed by the rest of the world. Make the world fear you and respect you, not the other way around.

You can use your race to your advantage. If you go to a white university and are a strong student, you can get scholarships like crazy. I received a scholarship nearly every semester because I had a 3.9 GPA. The fact that I was black somehow amazed them (as if they believed that a black man could not get a 3.9 GPA), so that brought much more attention to my application. Also, I still love, to this day, seeing the look on people's faces when they see a young black male with a PhD who is at the top of his game. They see me as an oddity, like a 4-headed giraffe. I simply see myself as another link of a long line of kings who were meant to control their destiny and their environment.

Ways to cope with the environment

Being strong all the time isn't always fun. You can get a little tired of always carrying the torch and fighting with fools left and right. Maybe you want to find a place on campus where you can relax and know that you are with a group of people who accept you and appreciate you for who you are. Here are some ways to make sure that you don't get lost in the crowd.

One way is to find a culture center or some place where students of your race like to kick it. There is always a place like this somewhere, and the nice thing about it is that even if there are only a few minorities on the entire campus, when you get them all together, it seems like there are a whole bunch of them. Find that place and hang, but don't get so attached to the place that you can't interact with other people. Some students become afraid, bitter and disassociated with the rest of the campus. This campus belongs to you too, even though the white folks got there first.

Secondly, try to do some things off campus that give you a chance to kick it with other people like you. There might be a church nearby that you can join. Also, there might be another university nearby that has a minority population of its own.

Look up minority professors on campus and go visit them, even if they are not in your major. Many of them will be glad to see you (ignore the ones who are not). This might be a chance for you to make a lifelong friend and find a good mentor. You can get great advice from these people. I met one of my best friends in the world during college, when he was the only black professor in the entire business school. We are best friends to this day.

Some of the elements of racism on white campuses

Some of the most racist folks out there have no idea that they are racist. Many of them are not even trying to be. It just sort of happens, like how you have always been breathing your entire life, or wiping your butt, but you have no idea why. That is just what you were taught and told to do, so that is what you do. If and when you experience racism on campus, try not to let it make you mad. Just realize that some people don't know that they are racist, and they are really trying to do the right thing.....SOMETIMES.

Another thing about racism is that it can become *institutionalized.* That means that you can have the racism, even when there is not a single racist person in the building. An example might be the case where you have a university where nearly every single professor is white. Of course, since they are all white, they are going to do white things and have an environment that best fits white culture. They are going to talk white, act white, have classes for white people and hire other white people. It's just a fact. Anything that involves other cultures is secondary, for example, the black history class is going to be an elective, whereas the American history class is going to be required and focus on the white heroes first. This is a form of racism because the institution is set up in a racist fashion, so it keeps racist traditions. So, even if all the white professors are not racist themselves, you are still in a racist environment. It's sort of like how if someone lets out a good fart and it still stinks long after they have left the room.

Of course things didn't get that way by accident. People of color were not allowed to go to most of these schools for the first 100 or so years they were in existence. So, there were a set of rules, traditions, regulations and environments created long before we even arrived on the dock. When we arrive on campus, we are forced to deal with the fact that none of our teachers are black, and that getting a black class on the curriculum is impossible because all the "essential" white classes have taken up all the space. That is what you have to deal with, and that is what they call institutionalized racism. That is also the biggest racism that there is. You probably won't have to worry about someone calling you dirty names in public. But you cannot believe for one second that the racism is gone.

When you are forced to deal with racism, whether it is institutionalized or blatant, make sure you look it square in the eye and conquer it. Dealing with racism is like walking to work in the rain: the rain makes it less comfortable to get there, but if you are focused, you are still going to get where you want to go. Minority students have lower graduation rates than other students on white campuses, and much of this has to do with racism in our society. But if you are focused on what you came to do, you will still succeed, no matter what.

Being the black voice of the class

One thing that happens sometimes in college is that the black student in class ends up becoming "the black voice" whenever there is a black issue raised in class. This can happen for other ethnic minorities as well. For some people, this is an opportunity, for others, it's a burden. Whatever your point of view, don't let any of this bother you. If you feel the need to speak up, don't be afraid to do so. Your voice does not need to be drown out, because it a very important one. You are giving the other students a chance to hear from a point of view that they may not get to hear otherwise. But if you are uncomfortable in this position, then do not feel like you have to say anything. It's up to you.

Time to blast off!

You are now ready to begin or complete your journey through college. You have all the weapons that you need to be the greatest student you can possibly be. What you have to remember more importantly than anything is that your greatest weapon is YOU. YOU are the one who writes your own story. YOU are the one who calls the shots for your life. YOU are the one who believes in yourself and is willing to pay the price for your own success. YOU are the one who will benefit from your hard work and perseverance.

Now that you understand the importance of your education, it is time that you put these principles into practice so that you can create the life that you want to have. There are obstacles in the world for minority students, but these obstacles can be overcome with hard work and lots of confidence. Your education and mental development are powerful tools in this world, so you should keep your weapons as sharp as you possibly can.

The Coco Rules

"The Coco Rules" are a set of short reminders of the things that you need to remember to succeed in college. All of the information in this book can be tough to remember. So, these rules provide a nice "cheat sheet" to help you remember the "dos" and "don'ts" of collegiate success.

Myths about College

Myth #1: You can either have fun or make good grades, but it is impossible to do both.

A person can make good grades AND have a great time in college, it's only a matter of proper time management. People get themselves into trouble when they don't understand <u>balance</u>. Doing too much of anything in college can be harmful, even studying. College is a place for you to get a complete, well-rounded experience, not for you to drink yourself into comas every weekend, or to stay in the library 24-7.

Myth #2: Everybody in college drinks.

For some reason, many students are convinced that drinking is just a natural part of the college experience and that everybody does it. That is ABSOLUTELY FALSE. Some students choose to drink, and many do not. If anyone ever feels like they can pressure you into drinking, then that is obviously a person who is not confident enough in who they are to do their own thing. Make sure that you don't make decisions just because somebody else is doing it, because if things don't work out, you won't be able to blame everybody else.

Myth #3: It is <u>supposed</u> to take 5 or 6 years to graduate.

Getting out of school in 4 years is not that difficult. Many of the people who do not make it in less than 6 years have either changed their major a million times or they are having some kind of problem that is slowing them down. It's like playing a videogame. If you have a map of where you need to go and what you need to do, you are going to get through the game faster than someone who has not taken the time to plan. No matter what anyone says, you don't have to be Superman to get out of college in 4 years, or even 3 years for that matter. You just have to be focused and know what you want to do.

Myth #4: You have to be incredibly smart to make straight As.

There is no magic formula for getting straight As. If you can get one A, you can get ten. The person who makes As in college is not the brainiac with a 200 IQ. It is usually that person who simply wants good grades and does what the teacher tells them to do. Also, the person who gets things done rather than waiting until the last minute is the one that is going to do well 9 times out of 10. So, good grades do not say that you are smarter than other people, it just says that you have done your job well.

Myth #5: People in college are smarter and better than those who are not.

People who go to college are usually there because they are from a family that encourages its kids to go to college. The people in college are no smarter than the people who choose to deal drugs, live with their mama, or work in grocery stores. Over the years, I've seen some college students do the dumbest things you can possibly imagine, some even worse than what you see on the street. Being smart is not a strong requirement for college, since there are families who send their kids to college no matter how smart they are. Don't let anyone tell you that you are not meant to go to college. You may not be a rocket scientist, but most people can go to college and eventually graduate if they put their mind to it (even if their minds are small).

Myth #6: Everyone who goes to college is going to make a lot of money when they graduate.

How much money you make when you graduate from college depends on what major you choose and how much education you get in your field. There are strong money majors, like business and engineering, and some less financially secure majors, like philosophy or English. The type of reward that you get from college may not be financial, and you have to choose your field and education level based on what you want from your life. There are trades that don't require college that can make more money than you would get with most college degrees, so make sure that college is what you want to do before you commit. Also, remember that getting the highest education level possible in your field may also be a good investment. Be sure to investigate all available options before you choose a major and decide on graduate school alternatives.

Myth #7: A college degree is everything you need in the job market.

The world is changing, and a college degree doesn't have nearly as much punch as it did back in the day. Most fields require you to have advanced education beyond the Bachelors degree before you can get the best jobs in your field. It is important that you find out what education level you need in order to do what you want to do. Only having a Bachelors degree when everyone else has a Masters degree is like bringing a dull knife to a gunfight.

Myth #8: You have to have a lot of money to go to college.

Most students don't pay their own way through college. Most of them use some kind of financial aid to get there. There are a lot of financial aid programs out there, especially for minority students. There are student loans, state and federal grants, scholarships and everything else. Also, there are schools with low tuition that you can afford with a part-time job. Money should not be the barrier keeping you away from college, the money is out there if you take the time to look for it.

The 10 biggest mistakes made by students who are preparing for college

Mistake #1: Listening to someone who says you are not "college material"

The term "college material" was pretty much meant to keep the "haves" away from the "have nots". There are a lot of kids in college who would have been kept away from college had they grown up in poor or non-white families. But these kids go to college, graduate and get higher paying jobs because they were <u>expected</u> to go on to college. If someone ever says that you are not "college material", this only means that you might need some work in certain areas to get up to speed. Even I was told that I was not "college material", and I am a professor! I also have a bunch of friends who are now professors that were told the exact same thing. For someone to tell you at the age of 18 that you are NEVER going to be smart enough to go to college is absolute bull.

Mistake #2: Waiting too long to take the ACT or SAT

You should get this over and done with early in your Junior year. That way, you can retake the test if you have to. Using this approach, you will be sure to have a valid score together before it is time for you to send off your applications. Before you head to college, you have to have a plan. Make the plan well in advance and stick with it.

Mistake #3: Not taking classes that will prepare them for college

You should make sure that whatever classes you take during high school are college prep classes that will meet the academic standards of college. It makes college a lot easier. It is not impossible to correct the problem if you don't have these classes in your background, but an ounce of prevention is worth a pound of cure. Have your parents talk to your counselor about making sure that your classes meet the needs of college. If they won't do it, then talk to the counselor yourself.

Mistake #4: Choosing a school that is too far away from home or too expensive

Sometimes college students just want to go as far away from home as they can. They don't worry about the expense, since they think that Mama and Daddy are made of money. If you really want to go to a school that is out of state, make sure that you know WHY you want to go to this school. For example, I had a friend from Tennessee who went to The University of Kentucky instead of The University of Tennessee, where her tuition would have been much lower (since she was a resident of Tennessee). She had no reason for wanting to do this other than the fact that she was from Tennessee and thought that it would be cool to go to a school in another state. That's stupid, because she ended up causing her mother to take out thousands of dollars in student loans only so that she could get the same quality of education for double the price. If you are comparing Harvard against some average state school, that is one thing, but if you are choosing some more expensive school across the country just for the "hulluvit", then that is a problem.

Mistake #5: Not applying to enough universities.

You should never put all your eggs into one basket. When you apply to college, you can't just send your app to one or two schools and hope for the best. You've got to spread yourself out there so that the world knows that you are going to college. You never know what kinds of special scholarships different schools have. Also, some schools may not offer you any money if they don't think that you have other options out there. You have to make sure that your interests are protected. Even if the school promises that you are a shoe-in to be admitted, you should still apply elsewhere.

Mistake #6: Not applying for every scholarship you can find

You should put your name on every dotted line that crosses your path. Serious scholarship searches can be very helpful in preparing financially for college. You have to work hard: buy books, use the internet, or whatever to make sure that you find a way to apply for as many things as you can, even if you don't think you can get them. A good way to motivate yourself might be to set a goal for the number of applications you should fill out. Try to make the number 30 or 40, or as high as you can. Then, when you've filled out that many applications, you will know that you've come close to doing your best.

Mistake #7: Choosing a school because your girlfriend or boyfriend is going to attend the same university

We all want to believe that love is eternal. Sometimes it is, but any divorce lawyer could tell you that it usually is not. This is especially true when you are young. But that doesn't mean that you should give up on your sweetie. It only means that you should be careful about how much you give up for this relationship. Also, you have to think about whether it is necessary to give some of these things up. Choosing a college just because your boyfriend or girlfriend is there is one of those things that can make you feel really silly later on. If they really love you, they will respect your decision, even if you choose to go to another school. If they don't respect your decision, then maybe they were never meant for you in the first place.

Mistake #8: Not keeping their grades high enough in high school

When I was in high school, I didn't spend too much time worrying about college. I would either not go at all, or I figured that it would take care of itself. So, I didn't do what I needed to do to keep my grades up. That was a terrible decision that I regretted later on. If your grades are not as high as you need them to be, you may want to talk to your teachers about how to get them up. You might also want to find out if there are places you can go to get help with your homework. Time management is especially important, so you should nail your assignments as soon as you get home from school. Good grades really pay off later in the process.

Mistake #9: Getting intimidated by the college admissions process

The whole college application thing can be really scary. But it's not as scary as you might think. You just have to look it square in the eye and say "I am going to make this happen, no matter what". Getting intimidated by the process is only going to make it that much harder for you to reach your goals. I know that you want a better life for yourself, so the hard work is something that you are going to have to do no matter what. Getting some help from adults is also a good thing. If you call a university, they are going to have people that can help you, and you also have your counselors and teachers, many of whom are going to be happy that you are thinking about going to college. Use these resources that are in front of you, and DO NOT BE AFRAID!

Mistake #10: Not studying for the ACT or SAT

Some people mistakenly believe that the ACT and SAT are measures of your intelligence. They are not. They are only measures of how well you do on a certain type of standardized test. You have to practice, and you have to study. The students who do well on these exams are not necessarily the smart ones. They are the ones who have practiced and practiced this thing until they know it backwards. They know the types of questions that are going to be asked, and they know how to figure out the right answers. Make sure that you are one of those people who studies for the ACT and SAT. It makes a tremendous difference.

Coco Rules for the aspiring college student

1) Make sure that you visit the schools you are thinking about attending

You don't want to have to spend 4 years in a place that you hate. Any school that is on your short list of places that you might want to attend should be a place that you've seen for yourself. You may get there and find that the campus is urban when you thought it was rural. Or you may find out that there are almost no minorities, when you thought there were going to be more. Any time you jump into such a big commitment, you should make sure that you protect your investment.

2) Try to live in the dorms, even if your parents are nearby.

Going to college is about a lot more than just getting a degree. It's about growing up and learning to be an independent adult. Living with your parents usually makes it harder to do that, since it is human nature for us to remain dependent on others if they are always taking care of us. In addition to that, you won't get as much out of college if you never know the thrill of living in the dorm with all your buddies. That is the part of college that everyone remembers for the rest of their lives. Your parents should understand if you want to live on campus, and they will probably be glad to see you get your own place. If they don't understand, explain to them that it is time for you to adjust to adulthood, and being on your own is an important part of that process.

3) If you move far away from home, make sure that you have money to come back and visit.

Going to college far away from home sounds really cool at first. But the thing is that if you are far away from home, coming back home is going to be very, very expensive. You probably won't be able to get back more than 2 or 3 times a year, and even those trips are going to be more expensive than most college students can comfortably afford. If you go far away to school, then you should either have some money available to travel home, have a plan to get some, or accept the fact that you are not going to be going home very much.

4) Don't choose a major because your parents want you to do it.

Sometimes, when we have loved ones who really care about us, they can end up trying to run our lives. That is because they have already gone through a lot of what you are going through, and they don't want you to make the same mistakes they made. But the problem is that there are some things we have to learn on our own. Also, what is right for your parents may not be right for you. Your dad may want you to become an engineer, and you may want to become an English Professor. If you spend your life doing things because other people want them for you, you are opening a door to life-long unhappiness. Take the advice of loved ones, and listen to their wisdom, but always make sure that you are the one making the final decision.

5) DO NOT drop out of college for any period of time, no matter how small, for any reason.

All through your life, you have to be careful about the things you do, for they are opening doors for you to end up doing something that you never planned for. Life has a set of chain reactions, and whatever you are today, you are always BECOMING something for tomorrow. Most people who have dropped out of school did not plan to drop out for good. Most of them left school saying "I am going to come right back, after ....(fill in the blank) happens". Before they knew it, a month turned into a semester, a semester turned into 5 years, 5 years turned into a lifetime. Do not put yourself at risk. Even if you have to bite, kick, creep and crawl to stay in school, make sure that you do it. Dropping out of school may solve a few short-term problems, but you could be creating a lifetime of regrets.

6) Apply to at least 15 different colleges, so that you can see what is out there.

Whether you think you are the hottest applicant in the world or the stankest, you HAVE to apply to as many schools as you possibly can. You never know what opportunities are out there and what certain schools are looking for. You also have to make sure that you go to the highest bidder. If you only apply to one place, then you are giving the school a lot of power. Many times, if they know that you have only applied to their university, they may not want to give you as much money because you have chosen to limit your options. Make sure that you always create as many options for yourself as you can, since that reduces the chance that you are going to be left out in the cold. Even if you have to get a part-time job to pay application fees, it is worth the trouble.

For community college and part-time students

1) Make sure that all your credits transfer BEFORE you take the class

Many students take classes at community colleges that don't transfer to the 4-year college that they decide to attend later. This leads to a lot of wasted time and frustration. Before you take anything, make sure that the class is going to transfer without a problem. You can find this information out by talking to the counselors at the school that you are trying to get into. Planning can help save a lot of time.

2) If you have a job while in school, be a <u>student who works</u>, not a worker who goes to school.

If you consider school to be a side activity, then you are not going to put it as your top priority. If something happens with the job, the kids or anything, school is going to be the first thing to go. Then, you will find yourself bouncing back and forth for years, spending 4 years to get through 1 year of college, until you eventually give up. You have to make sure that school is your top priority, since this is something that is going to build your educational, professional and financial future. Work can happen, but it has to be secondary so that you keep your focus and eventually find your way to graduation.

3) Draw a path for yourself on how you are going to get that college degree.

Remember the old saying: "We don't plan to fail, we fail to plan". When you go on a long trip, would you leave your house without looking at the map? How would you know which highways to get onto and not? The same applies for going to college. The students who are successful in college are the ones who go with a plan and know what they have to do to get their piece of paper. You have to be fully aware of what the requirements are for your major, and how you are going to get out of that school with a degree in your hand. Don't rely on counselors and other people to do this for you, because if you don't make it in the end, it is no one's responsibility but your own.

4) Start your family AFTER college, not during or before.

Having a family is a wonderful thing. But having one too early can limit your long-run options in life. When you are young, you have more flexibility than you will ever have in your life. Family takes time, and the more time you have to commit to family, the less you can commit to yourself. So, if you want to create the best life you can for your family, you can do that by creating the best life you can for yourself. Get this out of the way early; your children will thank you later!

5) Don't settle for an Associates Degree, keep your eye on the prize!

Associate Degrees are cool, but if you can get more, then go for more. Once you have completed the 2-year degree, the four-year is not much further along. In most fields, the

4-year degree can lead to a much higher salary and a many more job opportunities than the 2-year degree. If you decide you want a Masters Degree, you are in an even better position. When you set your educational goals, you should aim high. The worst that can happen is that you don't hit the highest mark, but you fall back on something that is still worthy of respect. That is how you win the game of life.

How to get ready for the ACT and SAT

1) Find a quiet, well-lit place to study.

When you are studying for any test, you should make sure that you are working in a place that is quiet and has lots of light. That usually means that studying at the kitchen table in your mama's house is not always the best idea. This is when you have your mother telling you to take out the garbage, or your little brother smacking you upside the head with a toy soldier. You need to be in a place that allows your mind to really focus, like a library. If you can't study in the library, then go to a McDonald's or something, and take some earplugs so you can screen out the noise.

2) Try to simulate test conditions as much as possible.

Taking any test, especially the ACT and SAT is like getting ready for a football game. You have to practice in the same conditions that you are going to take the test. That means you need an environment that matches the "game day" environment as much as possible. You should force yourself to sit through and take the entire exam in the amount of time that is going to be allotted on the actual test. Get a friend or relative to help you do that. Let them pretend to be the person giving the test: They can time you and tell you what section to start on next. Go through this process as many times as you can, so that when you take the real test, it is going to be just another practice for you. If you can't find a friend to help you with the test, just do it yourself. It only matters that you are exposed to the material as many times as possible.

3) Make sure that you study a certain number of hours every day (with some days off every now and then).

When you prepare for the SAT and ACT, you have to manage your time and make sure that you do something every day. Don't just buy the books and say that you are going to study whenever you have time. You should put yourself on a schedule where you put in 1 or 2 hours every day preparing for the exam. If you don't make sure that you do a little bit at a time, you are going to find yourself not prepared for the exam when the time comes.

4) Take as many practice tests as possible

Don't just study the stuff that is in the review books, make sure that you take practice tests. There is a difference between the two. The review books might tell you what types of questions to look for, but taking the actual practice test puts you in a position to see how the questions are going to come at you during the exam. You should make sure that you do plenty of both.

5) Try to take a Kaplan or Princeton Review course if you can afford one

Kaplan and Princeton Review courses are designed to professionally prepare you for standardized tests that you are going to need to take to get into college and graduate school. They are expensive, but worth it. Do whatever you can to get a good score, since it pays off in the long run.

6) Sign up for the tests early in your Junior year

Taking the ACT and SAT early is very important. You have to cover your butt in case you need to retake the exam. If you wait until your senior year to take the tests and something goes wrong, you are going to find yourself stuck with a bad score as you try to get into colleges. Find out the schedule of the exams during your sophomore year, and then try to make sure you take the tests during the fall of your Junior year, with the plan to take it again later on. But do not take the tests too early if that means that you have not had time to study.

7) Retake the test if your score is not high enough, but don't retake the test unless you have reason to believe that you are going to do better (they look at all the scores, not just the last one)

You may have good reason to repeat the ACT and SAT, but don't just take them over and over again to see if you can get a better score. Your score may actually decline the next time you take it. If you have no reason to believe that your score is going to improve the next time you take the test, then don't waste your time. Having a string of bad scores surrounding one score that is slightly better might hurt you more than help. If you think that you can be better prepared or if you were sick or something, then it might make sense to take at least one of the tests again.

8) Make sure you take both the ACT and SAT

Some students don't want to take both tests for one reason or another. But it is a good idea to have both of them on record in case you apply to a school that wants the other test. The last thing you need is to get into the last semester of your senior year and have them tell you that they need an SAT score that you don't have.

9) Don't be intimidated by the tests, and don't be discouraged by a bad score

If you don't do well on the tests, consider trying again with a different study strategy. It is not the end of the world. A lot of universities look far beyond the test scores to determine which students they are going to admit. You should not be intimidated by the tests, just determined to do your best. If you are determined to live out your dreams in the long run, no silly test is going to change that.

10) Have the tests sent to as many schools as you possibly can

You should spread your wings as far as you can. By sending your test scores to a lot of different schools (they usually give you an option to have them automatically sent to the schools you choose), you are making sure that a lot of places know that you are going to be heading to college soon. This may lead the schools to send you information or waive your application fees, especially if they happen to have a strong interest in recruiting minorities. Make sure that they know that you exist. You are a product, so you have to market yourself.

MONEY AND
FINANCIAL
AID

Where to get money for college

1) From yourself (savings)

Saving your own money is something that we all should learn how to do. You would be surprised at how much you can pull together with some hard work and diligence. Even if you are earning minimum wage, a healthy savings plan can put together enough money to pay your first semester of tuition at many colleges. Also, once you are on campus, that little extra job can be enough for you to keep money in your pocket, and also buy your books. But remember that if you don't have a ton of money, you should probably not choose an expensive school!

2) From a part-time job or work study

Work-study and campus jobs are all over the place. Manage your time wisely, and try to find a position that will allow you to make money without having to give up your entire life. The best jobs are the ones that let you study while you work. You should definitely make sure that you have a flexible job, so that you can take time off in the event that you have a class project or exam to take care of.

3) Getting a full-time job on campus with tuition breaks

On many campuses, full-time employees get tuition breaks. The thing is that it is usually tough to get these jobs. But if a person works it right, they can sometimes tweak the system and get around these little rules. These tuition breaks might be your only means of survival in college, but these jobs can be time-consuming. You also don't want to be tempted to make this job into your career, since that is not what you came for.

4) From your parents or relatives

If you've got parents or relatives with a little extra money, you may want to take up a collection for your college fund. You might be surprised by their willingness to help, or to at least buy you a little something here and there to help you out. You can also try going to them as an adult and asking if you can work out a loan agreement with them to cover your college expenses. They might be impressed by your maturity.

5) Scholarships (athletic or academic)

There are scholarship opportunities out there for almost everyone. You just have to do your homework and look for them. If you happen to be good at a sport, stick with it and see if that sport can cover part of your costs. But if you have a choice between an academic and athletic scholarship, you should choose the academic one, since that doesn't put you at the mercy of your sports team. Signing your name to every application you can get your hands on is also a very important part of obtaining a scholarship.

6) Grants

Most states have grant programs for college. Also, there are federal grants. If you choose a school with relatively low cost, you might find that the grants cover a big chunk of your total cost. Make sure you milk this cow to the fullest.

7) Student loans

Whatever grants don't cover, loans usually will. You should not be afraid to take out loans to go to school. Loans are a vehicle to get you to your goals, the same as a rental car can get you to work every day. If you don't rent the car, you can't get to work. So, taking out the loans is a good thing, as long as you only borrow what you need. They may take some time to repay, but at least you'll be repaying the loans by working at a higher paying job that you enjoy.

8) Your church

They're always passing the collection plate around TO you, this would be a chance for them to pass it around FOR you. If you belong to a church, there is nothing wrong with talking to the leaders of the church about your financial needs for college. Part of doing God's work involves helping those who want to help themselves. You certainly are in that category by heading off to college.

9) The school that you are applying to

The school that you are applying to may have internal scholarships available that you can apply for. Going to the Minority Affairs Office and other administrative offices on campus can help you find out where there are scholarships you can apply for. If you keep a good GPA while in college, you can usually have a chance to get more scholarship money.

10) The military

I don't recommend this option if you are not interested in possibly going to war or dying to get your money. Most people kinda forget that joining the military means that you are giving someone else the right to use your life for means that might differ from what you've intended. But if this is fine with you, then you might want to consider the reserves, or even active duty. One of the ways they entice young people to join is by offering money for college. Pay attention to their offers, and make sure that you are not just sweet-talked by an ambitious recruiter. Also, NEVER feel that the military is your only option for getting the money that you need. There are always other ways.

11) Summer pre-college programs

Summer pre-college programs are sometimes available for students to help them get ready for the rigors of college life. There are a lot of programs out there for black students. These programs may also be helpful when it comes to finding money for college. You might as well ask, since you might be surprised at what they have available.

12) Jobs that have tuition-assistance programs

There are many jobs off-campus that have tuition assistance programs. You have to dig around a little bit, but a lot of companies are willing to pay money to help their employees gain additional skill. The kicker is that many of these programs usually require you to take classes that they approve of. So, they may not be willing to cover the cost of that Far Eastern Philosophy class that you are trying to take. They also may not be as interested in supporting a History or Education major as they are in supporting a Business or Computer Science major.

13) Internships and co-ops while you are in college.

Summer internships and co-ops are not only something that you should do to get the experience you need for the job market, they are also good ways to make money. The key is that you have to work hard to search for the jobs that might be available.

Financial guerilla war-fare (OK, we've covered the money part in general, but this is what you can do if you get REALLY desperate!)

1) Never give up

This process can be tough sometimes. So, you have to be tougher than the process. That means that you have to go into the situation ready to work as hard as you can to solve your problems and reach your goals. Never ever give up, because giving up is the only way to guarantee that you have NO CHANCE to be successful.

2) Tuition payment plans

A lot of schools understand that students don't always have the money right then to pay their way through school. Check to see if your school has a payment plan you can use to cover tuition. This way, if you have a job, you can pay off your tuition in chunks, rather than paying it all off at the beginning of the semester. Many schools also allow you to pay your tuition in advance, so this could be something you use to reduce the burden later on.

3) Don't be afraid to borrow money

Loans are only bad if you are using the money for something silly. College is not silly. Don't be one of those people who never goes back to school because they are afraid of having loans. That makes no sense. You should be more afraid of not being able to get a good job or not having an education. That is when you are truly poor.

4) Get your grades up as high as possible, as soon as possible

Good grades make it easier for you to get scholarships. Also, a lot of scholarships pay special attention to minority applicants. Use this to your advantage by making sure that you have a GPA that is very competitive. This goes for both high school and college. You are either going to have to work hard at school or work hard at a minimum wage job. Take it from me, school is much easier!

5) If you have to pay for yourself, find the cheapest school you can

Colleges come in all different sizes, with many different costs. Don't choose a school that is going to break the bank. If you are bright and can get rid of your money worries by going to cheaper school, then go ahead and do it. A great college GPA will open the door for you to attend one of those expensive universities when you go to graduate school (That is what I did!).

6) Go to a community college if you have to, since they are cheaper. Also, going to school part-time is better than not going at all

If going to the least expensive school you can find is not the option for you, then consider going to a community college first, or going to school part-time. But only do this if you have to. Going the standard route gets you out and working much faster. But if attending part-time or through community college is the best route for you, then remember that getting some kind of education is better than getting nothing. Always keep yourself moving forward.

7) Find a job that lets you study while you work

Sometimes when you find yourself short on money, you may need to get a job, or even a second one. If that happens to you, your first pick should be a job that will allow you to study while you work. That way, you may actually be helping your grades by taking the job, since there isn't going to be anything else to do except study. Check for dorm monitor and security guard positions that might be available on campus.

8) Consider moving to the state that you want to go to school in and working there for a while to establish residency.

Most states have residency requirements, which allow you to pay in-state tuition after you've lived there for a while. Some students move to the state the year before they start school just so they can live and work in that state and make themselves residents. This can save a lot of money. But you can probably do better by just attending one of the public universities in your home state. However, there are some cases where it is cheaper to pay out of state tuition in a new state than it is to pay in-state tuition in your home state. Just make sure that you know the rules.

Rules for dealing with student loans

1) Make sure that you keep up with all the paper work that they give you when you sign up for the loan. Also, keep a running tab of how much you owe and keep up with your deferments.

Student loans tend to come with a big pile of paperwork with all kinds of details about the loans you have outstanding. It may be a bit of a pain, but make sure that you keep this information together. That way, you are always aware of how much you owe and whether or not you are in default. A lot of students don't keep up with this information, and it ends up piling up on them. Also, you should make sure that if you are still in school, you keep up with your deferments if necessary. A deferment means that you don't have to pay them right away (if you are still in graduate school or don't have a job yet). This can take some of the heat off until you are in a position to start paying the money. You may have to renew the deferment every semester, but it is definitely worth it.

2) Always get subsidized loans first, and then go for unsubsidized if you need the money

There are at least two different types of student loans: subsidized and unsubsidized. You should go for the subsidized first, since the interest on the loan is not going to be charged until after you graduate and start paying on the debt. This makes a huge difference in the amount of money you owe. The unsubsidized loans start charging interest as soon as you borrow the money. This option isn't bad either, since the government tends to charge relatively low interest rates. But this should be your last resort.

3) Borrow only after you've tried everything else. Free money is always better than borrowed money.

There are many grants and scholarships out there that you might be able to get access to. That should be your first choice, and the loans should be your last resort.

4) Borrow only what you need to pay your expenses

You have to repay your loans at some point, so it's a bad idea to just borrow till your head falls off. I recommend that you borrow enough money to cover your tuition and living expenses (room, board and books), and then maybe a few hundred more for savings or paying off credit cards. After that, you should stop. Borrowing up to your limit every single time will create a boatload of problems for you in the long run.

5) Make sure that your lenders always have your address when you leave school so that they can send the paper work to you.

Some people leave school and only think about moving on. They don't think about the fact that you now have obligations to take care of. The student loan people are like anybody else: when they give you their money, they expect to get it back. Most schools have an "exit interview" that you are supposed to attend, where you give them your personal information so that they can keep in touch with you and get their money. This is important, since you can cause yourself a heap of problems by not taking care of this stuff in advance.

6) If you get some extra money from your loans, make sure you save some of it.

This is simple: if you get a pile of money, learn to save by any means necessary. Not knowing how to save will cause you a lifetime of problems. Learn the skill of saving early.

7) Never take out a pile of loans just to go to an expensive college. Find a cheaper one that is going to cost less money.

College is not something that you should mortgage the house for. It is a means to an end: to get yourself an education that will open other doors for you later. It is better sometimes to get straight As at an average school than to get Cs at a highly-ranked university. No matter where you go to college, if you do a good job, you can open the door to get into any graduate school in the country. You can also work your way into a lot of great jobs. Spending tens of thousands of dollars to go to college is unnecessary, and can sometimes be disastrous.

Your path to complete and total academic domination

Lessons for the Get out quick student

1) Learn the path and put together a plan

Learn and study the program that you are entering and know exactly what you have to do to get out.

2) Get those difficult classes out of the way and don't procrastinate

No class is going to go away just because you delay it. If there is a tough class out there that you need to take, go ahead and get through it. If you don't, it's going to only seem scarier for you. Get a tutor if you have to, but get the class out of the way!

3) Don't spend an extra year in college getting an extra major or degree

Those extra degrees seem valuable and glamorous when you are earning them, but they don't mean much in the long run. In the end, you will wish that you had your time back, rather than that extra degree that takes up space on your Mama's living room wall. Getting out of college and getting the first degree is what matters, not how many Bachelors degrees you have. If you have extra time, put that time toward a Masters degree, PhD, MD or JD. That is a much better investment of your time.

4) Summer school is your friend.

Use your summer school opportunities to help yourself get out that much faster. You can kill an entire year of work and graduate in 3 years if you are diligent, or you can use the summers to make up for lost time. Try to get an internship if you can, and if you can't, summer school is your next best option.

5) Don't waste your time taking unnecessary classes: that is what electives are for.

It might seem tempting to take this extra class or that one, but in the long run, you are hurting your chances to graduate and get out of that place. Focus on fulfilling the requirements of your program, which probably already gives you plenty of room in your schedule for electives. Taking a bunch of extra classes is especially bad if you are paying your own tuition.

Top Ten Study mistakes

Mistake #1: Thinking that you don't have to study just because you have no homework

Most of the work that you do in college is probably not going to be homework. Usually, the work is going to require you to study at home and get ready for some big exam or quiz that's coming up. That can fool you, because you might think that because you don't have any homework, you don't have anything to do. That kind of thinking will cause you a lot of problems in college. There is ALWAYS something for you to read, study or go over, even when you have very little homework.

Mistake #2: Studying in the dorm room or with the TV on

You may not think that the TV is taking away from your ability to learn, but it is. Research shows that students who study with the TV on remember a lot less than those who do not. Don't catch yourself thinking that you are really working just because the book is open during the basketball game! You are probably not getting anything done.

Mistake #3: Cramming

You should spread out your studying, not do it all right before the test. Cramming will only make your life stressful, miserably and risky. If something goes wrong and you don't have time to cram, you are going to fail the test. Also, cramming increases the chances that you are going to study as hard as you can, only to get a failing grade. You should spread out your studying and force yourself to get things done in advance.

Mistake #4: Not going to visit your professors

Going to see your professor should be a CRITICAL part of your academic plan. Staying away from them is stupid, because you are giving up the chance to get valuable help and information. Professors also tend to give higher scores to the students that they see and like. Go see your professors at least once a week, and try to see them at least two weeks before the exam, since everybody and their mother is going to try to get into their office during the week of an exam.

Mistake #5: Not getting enough sleep before you study or before you take an exam

While you are studying, you should get plenty of rest. If you find yourself getting tired, you should take a nap. A fresh brain is the only kind of brain that can absorb, retain or recall information. A tired brain doesn't want to learn anything, and it is only going to make you dislike what you are studying. Push yourself hard, but be nice to yourself when you need to be. ALWAYS make sure that you get plenty of rest before you take an exam. Staying up all night before the test is just flat out stupid.

Mistake #6:   Only learning what the teacher gives you in class (not reading the book)

The teacher is going to go over a lot of things in class, but that isn't everything you need to know to do well on the exams. You have to find out your teacher's style for doing things, and then use that information to figure out what is going to be on the test. Usually, the teacher doesn't have time to go over every little thing in class. They are going to expect you to cover a lot of things on your own in the textbook. Keep a balanced approach to studying. The teacher is not going to spoon feed everything to you.

Mistake #7:   Not going to class on a regular basis.

You have to show up to class to get the information that the teacher is going to cover for the exams. Missing class is very tempting, but it is one of the dumbest things in the world that you can do. If you give in to the temptation to miss classes, you are going to find yourself falling further and further behind until you are unable to catch up with everyone else. At that point, not even Jesus can save you! Instead, he would probably let you fail and then tell you that you should have studied.

8) Studying with a bad group

Studying with a pack of people all the time is the easiest way to get a bad grade. It can sometimes be good to work in groups, but most of the time, a group is the easiest way to get caught up in random conversations. All that has to happen is for one person to start talking, and pretty soon, everyone else is in the conversation too. Most of the time, you are best off when you study on your own. Groups only work if you are very disciplined. But being with your best friends at a table for 4 hours without talking is tough for anyone. A good group is one where everyone is disciplined and quiet. The only exceptions are when there are tough problems to solve or you have a group project. But even in those cases, you have to be the one to keep the group focused.

Questions to ask your self when choosing a major

1) What do I like to do?

Never choose a job that you don't like. That is the quickest path to a lifetime of complete misery. My grandmother had a job for 30 years that she didn't like, and she regrets it to this day. She taught me that having a good education means that you give yourself the option to pick and choose what job you want, which increases your chances of finding your way to happiness. I agree with that 100%.

2) What are the factors that matter to me when I think about the kind of job that I want to have?

Every one of us has our individual set of things that we know are going to make us happy. The key is to find out what is going to make YOU happy. This a tough job, since we usually confuse what makes us happy with what makes everyone else happy. We have friends and parents who are influencing us, and they are always promoting their own beliefs when they tell you what you should do with your life. Don't get caught in that position. Find out what makes you happy and find a career that matches that. But you have to make sure that you figure everything in. How much does money matter? Does free time matter? Does prestige matter? This process requires a lot of soul-searching, and I encourage you to be honest with yourself, without worrying too much about what others are going to think (for example, if you really like money, then that is ok.

Don't let anyone tell you that you are a bad person because of it, because your life belongs to no one else).

3) How much time would I be able to spend with my family?

Different careers require different amounts of time away from home. Some jobs, like Wall Street Investment Banking, could potentially make tons of money, but you may not see your family for long periods of time. This may not matter when you are young, but it matters later when you decide to have kids. You may want to break your career into stages and figure out what you can do when you are young vs. what you plan to do when you are in your late 20s and 30s. As your life changes, your career should change also.

4) What is the demand in this field? Is it going to change?

If no one in the world wants to hire people in your field, then this may not be the way you want to make your living. The demand for people in your field means a lot more than how good you are when it comes to finding a job.

5) What is the level of education expected in this field to be successful?

You have to know what level of education you should go to in your field in order to be competitive. For example, Accounting and Engineering expect Masters Degrees. You can get along with a Bachelors Degree, but the money is not going to be quite as good, and you are going to miss out on a lot of jobs. The same is true for teaching. But some areas, like journalism, don't value Masters degrees as highly. Find out where you want to go, what kind of pull you would like to have, and what level of education you need in order to get into that position. If the field requires you to get a PhD before you can get a decent job, you may want to think about whether or not you want that much education.

6) What is my school good at producing?

Different schools have different things that they are exceptional at producing. Some schools produce great architects, and others might produce very good biologists. Find out what the strengths are for your school and if they lie in the areas you are interested in. This may affect your choice of major.

7) What can I do with this degree in case the field dries up?

The world is constantly changing. Sometimes the areas that are hot today are cold tomorrow. If the degree that you have has staying power, that means that even if the demand for a certain type of job goes away, you can use that degree to do something else. But you should always save your money and be ready to go back to school in the event that the opportunities dry up.

How to take a test

Rule #1: Jam, don't cram

Cramming is STOOPID. Yes, so dumb that I didn't even spell "stupid" the right way. You should spend your time studying hard early in the game so that you are not put in a position to have to cram later. If you don't think ahead, you are only going to set yourself up for serious disappointment. The students who wait till the last minute (to try to learn a month's worth of stuff in one night) are the ones who end up saying "I studied all night for the test, and I still failed it!" They are in that situation because they did not plan ahead. Instead of cramming, you should be "jamming". That is when you cram like crazy for the *next* test right after you finish the previous one. That way, you can get a heads up on the new material and impress your professors with the fact that you've gotten so far ahead of the rest of the class.

Rule #2: Get plenty of sleep the night before the test.

A lack of sleep only causes you to forget the stuff that you've already learned. Study hard the weeks before an exam, and then make sure that you get a good night's rest the night before the test. Not getting any sleep is like preparing for an Olympic marathon by trying to run a marathon a few hours earlier. That would be silly, because you would be too tired to run again. The time to prepare for the marathon would be the weeks before, and then you get plenty of sleep on the night before the big day. It is the same way for an exam, since you need a fresh brain for the performance.

287

Mistake #3: Don't miss any class the week before the exam, since important stuff is going to be covered.

Missing class in general is a bad idea, but it's especially STOOPID to miss class the week of the exam. This is the time that the teacher is giving out all the inside information on the test you are about to take. Do not miss class for any reason.

Mistake #4: Go to every single exam review that is being offered, and go see your teacher at least 3 times during the week before the test

If your teacher offers a review session, then make sure that you show up to it. Also, you should spend as much time in your teacher and the Teaching Assistant's office as you can right before the test. That is what they are there for, to help you figure out the things that you are stuck on. Also, they can see that you are working hard, and they will be that much more certain to remember your name and face.

Mistake #5: Set two alarm clocks the morning of the exam.

Relying on one alarm clock is just bad business in general. Your ears may become immune to the clock (in other words, you could sleep right through it), you may set it wrong, or it may just not work for some reason. If it plugs into the wall, that means that you are screwed if the electricity goes out. The bottom line is that your teacher is not going to want to hear any of these excuses, no matter how hard you try to convince him/her. Get at least two alarm clocks, both across the room from your bed, and make sure that at least one of them runs on batteries.

Mistake #6: Don't eat too much, since that is going to make you sleepy

Eating makes your brain tired. You don't need a tired brain when you go to a test. So, save the pancakes till after the exam. Don't walk into a test on an empty stomach though, since it's hard to think about physics when your stomach is growling.

Mistake #7: Make sure you know the location of the exam, what you need to bring, etc.

The little details can trip you up and make the process that much more stressful. Find out where the test is going to be held and when. Don't assume that it's being held in class at the same time the regular class takes place, because teachers are always switching up on that one.

Mistake #8: Try to find copies of the professor's old practice tests

A lot of frats and sororities keep test banks of old exams. As a professor myself, I don't agree with these test banks being in existence, but since they are........

Mistake #9: NEVER leave the exam early…..go over your answers a million times if you have to

If you get two hours to take a test, use the whole two hours. The worst feeling in the world is to lose points over something STOOPID. Go through your answers 2- 3 times to make sure that you did them correctly. If you go through for the third time and everything looks ok, then maybe it's all right to leave.

Mistake #10: Get to the exam at least 10 minutes early

Don't show up for a test at the same time the test is supposed to be given. Get there early so that you can find a seat and get comfortable. Also, don't sit next to people who cheat, it will only make you look bad in the end.

How to kick academic butt

1) Choose a major by the end of your sophomore year

Don't rush yourself when choosing a major, but if you wait till your Junior year to choose one, you are going to cause yourself to be in college longer than you need to be. The Junior year is when students start taking specialized classes in their major, and you don't want to be caught without a major at that point.

2) Try to find a job that lets you study while you work. If not, then don't work more than 25 hours per week

Working while you're in school definitely builds character. But don't get crazy with it. Earn enough money to pay for the things you need, and then chill. Try to find a job on campus that lets you study while you're working, because then you can work 40 hours per week and it will also help your GPA.

3) If you have repeat options, use them all. Quality is more important than speed

Some schools let you retake courses that you've done poorly in and then take the bad course out of your GPA calculation. If your school allows for this option, make sure you use it. Even if your GPA is already pretty high, you can always help yourself by getting rid of 1 or 2 courses that are holding down your GPA.

4) Make sure you know your academic program and all it's nooks and crannies. Draw a map for yourself and how you are going to get out of there

The first step to getting anywhere you want to go is to know where in the heck you are going in the first place. Figure out your path through your academic program, and then set a plan to make it happen. Don't blindly rely on hope or the advice of your advisors, that is the quickest way to get bamboozled. You must take responsibility for your own success because this is your life that you are dealing with, not anyone else's.

5) Try to get a good internship in your field during the summer. If not, then go to summer school. Make sure you are doing SOMETHING productive

Summers are not meant for slacking and chilling. They are meant for doing something productive toward your graduation. You can still chill, but you have to be doing *something* that is going to help you graduate from college. 25% of your life happens during the summers, do you really want to waste 25% of your life doing nothing?

6) Don't transfer to another school, unless you have a very good reason

Transferring schools is not for the faint of heart. It's something that you should only do if you absolutely have to. That means that switching schools because of a girlfriend, or just for the heck of it is not very cool at all. Once you've switched from school to school to school, you have to hunt all over the country to get your transcripts, you have to retake class after class, and maybe 7 years later, you've got a college degree! The quickest way to get through college is to find one school and stay there until they hand you your piece of paper. It's that simple.

7) Don't waste your time taking too many extra or unnecessary classes. There is already enough for you to do

Sometimes it can be tempting to sign up for this extra class or that one, maybe in tennis, aerobics, golf or whatever. Extra classes are fun, but that is what electives are for. Once you run out of electives to use, don't waste your time and money taking extra classes. You can learn to play tennis or golf by reading a book or playing in your spare time. You are in college to graduate, not to become Tiger Woods.

8) Participate like crazy in class. Most students don't like to talk, so this is a great way to stand out in the crowd

Don't just go to class and sit there. If the teacher asks for participation, use this as an opportunity to distinguish yourself. Other students are quiet and afraid to talk, so this is an opportunity for you to show the teacher that you know your stuff. Also, it is a great chance to get used to speaking in front of groups. Teachers are always impressed with students who participate.

Coco Rules for Studying Success

Study rule #1: Keep track of the number of hours you are studying every day, and make sure you are honest

Keeping track of the amount of time you spend studying helps you to make sure that you are working as hard as you think you are. There is no harsher truth than what we get from looking into the mirror. If you keep track of your study hours, you will know if you need to work harder or not. Also, make sure that you keep track of the number of hours you are <u>really</u> studying, not the number of hours you spend sitting at the table.

Study rule #2: Study in secluded, well-lit areas, not places that are loud or crowded

You need to be focused when you study. That means that you want to find the most boring, quiet place possible so that you can concentrate. Studying around a bunch of other people or in a place where there is noise is only going to make you have to spend more time with your face in a book. Be efficient with your studying and it will be over before you know it. After you've worked hard for a few days, it will be a breeze to sit and read for 4 or 5 hours straight.

Study rule #3: Begin your studying early in the day so that you can have it all done in time for the party

Get a jump on the gun and that will allow you to have all the free time to do whatever you want. *The party* is not what lowers your GPA, it's the party that you go to *when you haven't done any studying all day.* If you start work at 8 am, you can have a ton of stuff done by 2 or 3 p.m., with the rest of the day and night free to shake your butt till it falls off the hinges.

Study rule #4: Try to go over your notes right after the class in which you took them

The sooner you go over your notes, the more you are likely to remember them. Go through everything right after class, if you can, and that will make it easier for you when you have to go back through the stuff and prepare for your exam.

Study rule #5: Take a book with you wherever you go

You should always have a book with you, since you never know when you are going to have a bunch of free time on your hands. Why waste time standing in line at the grocery store or waiting on your friend to show up when you could be killing two birds with one stone? There is no worse feeling than wasting time that you could have used to get done with all the crap that is still waiting for you when you get home.

Study rule #6: Keep a lot of disposable earplugs in your book bag

It can be hard to study effectively with a lot of noise. You may think that it doesn't bother you, but your brain picks up every little sound and processes it. If your brain is processing outside noise, it has less energy to process what you are studying. Since you need to be focused, you should buy earplugs so that you can efficiently study, no matter where you happen to be. If you are in McDonald's, the mall, or on your break at work, you can study. The more studying you get done with, the less you will have to do when you get back to the dorm.

Study rule #7: Cram right after the previous test, not the week before the next one

Remember, "Jamming" is the best way to cram. That means that you study hard for a test, *right after the last one.* If you do this, you will get much more credit for your hard work because no one else will have read that far into the book yet. This would give you a chance to shine on every quiz, all class participation, and also on the exam. Remember that it's all a matter of timing. That is what gets you where you want to go. Yes, I am repeating what I said earlier, it's THAT important.

Study rule #8: Never get lazy, never give up.

Laziness is the worst disease in the world. Don't ever give in to laziness, for a person who is a slave to laziness will never get to live out their dreams. It may seem tough to sit your butt down and do your work, but force yourself to sit there, and after a while, you will get into a groove. You have to work hard to get good study habits, and then it becomes easy to study. Self-doubt is a horrible enemy as well. This means that you have to find a way to confront your failures and not allow them to affect your self-confidence. Learn to dig and dig and dig until you get what you came for. Nothing that is worth having is just going to fall into your lap. Great outcomes require hard work.

Study rule #9: Always attend every class, get there 5 minutes early and make sure you sit in the front row as close to the center of the room as possible

Never miss class. It can be tough to make sure you go to every single class, but missing classes is the quickest way to jack up your grade. You might miss a pop quiz, or you might miss some important information about the upcoming exam. Do not put yourself into that situation. Always plan get to class 5 minutes early, that way, if something happens along the way, you are still going to be on time.

Study rule #10: Make sure you visit every teacher at least once a week

Visiting your teacher is the easiest way to get free tutoring. Also, when someone knows your face, they are more sympathetic to you than if you are just a name on a piece of paper. Make sure that the teacher knows your face.

Study rule #11: Begin your day as early as possible

One of the best ways to study is to get it all done quick and early. If a person is disciplined enough to get up at, say, 8 am on a Saturday morning, they can have enough studying done by 3 or 4 to last for almost the entire weekend. That leaves a lot of time for naps, parties and Play Station. Where people get in trouble is when it comes to wasting time sitting on the phone, watching TV, or just "chillin". If you are "all about your business", you can work hard and play harder….that is what college is all about.

For the athletes

1) DO NOT let someone else choose your major

A lot of athletic departments attempt to choose the majors of their student-athletes. That's a problem, because they are going to pick the easiest major that doesn't get in the way of your sports schedule. You should have a problem with that because you are going to be the one stuck in a field that you are not happy with. The best thing to do is find out exactly how the program works before you sign with a school. That way, you don't have to suffer punishment for going against their team policy.

2) Make sure that you are still going to be allowed to stay in school if you can't play sports anymore. Try to get it in writing

If you are an athlete, there is a good chance that the school only values you for what you can do on the field. That means that if you can't perform for some reason, or you decide to quit, you have no value to them. You must protect yourself in advance from this kind of thing. Make sure that whatever school you take an athletic scholarship from gives you the right to quit the team and still keep your scholarship. If you can't do that, then try to find a way to get your scholarship money from some other source (a minority scholarship or academic scholarship) so that you are not owned by your sports team.

3) If you have to miss classes, make sure that you call each teacher every time you have to leave

If your sport puts you on the road a lot, you have to make arrangements with your teachers to deal with that. Some teachers can seriously have it out for you if you are never in class. Make sure that you talk to them personally every time you have to leave, to ensure that you are not missing anything important. If the professor is only getting emails from your coaches telling them what is going on, they may hold a grudge.

4) Do not leave school for any period of time without a college degree or guaranteed multi-million dollar contract in your hand

College is something that you came to finish. No matter what happens on or off the field, DO NOT leave school for any reason or period of time without either a degree or an amount of money that is going to set you for life. Some people start to feel that they don't belong in college for one reason or another. Then they leave. Even if you don't feel that you belong there, make sure that you stay until you graduate. Then you can leave forever if you want.

5) Don't choose a school just because they have a great athletic program. Don't transfer schools unless you absolutely have to

There are other qualities to a school besides its sports programs. Make sure you look into the other things your school offers, like graduation rates or quality of academic training and job opportunities after graduation. Sports may be important to you, but you can't focus on sports at the expense of your future.

6) Don't let your grades fall in the toilet, it will stay with you forever

It's easy to get caught up in sports to the point that nothing else seems to matter. There may be TV cameras all around and you may be led to believe that nothing else matters. This mentality will haunt you for life, and you will be struggling long after the lights have dimmed and the crowds have gone home. I've seen students let their GPA fall as low as 0.0 in the past, and it always caught up with them. Make sure that you use the same work ethic that you have in sports to keep your grades up. It is very important.

7) Learn your academic program well and do not rely on anyone else to tell you what you need to graduate.

Don't let your academic counselors be the only ones who understand the academic program you are trying to get through. You need to find a way to learn your own program so that YOU know exactly what you need in order to find your way to graduation. Relying too much on other people is the quickest way to destroy your academic career.

8) Watch out for creepy characters: gold-diggin women who might scream rape, friends who get a little too wild, or people who might be associated with gambling rings.

If you are a big-time athlete, you're going to find yourself with a lot of new "friends" who seem to get a thrill from hanging with the athletes. This is fine and good, but you need to be careful around anyone and everyone you encounter. College life can get kind of wild, so you should watch who you trust and only trust who you watch.

9) Talk to at least 4 other minorities over the age of 30 who have gone through the program who did not make it to "The League". They will be able to give you the inside scoop on how minority athletes are treated and what happens to you in the long run.

The sad thing about the way the NCAA treats its athletes is that most of them don't know if they've been screwed until after they graduate. They get older and look back in time to find out that they were mistreated and exploited. You can learn a lot from talking to people who have gone through your program already. Don't just talk to the ones who had good things happen, talk to the ones who didn't make it to the pros. If you find that there are many former athletes bitter about their experience at your chosen university, that might be a signal for you of things to come.

10) Use your position in the public eye for something positive. Conduct yourself with class and remember that you are a leader.

Don't be one of those athletes that gets arrested every week for weed possession or drunk-driving. Be a leader, or at least a model citizen. The world is waiting for you to screw up, so don't let them get what they are looking for.

Life
anyone???

Coco Rules for Life Success in college

1) Stay away from alchohol, drugs, promiscuity and gambling.

This issue depends on who you are. Some people think that a little drinking or sex in college is ok, some don't. The only thing that I DEFINITELY know is that too much of any of these things can be hazardous to your health or land you in jail. College is a breeding ground for all the little sins that tempt mankind. Enjoy yourself in college to the extent that you feel comfortable, but DO NOT get caught up in too much of anything.

2) Watch out for the credit card sales people - only get one card at most, and try not to spend more than you can afford.

The credit card vultures wait every semester for those naïve, unsuspecting freshmen who come through campus for the first time. You have a clean credit history, and they want to offer you what looks like free money. If you get a credit card, be smart with it. You should only use it if you have to, and only spend what you can afford. Financial problems are a major reason for students dropping out of college.

3) Don't pledge until you are done with your freshman year.

Pledging for frats and sororities is fine, if that is what you want to do. But don't do it during your freshman year. Also, if you are having GPA problems, then don't do it during your sophomore or junior year either. There is always the grad chapter!

4) Don't move off campus until your senior year.

Moving off campus creates a lot of new bills that will get in the way of your education. You have the rest of your life to live off campus. Stay on campus for now.

5) If you don't have a family yet, don't start one till you're both done with college.

Having kids is great, but not during college. Get your education first, so that you can use the benefits of that education to support a family. If you have kids and a spouse too early, you are going to be forced to either jeopardize your relationships with them in order to reach your goals, or you are going to have to give up your goals altogether.

6) Leave your Play Station, Xbox or Gamecube at home. These are serious time-eaters.

According to the Journal of Personality and Social Psychology, students who spend a lot of time playing videogames have lower grades than those who do not. Getting good at video games takes a lot of time, time that you don't have when you are in college. Leave the system at your parent's house, or only allow yourself to play your games after you've done a certain amount of studying for the night. Having that thing in your room is only going to distract you.

7) <u>Never </u> drop out of school for any period of time for any reason.

There are a billion folks who have dropped out of school "for just a little while" only to find themselves never ever going back to college. Don't let yourself get caught in that category. Only drop out if there is no other option, and remember that even when you think that there are no options, that usually means that you just haven't thought about all the possible solutions.

8) Don't go home too much, you will never get used to your new environment.

It is always fun to go back home and kick it with the family. But the only way you are going to grow as a person is if you get out there, have new experiences and meet new people. Get out there and live your life, don't spend all your time traveling back and forth to your home.

Coco Rules on Setting Goals and reaching them

1) Set long, medium and short-range goals

Goal setting requires that you focus on the long, medium and short-term horizons. Your medium and short-term goals should be pieces of the puzzle for you to fulfill your long-run objectives. Always make sure that you set goals so that your mind knows where you are trying to go. A person without goals is like a sheep out in the pasture just living from day to day. You don't want to be a sheep.

2) Read your goals every morning before you begin your day, and then think about what you have to do ON THIS DAY to reach them.

You have to make sure that you keep your mental connection between the long run objectives that you are trying to accomplish, and the things that you want to do every day to make them happen. Years are nothing more than a series of days, so if you waste each day, you will end up wasting months and years. That means you would be wasting your life. You should read your goals every morning so that you know EXACTLY what it is that you are trying to do and how you are going to work toward that objective on the day that lies in front of you.

3) Write down a careful long, medium and short-range execution strategy to meet those goals.

Goals are only the first step toward making your dreams come true. You then have to devise a strategy to turn your dreams into reality. Without a plan, a goal is just a bunch of hot air. Put together your goals, come up with a strategy to make it all happen, and then execute your strategy day-to-day until you are ready to go.

4) Don't be afraid to set high goals, just make sure you fully understand the price that is required to reach them.

Everything can be attained by the person who is a) willing to pay the price to reach that goal, and b) aware of what the price happens to be. Many times, we lie to ourselves about how committed we are to accomplishing something. It is much easier for a person to claim to be the hardest working person on the planet than it is for that person to actually follow through on their claim. Also, a lot of people get attached to the dream and don't recognize the level of hard work necessary to reach that dream. It is much more fun and glamorous to pretend to be Michael Jordan than it is to actually make the sacrifices necessary to become a Michael Jordan. Setting high goals is cool, but always be realistic when you think about what you have to do to reach them.

5) Never be afraid to fail, for that is the only way that you will ever succeed.

The reason that great success is so rare in our society is because most people are afraid to fail. Failure takes away confidence, which makes you not want to try again. So, usually people try and then give up, or they never try at all. The path to greatness is usually paved with failure. You have to know this right off the bat. But the great thing is that if you can deal with the failures and keep pushing, eventually you will get that great success that makes all the failures go away. For example, if a brother is trying to get a date for the prom. He may find himself rejected by 14 beautiful women. But if that 15th woman says "yes", then that makes all the failures go away. However, if he only asks out one of them and she says no, then he will give up and never experience the joy of success that makes all the failures worthwhile. When you start something, plan to pay a high price of disappointment along the way. Consider the price you pay to be the cost of that success that you will definitely get at the end if you never give up. The obstacles you face in your life will have a limit. If your determination has no limits, then you will always eventually win most battles.

6) Set goals for *every* part of your life, not just for school.

One important part of your development as a human being is that you remember to be well rounded. You can't just work like crazy on one thing and ignore everything else. If you do that, you end up being a geek who can't relate to people, or a person who ignores his/her family all for the sake of earning that extra dollar. The dollars are fine, but the fact is that you have to think about what is going to make you happy in the long run. One way to keep your balance is to incorporate your family and friends into your goals. You can have goals related to school, but you can also have a goal related to spending more time with your family, making new friends, or losing weight. If you have a relationship, you can set a goal related to making your relationship work or at least learning to be nicer to your boyfriend. Think about all the things that make you happy in your world, and work hard to get them all right. The actor Will Smith mentioned that not setting goals in every area of his life led him to have tremendous success on the big screen, but failures in his personal life. You don't want to have that same kind of pain.

7) Review your goals on a regular basis and think about whether you are doing what it takes to reach them.

Every goal you set should also be accompanied with a strategy for achieving that goal. You have to not only know where you want to go, but you must also have a map for getting there, and a vehicle that you are going to use. Keep checking the map every couple of days to make sure that you are headed in the right direction. You have to remind yourself of your goals every day, what the requirements are, and whether or not you are meeting those requirements. That is how you get to the finish line.

8) Never let failure get to you or take away your confidence

Many great people have strong confidence that carries them through the embarrassment of their failures. Remember that "being great" is not something that describes a person, it is a choice that a person makes. That means that "great" people are not usually born with greatness, they go out and get it. They make a day-to-day choice to go that extra mile, no matter what. They also understand that failure is just a bump in the road on their way to success. The more you can adopt that mentality, the more likely you are to succeed.

9) **Be happy no matter what**

It means nothing to reach your goals if you are not happy. No matter what happens, what you go through, or how things work out, you must ALWAYS find a reason to be happy and smile. We are all blessed with life and have many things that are very valuable to us: maybe it's our family, our health, the chance to go to school, or just having both legs! Don't ever get so caught up in your desire to achieve that you forget to be happy. If you don't reach your goal, just try again, but remember that while you should take your goals very seriously, it is not the end of the world if you don't reach them.

10 things that college students do to ruin their lives

1) Sex, drugs, alcohol and gambling

College is a great place to pick up a lot of really bad habits. The worst thing is that people tell you that these things are ok. It's not that all of these are bad things to do, but at the very least, they should be done in moderation. It doesn't matter if you are in college: If you have sex with too many people, you are going to catch a disease or get pregnant. If you use drugs, you are going to become a drug addict. If you drink too much, you will become an alcoholic. Gambling can also ruin your life as much as drugs or alcohol.

2) Falling for the credit card scams and ruining your credit

There are no serious credit card scams in college, only the little people who stand out in front of the bookstore trying to get you to take their "free money". Credit cards are very tempting when you are in school, especially since you are broke. If you decide to take one, make sure that you are very careful with how much you buy with the card, and that you have a careful plan to pay it all back. Putting yourself in over your head can easily destroy your credit. That is not a good cycle to get into. Not taking care of your student loan obligations can ruin your credit as well.

3) Working too much outside of school and forcing yourself to drop out

Getting a job in school is not a bad thing to do. In fact, it builds character. But you should work only to support your basic needs. If you find yourself working non-stop in order to pay for things that you shouldn't be buying in college, then that is when it is time for you to settle down and reconsider your priorities. Your professors are not going to care if your grades are in the toilet because you are engaged in too many outside activities. It is your responsibility to keep up in class

4) Screwing up their freshman year

There are a ton of students out there who are spending every waking moment of their Sophomore, Junior and Senior years trying to compensate for the screwing up they did during their Freshman year. If you get off to a bad start, you're asking for serious trouble all through college. You will have to do 10 miles of work to get 5 miles of reward. Don't put yourself into that position if you can avoid it.

5) Pledging too early

The quickest way to ruin your GPA and put yourself on a downward spiral in college is to pledge during your freshman year. Some frats and sororities are responsible enough to make sure that they don't allow freshmen to pledge. But even if they are not, you should not allow yourself to pledge until you've had a good freshman year. If you are still struggling academically after your freshman year, you should wait and pledge grad chapter.

6) Choosing a major you hate or one that doesn't make as much money as you would like

You should not choose a major just because it makes money. You also should not choose a major just because it is exactly what you want to do. The best way to choose a major is to figure out what combination of things are going to make you happy in the long-run. I LOVE playing basketball, but I would not enjoy being a broke brother who was not good enough to get to the NBA. So, I play basketball in my spare time and I work as a finance professor, which I enjoy, but also pays the bills. You should choose a major based upon the ability of the major to take care of your long-term financial needs, as well as provide you with a job you can enjoy. So, don't pick something just because you love it, and don't pick it just because you have money or prestige. Find out what is going to be important to you in the long run and let that be the basis for your choice. You should also factor in what kind of life you want to have when you are older, say, 30, and how this job fits into that. Do you want to have a family? Well, they are going to need time and financial support. Does your job give you that? Also, you should never let anyone choose a major for you. That is usually the world's quickest way to unhappiness.

7) Getting too caught up in things that don't have anything to do with academics

It's great to be involved with extracurricular activities, it is a very important part of the college experience. But anything that gets too much in the way of academics should be reduced. You are there for your education, and you don't want to ruin your GPA over something silly. Make sure that you manage your time properly and that you make others respect your time. If you are not taking care of things on the academic front, then everything is going to fall apart for you.

8) Going home too much

College is a time for you to grow up and learn to be an adult. Don't catch yourself going home every single weekend. The umbilical cord that you shared with your mother at birth should be cut by the time you are 18. By going home too much, you are simply extending the cord down the highway. Visit your family, but don't spend too much time leaning on them. You will never learn to take care of yourself, and you will find yourself in your mid and late twenties asking your parents for money.

9) Not thinking about going to graduate school

Any person with a Bachelors Degree who is in a field where graduate degrees have value should definitely go on to graduate school. The marketplace is changing, and the Bachelors Degree doesn't carry the same heat that it did back in the day. You have to be able to compete with those out there with better credentials, and you are seriously hurting yourself if you do not go to graduate school. It can also have a big impact on your salary and job opportunities. Finally, the world economy is integrating, so you are going to have to compete with people all over the world, in addition to those in the U.S. You don't want to be left behind.

318

Odds, ends, and in-betweens

Top 10 coco tasks that you can do in the summer (ranked in order of preference):

1) A paid internship to give you experience, preferably abroad.

Getting experience is critical, and it's always best to get paid for it. Having something international further adds to what you've accomplished. As one of my professor friends explained to me "People just don't look at you the same when you've gone overseas." Students with overseas experience are valued at a premium by potential employers.

2) A paid internship in the U.S.

If you can't go overseas, there are a lot of good programs here in the U.S. Try to get with a reputable company so that it all looks good on your resume.

3) Study abroad programs.

If you can't find a good internship that pays, study abroad programs let you kill some college credits, have some fun, and also get a good international experience to put on your resume. I highly recommend study abroad programs.

4) Unpaid internship in the U.S.

If you can't get paid to get experience, then get it for free. This isn't the best of the lot, but the bottom line is that having experience before graduation is very, very important. Also, since they are not paying you, that means that you can claim to work for this company for a while, but you don't have to put in mandatory hours. The best thing about no one paying you is that no one owns you.

5) Academic summer programs that will help you get ready for your graduate program.

If you are going to graduate school, there are a lot of summer programs out there designed to help you get prepared for your field. Graduate school is a big step and a lot of things change, so it's best when you get the chance to see it up close before you step into the fire. Also, you can make contacts with other students and professors in your field. If you are getting a PhD, these contacts come in handy later on.

6) Research position (paid or unpaid) with a professor.

If you are interested in research or the sciences, a research position with a professor is a productive way to spend your summer. Having a good professor back you is very helpful if you are trying to go to medical school or get a PhD. Also, working with a professor will be helpful when you are trying to get letters of recommendation. They know you personally, so they are likely to go out of their way to help you.

7) Go to summer school on your current campus.

Summer school is a great way to propel you toward graduation. If the other options I've mentioned are not available, then summer school is a great alternative.

8) Go to summer school in your hometown while working at the same time.

If you can't go to school on your campus, then find a community college in your hometown that will let you take a few classes. They are usually cheap, and you should do whatever it takes to get closer to obtaining that degree. Check before hand to make sure that the credits are going to transfer, so that you don't waste your time. Also, if the job is not the kind that is going to help you get valuable experience, at least make sure that they offer you a flexible schedule that is going to allow you to be free when you have a test or other important things to do.

9) Find a regular summer job at home.

This should be your last resort. A job should build toward something for the future, or you should at least try to do something else that is going to enhance your future. If you just take a dead end job that doesn't build toward anything, you are probably wasting your time. Only go this route if you absolutely have to. If you do this, at least be smart and save your money. You're going to need it when you get back to school.

Coco rules for the job search

1) Make sure that you practice: Mock interviews, resume-writing books, etc.

Don't just go into an interview cold turkey, or you'll be eating cold leftover turkey when you don't have a job. Like anything else, you should plan your interviewing techniques and be prepared to handle the types of questions that you are going to receive. You can get some of this practice by going to the career center and seeing what resources they have. You should also go to the Internet and find information on job hunting and interviewing techniques. Don't try to just wing it, or you may end up looking bad.

2) Get good internship and other experience, even if you have to volunteer.

Experience is critical for job hunting. Internships are the way to get that experience. Try to get good internships with companies that have a strong reputation. Seeing that big company name on your resume makes a difference when hunting for jobs. Even if you have to volunteer, think of the internship as just another class that you have to take before graduation.

3) If in doubt, always go for more education

If there are no jobs on the horizon, or you are just unsatisfied with what is out there, then consider holding out to get more educational credentials that might open doors for you. If everyone in your field seems to have a Masters Degree, then you should make sure that you have one also. If you have to go to certain types of schools to get a job in a given field, then try to go to graduate school at one of those places. The key is that you keep your grades up so that you can go to graduate school if you choose to.

4) Start the search early in the year

When you are searching for a job, you need to start the search very early in the school year. Waiting until the spring is a sure-fire recipe for disaster. By then, all the good jobs are going to be gone.

5) Go beyond the career center, use the Internet.

The career center at your school and the Internet are your best resources. Use them diligently to not only get information on how to find a job, but also to find places to send your resume.

6) Go to every career fair that you can find.

There are career fairs held all over the country, where employers come and show you their stuff. Go to as many of these things as you can. This is another place where you can find leads for jobs.

7) Use the connections you might have

If you have a friend or neighbor who works in your field, try calling them to see if they know of jobs that might be available. Also, if there are ex-students who work for the company you are trying to work for, go with them also. Your professors may also know a few things that can help you land jobs.

8) Keep the GPA high so that you can have your pick of jobs.

Keeping your grades up is important. This makes the difference between begging for jobs, and having a potential employer begging you to come work for them.

Graduate school

1) Study hard for the standardized tests, do not take them for granted. Take a Kaplan course, even if you have to borrow or save money well in advance.

Don't try to just take these tests with what you already know. You have to study and prepare for these things, and your level of preparation will surely show itself when you get your final score. Also, you should do whatever you can to take a Kaplan course, since this can be helpful when it comes to improving your score.

2) Contact as many people as you can in your field to get information on which schools are best, then create your own ranking

Some fields are very specialized, where the rankings are not made public. But academic-types tend to know which schools have the best reputation in their area. You have to go where the information lies and put together your own ranking in the end. For law, medicine or business school, you may already have rankings out there that are pretty good. But in the end, you have to make sure that the school is good at what YOU want to do, not what someone else wants. For example, if you want to study entertainment law, you have to find out which schools produce the best entertainment lawyers. If you want to work in Nebraska, you may be better off going to graduate school in Nebraska than anywhere else.

3) Apply to at least 12 –15 schools, you have to diversify

When you apply to graduate school, you have to spread out your application to as many places as you possibly can. You never know what certain schools are looking for and what they are willing to offer to get it. Creating options for yourself is critical, since it increases the chances that you are going to be successful. Market yourself widely to the world so that you can see how much they are willing to do to have you.

4) Visit every single school that you are thinking about attending – bring good questions

Make sure that before you commit to a graduate school, you visit the place that you are going to spend the next stage of your life. A place is always going to look good in a brochure, but you have to make sure that you see things first hand. Also, bring a long list of questions before you visit the campus. Get full information before you commit.

5) Talk to the students at the school at all levels of the game to get a feel for what the school is all about.

If you go to visit a school, they are going to try to make sure that you only get a chance to talk to people who are going to say good things. That's all fine and good, but you have to get around and talk to everybody. Talk to students, professors, even janitors to get a feel for what the school is like, particularly from the black perspective. Don't take anyone's answer as gospel, since one person's opinion may be biased in some way. But if you talk to enough people, you will eventually have a strong feel for the environment.

6) Clearly define an area of interest before you start, even if you don't really have one. Focus looks good.

Even if you don't know exactly what it is that you want to do, at least try to think of something good to say on your application. Not having focus by this stage of your career looks very bad. Also, having some kind of focus might lead a professor to identify with you and your goals, which could make the difference in terms of getting you admitted.

7) Make sure you find out what the professor is going to write about you before you let them give you a letter of recommendation – some of them can be kinda shady.

If you are going to get a letter written about you by a professor, don't assume that every professor is planning to write great things about you. You should first ask the professor if they feel comfortable writing a letter for you, and then you should ask them what they are going to emphasize in the letter. After a while, you will get a feel for what they are going to say. Some students also make sure that they do not waive their right to read the letter (you check a little box on the form) so that they can see what their professor has written about them. If a professor is afraid to let you see what they wrote about you, you better make damn sure that the person is going to write something good!

8) Follow up regularly on every letter of recommendation to make sure that the professor did not forget to do it.

If you have a professor writing a letter for you, don't assume that the professor is going to handle every point of their business. Most professors are responsible, but they have a lot of things to do and can sometimes forget. This is YOUR life, so it's YOUR responsibility to make sure that everything gets done on YOUR application. If the professor screws up, you have no one to blame but yourself. Stay on them without being a "bugaboo", calling them about once every week or so. The closer you are to the deadline, the more you want to stay on them.

9) Find out what people are doing and earning after they leave *your specific program*. This can vary from school to school.

Don't just pick a school because their program has a strong reputation. Make sure that they have a strong reputation in helping people to do what you want to do. For example, you may want to work in the east coast after graduation, so choosing a west coast school might not be the best idea. Or if you are good in one area of business, then a top ranked MBA program may have developed its reputation in another area. The best way to find out what is going to happen to you after you leave a graduate program is to find out what happens to other people who *do exactly what you do*. If they are all unemployed, there is a good chance that you may be also.

10) Apply very early and have your materials organized months in advance of the application deadlines.

As with most things, going to graduate school requires that you plan ahead and know what you want to do well in advance. If you try to do everything during the second half of your senior year, you are going to be in big trouble. Remember: get your standardized tests out of the way during your Junior year, pick up the apps, arrange your letters and get the transcripts together during the summer before your senior year. You should send out the applications during the fall.